31.50

PUBLIC INFRASTRUCTURE PLANNING AND MANAGEMENT

Volume 33, URBAN AFFAIRS ANNUAL REVIEWS

PUBLIC INFRASTRUCTURE PLANNING AND MANAGEMENT

Edited by
JAY M. STEIN

Volume 33, URBAN AFFAIRS ANNUAL REVIEWS

SAGE PUBLICATIONS
The Publishers of Professional Social Science
Newbury Park   Beverly Hills   London   New Delhi

For information address:

SAGE Publications, Inc.
2111 West Hillcrest Drive
Newbury Park, California 91320

SAGE Publications Inc.   SAGE Publications Ltd.
275 South Beverly Drive   28 Banner Street
Beverly Hills   London EC1Y 8QE
California 90212   England

SAGE PUBLICATIONS India Pvt. Ltd.
M-32 Market
Greater Kailash I
New Delhi 110 048 India

Printed in the United States of America

Library of Congress Cataloging-in-Publication Data

Public infrastructure and planning management / edited by Jay M.
   Stein.
          p.   cm. — (Urban affairs annual reviews ; v. 33)
       ISBN 0-8039-2690-1. ISBN 0-8039-2691-X (pbk.)
           1. Infrastructure (Economics)—United States—Planning.
   2. Municipal services—United States—Planning. I. Stein, Jay M.
   II. Series.
   HT108.U7 vol. 33
   [HC10.C3]
   307.7′6 s—dc19   87-18353
   [363]   CIP

HT
108
.U7
vol. 33

Contents

Preface

The center of a 540-foot bridge on the Governor Thomas E. Dewey Thruway collapsed without warning this morning, sending at least two cars and one truck plunging into a swollen creek. The cause of the collapse was unknown, but it followed two days of heavy rains.

Authorities could not say tonight how many people might have been killed or injured in the accident. It occurred in a light rain and left a 330-foot gap in the steel reinforced concrete bridge in the village of Fort Hunter, just west of Amsterdam, about 40 miles northwest of Albany (New York). [*New York Times*, April 6, 1987]

The collapsed Thruway bridge was only thirty-one years old, had undergone a major rehabilitation less than five years ago, and had been inspected less than one year ago. Moreover, this is not an isolated incident. Less than four years earlier, a 100-foot section of a Connecticut Turnpike bridge spanning the Minus River collapsed sending several people to their deaths. Such incidents occur with alarming regularity for a wide range of infrastructure facilities in all regions of the country.

Infrastructure failures are not just tragic events involving the senseless loss of life and property. They are also vivid symbols of our nation's lack of adequate planning, management, and financial commitment to public infrastructure facilities.

This book examines the very complex set of issues and problems involved in contemporary planning and management of infrastructure facilities. Its overall perspective is that public infrastructure is an integral part of a community's landscape affecting form, shape, quality of life, economic development, and land use patterns. Moreover, the local need and ability to pay for infrastructure facilities are increasingly a function of national and international economic conditions and restructuring.

ORGANIZATION OF THE BOOK

The book contains four major parts. First, it describes the larger economic context determining the current U.S. infrastructure crisis.

Stein argues that changes in the rate, structure, and distribution of economic growth play an important role in the demand for and ability to support infrastructure investments. As economies move from reliance on heavy industry toward service and high-technology activities, the required mix of infrastructure facilities also changes. Thus communications and data networks have become as important to modern economies as road and bridge facilities. Moreover, economic restructuring and sectoral shifts have contributed to uneven spatial growth and decline. Thus some communities experience intense pressure to expand public facilities while others have excess capacity and must consolidate or close facilities. Ultimately, the rate and distribution of economic growth affects the ability of federal, state, and local tax bases to generate revenues in support of public investment.

Part II examines the issues involved in measuring infrastructure needs. It begins with results from Kaplan's study for the *Joint Economic Committee of Congress*, which analyzed national infrastructure needs and revenues to the year 2000. The study's final report, *Hard Choices* (Kaplan, 1984), estimated that there is a $400 billion funding "gap" to the year 2000. However, as Kaplan notes, there are considerable methodological problems with this estimate. The quality of local record keeping is poor and unreliable, widely accepted standards for measuring infrastructure conditions do not exist, and perceived needs are largely a matter of tastes. Up to what point are traffic delays tolerable? At what point is there a need for additional facilities?

Lee's study of highway needs offers a technical definition of needs that avoids value-laden connotations—an infrastructure need is any capital project for which the benefits exceed the costs. His definition construes benefits and costs quite broadly to include positive and negative influences of value, including social or opportunity costs of all resources consumed.

Newton's focus on infrastructure decay in Great Britain and Western Europe takes the perspective that the link between urban change and financial crises are mediated by the special features of each nation's local government and political system. Social, economic, and political variations cause different patterns of growth and decline in different regions and nation states. Nevertheless, Newton argues that cities of the Western world retain the means to refurbish and develop their urban infrastructure.

Part III contains five chapters that focus on the planning and financing of public infrastructure. Catanese views infrastructure planning as an effective tool in guiding and controlling the timing, direction, and magnitude of growth. He argues, however, that the provision of infrastructure is no longer a public monopoly, but increasingly involves public/private partnership. Peterson also explores creative ways to pay for infrastructure. Since the current dollar value of federal grants is unlikely to grow, and very likely will decline in real, per capita terms, Peterson concludes that either financing from current revenues will have to expand or there must be greater reliance on debt instruments. However, the increased use of debt means that total costs of infrastructure investments are highly vulnerable to interest rate levels. Projects that have a favorable benefit-cost ratio when interest rates are low, may have to be abandoned when rates are high.

Finally, Nelson explores the growing use of development impact fees to shift the burden for new infrastructure to developers and/or new community residents. Impact fees are most effective in rapid growth communities with strong housing demands. Such fees, however, have serious equity implications and may be viewed as a form of exclusionary zoning.

The next two chapters focus on the planning issues involved in the specific areas of recreation and transportation planning. Eplan examines a Charleston, South Carolina park plan as a model of recreation planning. Rather than focusing on discreet needs, interests, and spaces of specific user groups, Eplan advocates that parks be viewed as part of a system of leisure activities. Moreover, the park system can be part of a process for realizing larger community goals of growth, change, and revitalization.

Finally, Ross examines transportation planning issues by first expanding Lee's discussion of "needs" to include not only highways, but also mass transit. She then concludes that federal grants should be more flexible to allow for greater investment in maintenance and repair, rather than new facilities; and suggests innovative practices for state and local governments.

The book's final section focuses on political, environmental, and equity issues involved in infrastructure planning. Lines and Parker provide a case history of the planning of New York City's Verrazano Narrows Bridge. Their chapter shows the institutional politics involved in the planning of a major infrastructure project.

Beginning with the National Environmental Policy Act of 1969 (NEPA), environmental assessment of proposed infrastructure projects has been required of all projects with federal government participation. NEPA also has been an influential model for state and local government planning efforts. Ortolano's chapter focuses on an often ignored concern in environmental impact assessments—indirect effects of infrastructure on land use. The chapter explores the nature of these impacts and then examines the relative advantages of two principal land use prediction strategies: expert judgment and mathematical models.

Beatley discusses how public investment decisions affect people's lives in fundamental ways and raises basic questions about how society is organized and how public decisions are made in a representative-democratic context. Certainly a minimum investment rule is that public investment decisions should not further exacerbate already existing income and wealth inequities. The chapter identifies a number of ethical principles and concepts that should be useful to planners and policy-makers in formulating infrastructure decisions in ethical terms.

Based on his own field experience, Lucy discusses problems involved in implementing equity in the capital improvement planning process. He concludes that equity is more difficult to operationalize for large, special facilities, such as airports and sewage disposal plants, and is most readily applied where geographic and neighborhood comparisons are feasible.

An infrastructure crises does exist in the United States. However, its definition as well as solutions involve far more than closing a projected gap between needs and resources. It involves understanding that the infrastructure problem stems from a complex array of economic, social, and political forces. These include international economic restructuring and technological change, federal monetary policies, and budget priorities—the vast investment in defense as opposed to domestic programs, and the absence of national economic planning and development policies.

As a result of the rapid population movements that the United States has experienced since the end of World War II, some regions have excess infrastructure capacity while others are in desperate need of additional facilities. Moreover, this is true not just on a regional basis, but also within metropolitan areas. Many central cities have been closing schools, while their neighboring suburbs operate on double session and struggle to pass bond issues to finance new construction. Yet there is no national planning effort to mitigate these impacts. Instead, the approach is to bemoan the lack of resources for new facilities, rather than to manage infrastructure needs by directing growth.

Infrastructure problems cannot be effectively solved unless viewed as part of wider system issues and failures. This requires addressing the larger policy contexts of federal budget priorities, national growth strategies, and economic development planning.

—Jay M. Stein
Buffalo, New York

Acknowledgments

I am greatly indebted to the U.P.S. Foundation's financial support for developing this book while I served as Visiting Professor in Stanford University's Infrastructure Planning and Management Program, Department of Civil Engineering, in 1984-1985. The students and faculty, especially Leonard Ortolano, provided valuable insights about infrastructure problems and issues.

My colleagues and students in the Department of Environmental Design and Planning at SUNY/Buffalo also gave important support to this effort. I am especially indebted to Catherine Ross, and Anthony J. Catanese for their very special friendship and constant professional encouragement.

Debbie Sponholz of SUNY/Buffalo typed the manuscript and showed great patience and perseverance. Ann West of Sage gave valuable editorial assistance. My wife Karen provided much emotional sustenance, patience, and encouragement.

Part I

Introduction

1

The Economic Context of the Infrastructure Crisis

JAY M. STEIN

COLLAPSED BRIDGES, highway cave-ins, and dam breaks are headline grabbing events that have focused considerable attention on the deteriorated condition of our nation's public infrastructure facilities. Failed infrastructure facilities, however, are not the result of a lack of technical knowledge or expertise on how to construct or maintain capital facilities. Rather, they are the result of inadequate investment in maintaining, replacing, and/or expanding the nation's infrastructure stock. While several studies have examined the shortfall between projected infrastructure needs and revenues (Choate and Walter, 1983; Kaplan, 1987), little attention has been paid to the larger economic context that determines the fiscal condition of infrastructure investments.

The perspective of this chapter is that the accounting approach, which measures needs and projects revenues, does not provide sufficient insight and information about the infrastructure crisis to yield long-term solutions. For effective policies and programs to be developed, it is necessary to view the infrastructure crisis as part of a larger, more complex set of economic problems. Ultimately, for infrastructure strategies to succeed, they must take into account the economic world that determines both the demand for facilities and affects the ability of governments to generate revenues.

This chapter's first section discusses the role of economic growth in the demand for and support of infrastructure. Section two focuses on the importance of federal government policies and budget priorities—especially the tradeoffs between defense spending and domestic programs. The next section examines the current fiscal condition of state and local governments—the major purchasers of capital improvements. Conclusions and recommendations are in the final section.

THE IMPORTANCE OF ECONOMIC GROWTH

Changes in the rate, structure, and distribution of national economic growth play an important role in both the demand for and ability to support infrastructure investments. These impacts are discussed below.

INFRASTRUCTURE DEMAND

Economic growth has several effects on infrastructure demand. First, the rate of growth influences the intensity of infrastructure use and, consequently, the extent to which capital facilities deteriorate over time and need to be replaced. In rapid growth periods, for example, the volume of goods produced and transported increases. Highways are then more intensely used, especially by heavy trucks, resulting in more rapid deterioration. This, eventually, creates a need for increased expenditures to repair or replace roads and bridges.

Second, growth is not uniformly distributed across all sectors of the economy or regions of the country. Different types of economic activity will generate different sets of demands for infrastructure facilities. Several studies have portrayed the U.S. economy as in a period of rapid change and transition as it moves from reliance on heavy industry and traditional manufacturing to a high technology, knowledge-intensive, and service-based economy (Noyelle, 1984; Birch, 1984; Knight, 1984). Such dramatic changes affect the economic well-being of individuals, as well as communities, states, and regions. It also alters the required mix of infrastructure facilities and results in new capital demands. For example, to accommodate the travel requirements of executives involved in the supervision of global production processes, such as in the manufacture of "world cars" (Grumwald and Flamm, 1985; Lawrence, 1984), many communities have built new airports or expanded existing facilities and runways to handle the larger planes used in international flights. Similarly, the need for public regulation of cable networks has greatly increased as data transmission and computer communications have grown in importance. Thus Nicol (1985: 192) has stated: "In a very real sense communications is becoming the most important component of the economic infrastructure. The future of the information economy hinges on building an adequate communications infrastructure." Nicol speculates that eventually communications planning will develop into a field comparable in scope to transportation planning.

Third, economic restructuring and sectoral shifts have combined with other factors to create uneven spatial growth. Some areas of the country, experiencing rapid population and economic growth, generate intense pressures to expand infrastructure facilities. Simultaneously, other areas are suffering from population and economic decline and must struggle just to maintain facilities and to manage excess capacity. Thus from an infrastructure perspective a highly inefficient situation has emerged. Some communities struggle to expand their infrastructure facilities, while others must consolidate or close facilities, such as schools or police stations, to reduce excess capacity.

In summary, the rate and distribution of economic growth influences infrastructure demand in three important ways. First, it affects the intensity at which facilities deteriorate and need to be replaced. Second, it alters the mix of required capital investment. As the economy restructures and new production technologies develop, demand patterns change and evolve. To the extent that the rate at which infrastructure becomes outdated is the result of economic transformation and not neglect, it can be an important indicator of economic vitality. Moreover, as economic growth generates higher living standards, a community's tastes and preferences may call for a higher quality of infrastructure facilities. Affluent communities are less tolerant of potholed streets and more willing to pay for their repair. Furthermore, the opportunity cost of travel delays and car repair is probably greater in wealthier communities. Finally, since economic growth is distributed unevenly, some areas of the country require additional infrastructure to serve growing populations, while others face the often painful and politically controversial choices involved in closing and/or consolidating public facilities. As discussed below, the sectoral and spatial restructuring also has significant effects on the fiscal capacity of local governments to finance infrastructure demands.

TAX REVENUES TO
SUPPORT INFRASTRUCTURE

The rate and distribution of economic growth directly affects the size of the federal, state, and local tax bases available to generate revenues. These tax bases ultimately support infrastructure as well as other forms of public investment and consumption. As Denison (1985: 1) notes: "Expenditures for one or more of these purposes must be curtailed when

TABLE 1.1
Government Receipts as a Percentage of GNP,
Selected Years 1929-1985

Calendar Year	Total Public Sector Receipts	Total Federal Receipts	From Own Sources State and Local			Federal Aid
			Total	State	Local	
1929	10.9	3.7	7.3	2.2	5.0	0.1
1939	16.9	7.4	9.6	3.4	6.2	1.1
1949	21.6	15.0	6.7	3.4	3.2	0.9
1959	26.5	18.4	8.1	4.0	4.1	1.4
1969	31.4	20.9	10.6	5.8	4.8	2.2
1974	31.7	20.1	11.7	6.6	5.0	3.1
1976	31.3	19.3	12.0	6.9	5.1	3.6
1978	31.5	19.9	11.6	6.9	4.7	3.6
1980	31.9	20.6	11.3	6.9	4.4	3.4
1981	32.4	21.1	11.2	6.8	4.4	3.0
1982	31.8	20.1	11.7	7.0	4.7	2.7
1983	31.3	19.4	11.9	7.1	4.7	2.6
1984	31.0	19.2	11.8	n.a.	n.a.	2.5
1985	31.5	19.5	11.9	n.a.	n.a.	2.6

SOURCE: Advisory Commission on Intergovernmental Relation (1986: 10-11).
n.a.—not available.

there is less output to be distributed, and in practice all are likely to be reduced."

From 1929 to 1969, rapid Gross National Product (GNP) growth combined with an increase in the percentage of GNP allocated to public sector revenues to produce significant increases in per capita constant dollar government revenues. Despite interruptions from the Great Depression and World War II, the 1929-1969 economic period generated high rates of resource utilization and rapid productivity growth. Average potential national income grew at a 3.9% annual rate in this period (Denison, 1985: 1-5). At the same time, government receipts as a percentage of GNP increased from 10.9% in 1929 to 31.4% in 1969. As a result, total government constant dollar (1972) revenues increased at an average annual rate of 7.64% from the period 1929-1949; 5.10% from the period 1949-1959; and 5.65% from the period 1959-1969 (Office of Management and Budget, 1985: 2.1-2.2) (see Table 1.1).

Since 1969, however, reflecting slower GNP growth and public resistance to expanding the tax share of GNP, constant dollar (1972) tax receipts have grown more slowly than in previous periods. From 1969 through 1978, constant dollar (1972) per capita tax receipts increased at an average annual rate of only 2.26%; from 1978 through 1984, only 0.76%.

The 1978-1984 period has been characterized by slow economic growth with a sustained deterioration in productivity. In the 1982 business cycle trough, unemployment reached a post-World War II high of 9.7%, with actual output falling 11.9% below potential output. The growth rate in national income was a -0.5% in the period 1979-1982. From 1979 to the first quarter of 1985, which includes a brisk cyclical recovery, national income still averaged only a 1.9% annual increase.[2] Combined with a leveling off in the public sector receipts share of GNP at around 31.5% (the result of federal income tax cuts and state/local tax-expenditure limitations), the result has been a marked slowdown in total government revenue growth. Given the Reagan administration's commitments to constrain or even contract the public sector, an increase in the federal tax share of GNP is very unlikely. Thus future federal support of infrastructure investment will be inexorably linked to either changes in budget priorities or accelerated economic growth rates. It is very unlikely that the total government share of GNP growth will increase as it has in past decades.

ECONOMIC GROWTH PROJECTIONS

Thus the rate of future economic growth is important to budget projections and planning for infrastructure needs. Unfortunately, economic forecasting is a highly uncertain science—or perhaps art. Even short-term forecasts are subject to considerable error. Although numerous private economic consulting firms and government agencies engage in forecasting, no clear consensus exists about "best practice" procedures or what may be expected over the next five, let alone twenty, years.

Both the Congressional Budget Office (CBO) and the Reagan administration now base their projections on the simple rule of thumb of historical experience. Their projections are based on "static" or "direct" budgetary impacts of changes in spending and tax provisions, rather than the interaction between changes in the economy and consequent budgetary impacts (Congressional Budget Office, 1985a: 2-5).

The CBO and the administration, however, differ in the assumptions governing their forecasts. The administration's forecasts generally include more optimistic projections about growth rates in real output, unemployment, rates of inflation, and real and nominal interest rates.

TABLE 1.2

Administration and CBO Federal Revenues and
GNP Projections (by fiscal year, in billions of dollars)

	1985	1986	1987	1988	1989	1990
Real GNP (percentage change year over year)						
Administration	3.9	4.0	4.0	4.0	3.9	3.6
CBO	3.5	3.2	3.3	3.4	3.4	3.4
Total Revenues						
Administration	737	794	862	950	1,030	1,108
CBO	735	789	855	934	1,007	1,090
Revenues as Percentage of GNP						
% Admin. GNP	19.0	18.9	18.9	19.3	19.4	19.5
% CBO GNP	19.1	19.0	19.1	19.3	19.3	19.4

SOURCE: Congressional Budget Office (1985: 8-9).

Consequently, the administration's revenue forecasts are higher than CBO's—by $23 billion in 1989 and $18 billion in 1990.

Table 1.2 shows the administration's and CBO's projections for GNP, total revenues, and revenues as a percentage of GNP for 1985 through 1990. Although the administration is more optimistic than CBO, both are forecasting moderate real GNP growth in the 3% to 4% annual range, a small increase in revenues as a percentage of GNP and, thus, moderate revenue growth.

Outlays, however, are projected to grow even more slowly than revenues as the federal government attempts to narrow the deficit. The deficit is projected to decline from 6.4% of GNP in 1983 to 1.4% in 1990 (Office of Management and Budget, 1985: 1.2). Thus virtually no increase is projected in total real dollar (1972) budget outlays—from $397 billion in 1985 to $402.2 billion estimated for 1990 (Office of Management and Budget, 1985: 6.1). Thus infrastructure investments will be competing with other budget demands in virtually a zero-sum game situation.

In a less optimistic, static economic growth scenario for the 1986-1990 period, total real dollar federal outlays would decline substantially. Total budget authority for the cumulative five-year period would total $1.69 trillion, versus $2 trillion under current CBO baseline projections—a cumulative difference of approximately $300 billion in budget authority (Congressional Budget Office, 1985b: 22-25). Under such a scenario, the probability of additional funds being allocated to infrastructure is extremely low. It is more likely that the current level of investment would be difficult to sustain.

THE ROLE OF THE
FEDERAL GOVERNMENT

The federal government affects infrastructure investments in four important ways. First, federal fiscal and monetary policies have major impacts on the rate and distribution of economic growth. Expansionary policies accelerate economic growth, which generates tax revenue. At the same time, it also increases the rate of change and alters the mix of required infrastructure. The distribution of federal outlays, the incidence of taxes—including the differential treatment of economic sectors (still contained in the tax codes despite recent tax reform legislation), and budget priorities all contribute to sectoral and spatial restructuring. Moreover, the influence of the federal government on interest and inflation rates ultimately affects the actual cost of completing capital projects.

As discussed in the next section, the recent increase in the defense budget and the uneven regional distribution of defense outlays also significantly influence the economic bases of different communities. Eventually, this affects the ability of state and local governments to generate tax revenues to support infrastructure and other public activities.

Second, the federal government makes direct investments in public physical capital assets. Table 1.3 shows that as both a percentage of total federal outlays and of GNP, infrastructure investments peaked in the mid-1960s and have declined ever since. In 1964, federal spending for major nondefense capital investments was 2.5% of total federal outlays, but fell to an estimated 1.2% by 1986. In constant 1972 dollars, outlays declined in the 1970s and have only slightly recovered in the 1980s. Thus direct capital nondefense outlays totaled $4.2 billion (1972 dollars) in 1966 and an estimated $4.6 billion (1972 dollars) in 1986. In contrast, direct capital defense outlays in the same period have increased from $21.5 billion to an estimated $33.9 billion in 1972 dollars (Office of Management and Budget, 1985: 9.2).

Third, federal regulatory policies affect the direct costs of infrastructure. Federal environmental standards have raised costs in many infrastructure-related areas. Meeting standards, often a prerequisite

TABLE 1.3

Direct Federal Outlays for Major Nondefense

Capital Investments, 1954-1986 (selected years)

	Current Prices	Constant Prices (1972)	% of Total Federal Outlays	% of GNP
	(in billions of dollars)			
1954	1.4	2.4	2.0	0.4
1956	0.9	1.4	1.3	0.2
1958	1.3	1.9	1.6	0.3
1960	1.9	2.6	2.1	0.4
1962	2.3	3.3	2.2	0.4
1964	2.9	3.8	2.5	0.5
1966	3.3	4.2	2.4	0.5
1968	2.9	3.4	1.6	0.3
1970	2.5	2.8	1.3	0.3
1972	3.6	3.6	1.5	0.3
1974	4.0	3.7	1.5	0.3
1976	5.2	3.7	1.4	0.3
1978	6.7	4.4	1.5	0.3
1980	8.1	4.2	1.4	0.3
1982	8.4	3.7	1.1	0.3
1984	9.8	4.2	1.2	0.3
1986 est.	11.7	4.6	1.2	0.3

SOURCE: Executive Office of the President, Office of Management and Budget (1985: Tables 9.1, 9.2).

for state and local governments to receive grants, have resulted in higher per unit costs of many infrastructure investments.

Costs of public capital facilities are as sensitive as other sectors of the economy to general price increases. Thus in periods of rapid inflation the costs of constructing facilities will increase and may unfavorably alter the expected ratio of benefits to costs. Project costs are also especially sensitive to changes in interest rates. Since state and local governments rely on debt instruments for approximately 40% of their sources of funds for capital projects (Peterson, 1988: Table 2), interest expense is a major component of project costs. When interest rates are high, as in the late 1970s and early 1980s, state and local governments may curtail or cancel capital improvement projects. Moreover, since several state constitutions contain provisions that prohibit borrowing above certain rates, many governments and authorities may effectively be "shut-out" from the credit markets during high interest rate periods.

Congressional debate over tax reform has also created uncertainty in recent years over the status of tax-free bonds. This has resulted in higher interest expense for government borrowers. The Tax Reform Act of 1986's lowering of marginal tax rates, as well as its curtailing or even eliminating in certain circumstances the tax-exempt status of interest income on municipal bonds, have reduced the relative attractiveness of tax-exempt investments. Thus state/local borrowers to provide investors with competitive after-tax yields, have been forced to issue debt with relatively higher yields than they did prior to tax reform.

Finally, the federal government provides direct grants to state and local governments for capital outlays. Although federal assistance has varied in importance by functional category, since 1977 it has accounted for approximately 40% of state and local government funds for fixed capital formation (Peterson, 1988: Table 2). Indications are that such federal assistance will decline significantly in forthcoming years in response to slower economic growth and changes in budget priorities.

FEDERAL BUDGET PRIORITIES

Major shifts in the composition of federal sector expenditures occur over time. The change in priorities and the competition among programs have a major impact on infrastructure investment.

Beginning in the last two years of the Carter administration, and accelerating in the Reagan administration, a major shift in federal spending priorities occurred—large cuts in domestic programs and rapid increases in defense spending.

THE DEFENSE SPENDING PRIORITY

The extent to which tradeoffs exist between domestic and defense programs has been a long debated public policy issue (Russett, 1982; Domle et al., 1983). That is, do domestic and defense programs directly compete for funds in a zero-sum type game, or is each category driven by its own unique set of determinants? Regardless of how this is resolved, the bottom line is that in the six years of the Reagan administration, domestic programs have been significantly reduced and defense spending has increased enormously.

U.S. defense outlays are projected to reach $398.8 billion by fiscal year 1989. Total defense outlays are estimated to total $1.7 trillion for fiscal years 1985-1989, or approximately $8,000 for every man, woman, and child in the country. Moreover, these are conservative expenditure estimates that do not include Veterans Administration outlays (costs of past wars), interest payments on the defense portion of the national debt, and the undetermined sums spent by state and local governments in tax expenditures to lure defense contractors to their communities (Stein, 1985).

The current buildup reverses a long-term trend that began at the conclusion of the Korean War of lower defense expenditures relative both to GNP and to total federal outlays. From the end of the Korean War to 1980, defense purchases of goods and services declined from 69.5% (1954) to 22.7% (1980) of total budget outlays. Although this trend temporarily reversed during the Vietnam War, by 1970 the defense share was back to below the pre-Vietnam percentage. Thus Kamlet and Mowery (1984), using a simultaneous equation model of federal budgeting, have found Reagan administration defense expenditures to be higher, and nondefense expenditures to be lower, than would be predicted by current fiscal conditions and the behavior of six previous presidential administrations. These findings are noteworthy, given the evidence in the public budgeting literature of incremental change and long-term stability in federal expenditure categories (Wildavsky, 1964, 1977).

It is beyond the scope of this chapter to discuss whether the size of the defense budget is appropriate for our military requirements. The subject of waste and inefficiency in defense, however, has recently received considerable public attention. Thus Kaufman (1984: 41-47), for example, has estimated that with a more relaxed U.S. military posture, but maintaining hedges against major threats, $266.7 billion could be saved from current Reagan administration projections over fiscal years 1985-1989. Kaufman's "efficient" budget, which involves no changes in military strategy, but assumes improved management and reductions in weapons duplication among the services, yields estimated savings of $174.3 billion over fiscal years 1985-1989. If such savings were realized, they would obviously not all be available for infrastructure projects. Even some share of those savings, however, could go a long way toward closing the estimated infrastructure gap of $400 billion, or $20 billion annualized, for the twenty-year period of 1980-2000.

In addition to the possible opportunity cost in reduced infrastructure investment of the defense buildup, there is also the issue of the impact of defense spending on economic development. Although enormous in total size, defense expenditures are not uniformly distributed across the country. Defense spending has played an important role in uneven regional growth, eventually contributing to differences in fiscal capacity to pay for capital facilities. Stein (1985: 8-9) has calculated that the highest total defense outlays in the nation go to the Pacific region—$56.7 billion. This is 66% higher than the national per capita average. The South Atlantic, Mountain states, and New England regions all receive per capita allocations above the national average. The other five regions receive below average per capita allocations, with the East North Central the lowest. This area (Michigan, Ohio, Indiana, Illinois, and Wisconsin), once the industrial heartland and now economically struggling, receives 43% of the national defense per capita average. It is the major loser in the defense distribution game and has hurt the area's economic growth. Clearly, an area is hurt if it does not receive its fair share of the estimated $1.7 trillion spent on defense from 1985 through 1989. Defense spending is the largest public works project administered by the federal government.

DOMESTIC PROGRAMS

Federal expenditures for domestic programs show a pattern almost completely opposite that of defense expenditures. Transfer payments to individuals—either direct or through grants to state and local governments, have increased from 17.8% in 1954 of total federal outlays to 47.0% by 1980. The state and local government grants component increased from 2.0% to 5.4% in the period. Most of the nondefense increase resulted from more generous retirement and social insurance programs, automatic increases in benefit levels tied to inflation rates, a larger pool of beneficiaries, and expansion of the Medicare program.

Beginning in 1981, the Reagan administrative initiated a number of cuts in domestic programs. These reductions are not evenly distributed, but are most drastic in social programs for low-income recipients. Entitlement programs lacking means tests, mainly Social Security and Medicare, have remained largely unscathed (Palmer and Sawhill, 1982, 1984). However, under the recently enacted Gramm-Rudman-Hollings deficit reduction legislation, a 4% reduction in programmatic budget spending by fiscal year 1987 is required. By 1991, a $104 billion reduction in baseline expenditures must be achieved. However, under the balanced budget legislation, only 35% of total government spending, including interest, is subject to automatic cuts (Cunningham and Cunningham, 1986: 19-24).

Thus a very small portion of the overall budget will absorb substantial spending reductions. Nondefense discretionary spending, which refers to programs without established entitlements or benefits, is especially vulnerable. This spending, subject to annual appropriations or to loan limits imposed in appropriations acts, supports a wide variety of activities. The bulk of infrastructure appropriations, either for direct federal purchases or in the form of federal grants to state and local governments, are in the nondiscretionary category. Included are transportation, air, water energy, land and park management, pollution control, and agriculture programs.

Since 1980, nondefense discretionary spending has declined in real terms, as a percentage of the federal budget, and as a share of GNP (Congressional Budget Office, 1985b: 38-42). This decline is likely to accelerate.

A National League of Cities survey shows the recent experience of cities with federal, general, and categorical aid for all purposes (Vincent, 1985: 42-43). In total, 60% experienced real declines in federal aid in fiscal years 1983-1984 and 66% expected a real decline for fiscal years 1984-1985. By regions, 92% of northeast cities reported a real decline in fiscal years 1983-1984. In contrast, 50% of western cities responding to the survey reported a decline for the same period. Peterson (1988) estimates that under the Gramm-Rudman-Hollings legislation, total federal assistance to state and local government would be reduced by 20% in current dollar terms by 1988, with a 55 billion cut in federal capital assistance.

THE FISCAL CONDITION OF
STATE AND LOCAL GOVERNMENTS

State and local governments are the major purchasers of our nation's public, nondefense capital facilities. While federal direct outlays for major infrastructure totaled $9.8 billion in 1984 (Table 1.3), state and local government-fixed capital formations expenditures equaled $59.4 billion (Peterson, 1988: Table 1.2). Although federal grants accounted for approximately 40% of state/local fund sources to support these expenditures, the remainder is financed by state/local debt offerings and from current revenues.

With the projected decline in federal assistance, the nation's ability to meet its infrastructure needs adequately is largely dependent on the economic health and fiscal capacity of state and local governments. In turn, this is largely determined by international and national economic trends, spatial, cyclical, and sectoral restructuring, and the success and aggressiveness of community economic development programs. Healthy, growing state/local economic bases provide an expanded potential for generating revenues; declining bases limit revenue raising ability. These conditions also affect bond ratings and, ultimately, the interest rates paid by state/local borrowers. That is, the weaker the local economy, generally the lower its bond ratings, and the higher the interest costs.

Economic growth in the United States has been quite unevenly distributed. While many areas have been growing and prosperous, others are declining and distressed. Several prominent academic, research institutions and government agencies have developed indices to measure and compare the economic, physical, and social health of communities. The Brookings Institution's Urban Conditions Index, for example, measures community physical development needs relative to population changes and socioeconomic conditions (Nathan and Dommel, 1981). Indices developed by government agencies include the Urban Needs Index (Congressional Budget Office), Community Needs Index (Department of Housing and Urban Development), and the Urban Fiscal Strain Index (Department of the Treasury). Several of these indices have been incorporated in the distributional formulas of such major federal programs as Urban Development Action Grants, Revenue Sharing, and Community Development Block Grants.

Despite differences in variable selection, models, and approaches, the indices cover essentially similar community characteristics—socio-economic, physical, fiscal, and economic development. A complete portrayal of community distress would cover these four categories. However, for our purposes the fiscal dimension is most important and is briefly discussed below.

There are both short-term and long-term measures of fiscal stress. A useful short-term indicator is government difficulty in balancing its current budget. That is, its ability to collect the revenues necessary to pay for a basic package of public services. Long-term or "structural" fiscal distress can be defined as a long-term imbalance between responsibilities and revenues. The imbalance could stem from an unfavorable combination of six major factors: size of the tax base, level of intergovernmental aid, tax collections of overlying governments, range of service responsibilities, costs of local production, and level of service needs (Advisory Commission on Intergovernmental Relations, 1985: 12-14).

Table 1.4 contains data for three dimensions of budgetary distress: the current balance between revenues and expenditures (surplus or

TABLE 1.4
Budgetary Fiscal Distress Measures

	All	Northeast	Central	South	West
Number of cities	153	28	41	52	32
(1) Average current account surplus or deficit as percentage of budget (higher is better)					
1972	14.5	9.4	14.3	15.0	18.3
1977	13.7	0.1	14.9	17.8	17.2
(2) Average short-term debt as percentage of total revenues (lower is better)					
1972	17.3	31.6	21.7	11.4	8.6
1977	8.4	15.7	13.7	3.7	2.7
(3) Average debt service cost as percentage of total revenues (lower is better)					
1972	30.3	40.9	35.6	27.9	18.1
1977	19.6	25.7	25.5	16.1	12.6

SOURCE: Advisory Commission on Intergovernmental Relations (1985: 13). Based on Bradbury (1982: 33-43; 1983: 32-43).

deficit), average short-term debt as a percentage of total revenues, and average debt service costs as a percentage of total revenues. As the data show, the northeast had the worst scores on all measures in 1972 and 1977. That is, the lowest budget surpluses, highest dependence on short-term debt, and the largest debt and debt service costs of all cities (Advisory Commission on Intergovernmental Relations, 1985: 11-13).

Similarly, a study by the Joint Economic Committee (U.S. Congress, 1981) shows that fiscal distress in U.S. cities is still quite substantial. The study found that for all cities with populations of 10,000 or more, the average increase in revenues and expenditures did not match the inflation rates in 1979 and 1980. In total, 70% of the largest cities experienced deficits in 1980. The economic recovery of recent years has certainly improved these conditions. Nevertheless, several cities are still experiencing considerable distress. Nor can cities necessarily expect to receive help from the states. Although the Reagan administrative has sought to shift responsibility from the federal government to the states, several of the latter are also experiencing difficulties. At the end of fiscal year 1983, nineteen states had projected budget deficits and 35 states had reduced their spending levels to below that year's proposed budget (Advisory Commission on Intergovernmental Relations, 1985).

Given the fiscal conditions of many state and local governments, it is therefore not at all surprising that state/local capital outlays in constant 1972 dollars fell by 10% in fiscal year 1980-1981 and 6.7% in 1981-1982 (Advisory Commission on Intergovernmental Relations, 1984: 10). State and local governments cannot be expected to even maintain, let alone increase, expenditures for infrastructure, unless their fiscal conditions significantly improve.

CONCLUSIONS AND RECOMMENDATIONS

An infrastructure crisis does indeed exist in the United States. In the interests of public safety, economic development, and the effective delivery of services, there is a need for considerable investment in the repair, maintenance, and new construction of our capital stock. Depending on stage of economic development, demographics, previous levels of investment in construction and maintenance, age and condition of facilities, and fiscal capacities, there are considerable differences among communities in level and type of needs—and their ability to respond to them. The crisis is not in our lack of knowledge/expertise on how to build capital facilities, but in our lack of resource commitment to public facilities.

Improvements in planning, management, and infrastructure technologies have the potential to reduce both the level and cost of needs. However, such improvements can only make a small dent in the projected $400 billion shortfall to the year 2000 (Kaplan, 1988).

This shortfall is not simply the result of an unwillingness to increase taxes. Instead, it stems from a complex array of economic, social, and political factors. Economic cyclical and structural forces—at a national and international level, federal fiscal and monetary policies, budget priorities, and spatial development patterns have all combined to produce the current "crisis" in infrastructure.

The infrastructure problem cannot be solved if it is viewed as an isolated problem. It must be addressed in the larger policy contexts of national growth strategies, economic development planning, fiscal and monetary policies, and federal budget priorities.

NOTES

1. The national infrastructure study covers only the capital requirements and revenues for highways, sewerage, water, and other transportation (Kaplan, 1988). A broad

definition of infrastructure would also include facilities such as schools, hospitals, airports, libraries, parks, and so on. A study by ABT Associates (1980) identified 37 categories of infrastructure facilities.

2. Denison (1985: xxi) contains a lengthy discussion on the concept of potential output. He defines national income in 1972 prices in any year, "as the value that national output in 1972 prices would have taken if (1) unemployment had been at 4% of the civilian labor force sixteen years of age and over; (2) the intensity of utilization of resources that were in use had been at that rate every year, namely, that which on the average would be associated with a 4% unemployment rate; and (3) other conditions had been those that actually prevailed in that year."

REFERENCES

ABT Associates (1980) "National rural community facilities assessment study: pilot phase." Final report, Cambridge, MA.

Advisory Commission on Intergovernmental Relations (1984) Financing Public Physical Infrastructure. Washington, DC: author.

Advisory Commission on Intergovernmental Relations (1985) The States and Distressed Communities: The Final Report. Washington, DC: author.

Advisory Commission on Intergovernmental Relations (1986) Significant Features of Fiscal Federalism, 1985-86 Edition. Washington, DC: author.

BIRCH, D. (1984) "The changing rules of the game: finding a niche thoughtware economy." Economic Development Commentary 8: 12-16.

CHOATE, P. and S. WALTER (1983) America in Ruins: The Decaying Infrastructure. Durham, NC: Duke Press.

Congressional Budget Office (1985a) An Analysis of the President's Budgetary Proposals for Fiscal Year 1986. Washington, DC: Government Printing Office.

Congressional Budget Office (1985b) Reducing the Deficit: Spending and Revenue Options: A Report to the Senate and House Committee on the Budget—Part II. Washington, DC: Government Printing Office.

CUNNINGHAM, T. and R. CUNNINGHAM (1986) "Projecting federal deficits and the impact of the Gramm-Rudman-Hollings budget cuts." Economic Rev., Atlanta, Federal Reserve Bank of Atlanta (May): 19-24.

DENNISON, E. (1985) Trends in American Economic Growth, 1929-1982. Washington, DC: Brookings Institution.

DOMLE, W., ECHENBERG, R., and C. KELLEHER (1983) "The illusion of choice: defense and welfare in advanced industrial democracies, 1948-1978." Amer. Pol. Sci. Rev. 77: 19-35.

GRUMWALD, J. and FLAMM, K. (1985) The Global Factory. Washington, DC: Brookings Institution.

KAMLET, M. and D. MOWERY (1984) "Upsetting national priorities: an analysis of the Reagan budget." Presented at the conference on Allocation and Distributional Impacts of Reagan policies in Alexandria, Virginia.

KAPLAN, M. (1988) "Infrastructure needs assessment: methodological problems and opportunities," in J. M. Stein (ed.) Public Infrastructure Planning and Management. Newbury Park, CA: Sage.

KAUFMAN, W. (1984) The 1985 Defense Budget. Washington, DC: Brookings Institution.

KNIGHT, R. (1982) "City development in advanced industrial societies," in G. Gappert and R. Knight (eds.) Cities in the 21st Century. Newbury Park, CA: Sage.

LAWRENCE, R. (1984) Can America Compete? Washington, DC: Brookings Institution.

NATHAN, R. and P. DOMMEL (1981) "Issues and techniques for federal grant-in-aid-allocations to distressed cities." Urban Affairs Papers, pp. 21-34.

NICOL, L. (1985) "Communications technology: economic and spatial impacts," pp. 191-209 in M. Castells (ed.) High Technology, Space and Society. Newbury Park, CA: Sage.

NOYELLE, T. (1984) "The service era: focusing public policy on people and places." Economic Development Commentary 8: 12-17.

Office of Management and Budget (1985) Historical Tables: Budget of the United States Government. Washington, DC: Government Printing Office.

PALMER, J. and I. SAWHILL (1982) "Perspectives on the Reagan experiment," pp. 1-30 in J. Palmer and I. Sawhill (eds.) The Reagan Experiment. Washington, DC: Urban Institute.

PALMER, J. and I. SAWHILL (1984) The Reagan Record. Washington, DC: Urban Institute.

PETERSON, J. E. (1988) "Infrastructure financing: examining the record and considering the options," in J. M. Stein (ed.) Public Infrastructure Planning and Management. Newbury Park, CA: Sage.

RUSSETT, B. (1982) "Defense expenditures and national well-being." Amer. Pol. Sci. Rev. 76: 767-777.

STEIN, J. (1985) "Military spending, economic development and conversion planning." Presented at the Association of Collegiate Schools of Planning (ACSP) conference, Atlanta, Georgia.

U.S. Congress, Joint Economic Committee (1981) "Trends in the fiscal condition of cities, 1982." Washington, DC: Government Printing Office.

VINCENT, F. (1985) City Fiscal Conditions and Outlook for Fiscal 1985. Washington, DC: National League of Cities.

WILDAVSKY, A. (1964) The Politics of the Budgetary Process. Boston: Little, Brown.

WILDAVSKY, A. (1977) Budgeting: A Comparative Theory of Budgetary Processes. Boston: Little, Brown.

Part II

Perspective on the Infrastructure "Crisis"

2

Infrastructure Needs Assessment:
Methodological Problems and Opportunities

MARSHALL KAPLAN

INFRASTRUCTURE WAS "in" during the late seventies and early eighties. The media had made the status or condition of America's streets, highways, transit and water systems a popular subject in the Halls of Ivy as well as the halls of Congress. We were told that our nation's economic productivity and quality of life would suffer if we didn't respond to infrastructure problems.

In response to these concerns, the Joint Economic Committee of Congress created the National Infrastructure Advisory Committee (NIAC), a representative group of academic, public, and private sector leaders. As staff director, I headed the effort to prepare a comprehensive analysis of the nation's infrastructure needs.

Absence of national data regarding infrastructure at the federal government level led to the development of a bottoms-up or state-by-state approach to the NIAC study. All fifty states were asked to participate, but only twenty-three states responded positively. Fortunately, they were located in all regions of the nation and illustrated a reasonable array of policy concerns and characteristics.

Universities from participating states, selected by the coordinating core staff, were asked to prepare snapshot analyses of then current infrastructure conditions in their state and to estimate anticipated needs and revenues through the year 2000. Comparative analyses among and between studied states were prepared by core staff. They were combined with extrapolation of aggregate state data to generate national findings.

NIAC submitted its final report, *Hard Choices*, to the Joint Economic Committee of Congress in the Spring of 1984 (Kaplan et al., 1984). The report provided an aggregate national estimate of infrastruc-

TABLE 2.1

Total Projected Per Capita Capital Requirements
and Revenue for Highways, Sewerage, Water, and
Other Transportation (in dollars)

Region	Needs	Revenue	Shortfall
Northeast	262	139	123
Midwest	351	175	176
South	245	163	82
South-Central	266	173	93
West	222	136	86

ture needs through the year 2000. According to the Committee, America will have to spend close to $1.15 trillion to repair, maintain, and develop basic infrastructure—transportation, water, and sewer systems—to avoid major quality of life and productivity problems. Because nearly $714 billion will be available from federal and state revenues, the infrastructure funding "gap" requiring policy attention will total $400 billion or, if annualized, nearly $20 billion each year (1982 constant dollars). However, as explained later in the chapter, because of various methodological problems, including unreliable data and lack of a widely accepted definition of needs for each category of infrastructure, these estimates are subject to considerable error.

Clearly, NIAC's numbers were politically and substantively compelling. Contrary to media accounts of a three trillion dollar infrastructure bill, the Committee's projected deficit seemed manageable.[1] Moreover, the Committee's analysis portrayed significant infrastructure needs in all regions of the country—not just in the older northeast and midwest states as generally believed. For example, in Maine, nearly two-thirds of the highway system required immediate improvement; in Alabama, 53% of the county-maintained bridges were in trouble; and in Washington, only 14% of the population was served by facilities providing secondary waste water treatment. The annual per capita gap between needs and available resources through the year 2000 will be $86 in the West, $82 in the South, $123 in the Northeast, $88 in the South Central states, and $176 in the Midwest. These results are shown in Tables 2.1 and 2.2.

Averages oftentimes blur or hide variations regarding infrastructure needs internal to regions. Indeed, from a national policy perspective, differences within regions often appeared more relevant than differences between regions. Table 2.3 illustrates both average per capita and the range of per capita needs by region.

TABLE 2.2

Ranking (Highest to Lowest) of States According to Real Annual Per Capital Needs
1983 to 2000, by Functional Category

Rank	Highways State	Highways Per Capita Need	Other Transportation State	Other Transportation Per Capita Need	Sewerage State	Sewerage Per Capita Need	Water State	Water Per Capita Need	Subtotal State	Subtotal Per Capita Need
01	Indiana	$309	Alabama	$188	Indiana	$88	Oklahoma	$68	Indiana	$405
02	Kentucky	279	New York	126	Massachusetts	81	Oregon	59	Alabama	380
03	Tennessee	273	Massachusetts	80	Maine	79	New Mexico	44	New York	363
04	Ohio	244	Colorado	66	Washington	73	Colorado	30	Kentucky	344
05	Louisiana	227	New Jersey	41	Oregon	60	California	28	Ohio	321
06	Missouri	218	California	31	New York	58	New York	24	Tennessee	314
07	Montana	199	Oregon	23	Ohio	56	New Jersey	22	Missouri	289
08	Oklahoma	197	Ohio	21	New Jersey	44	Kentucky	19	Oklahoma	272
09	Maryland	194	Missouri	19	Kentucky	42	Missouri	19	Louisiana	258
10	Texas	185	Maryland	17	California	34	Texas	19	Oregon	258
11	Alabama	166	New Mexico	14	Missouri	34	Washington	19	Massachusetts	257
12	North Carolina	162	Maine	13	Louisiana	28	North Carolina	16	Colorado	252
13	New York	154	North Carolina	9	Tennessee	22	Tennessee	13	Maryland	239
14	Colorado	138	Indiana	8	Maryland	20	Maryland	13	New Jersey	239
15	Washington	135	Florida	6	Colorado	18	Alabama	12	Washington	227
16	New Jersey	132	Montana	6	Texas	18	Massachusetts	11	Texas	222
17	Oregon	116	Tennessee	6	North Carolina	15	Maryland	8	Montana	218
18	Florida	111	Kentucky	4	South Carolina	15	Florida	5	North Carolina	202
19	New Mexico	96	Louisiana	3	Alabama	13	Montana	5	California	184
20	California	90	South Carolina	3	New Mexico	13	Indiana	N/A	Maine	169
21	Massachusetts	86	Oklahoma	2	Florida	7	Louisiana	N/A	New Mexico	167
22	South Carolina	84	Texas	N/A	Montana	7	Maine	N/A	Florida	129
23	Maine	77	Washington	N/A	Oklahoma	5	Ohio	N/A	South Carolina	109
	avg.	168	avg.	33	avg.	36	avg.	23	avg.	271

NOTE: The table is based on simple averages. Weight in needs by population would result in per capita needs as follows: Northeast, $306; Midwest, $350; South, $182; South Central, $243; and West, $205. Table dated December 27, 1983.

37

TABLE 2.3
Summary of Annual Per Capita Needs by Region

Category	Northeast	Midwest	South	South-Central	West
Highways					
Average	$112	$257	$181	$203	$129
Range	77-154	218-309	84-279	185-227	90-199
Other transportation					
Average	$65	$16	$33	$3	$28
Range	13-126	8-21	3-188	2-3	6-66
Sewerage					
Average	$65	$59	$19	$17	$34
Range	44-86	35-91	9-47	6-32	8-89
Water					
Average	$19	$19	$11	$44	$31
Range	11-24	N/A	5-19	19-68	5-59
Total					
Average	$262	$351	$245	$266	$222
Range	239-363	N/A	109-380	N/A	167-258

Because NIAC's numbers show infrastructure to be a national problem, Congress would not have to fight the Frostbelt/Sunbelt war to achieve consensus on new initiatives; neither would it have to contemplate expenditure estimates that placed the subject in an "Alice in Wonderland" category. Thus NIAC's report kept the infrastructure issue alive and served Congress well. The estimates of needs, revenues, and gaps, were important in generating long overdue national policy debates about appropriate policy responses.

INSTITUTIONAL AND
METHODOLOGICAL PROBLEMS

An important lesson learned from the NIAC study is that there is a need for much more analytical work to be done before Congress and respective state and local governments can manage infrastructure problems. Regrettably, very few states and local governments have seen fit to initiate comprehensive inventories of infrastructure, analyses of infrastructure needs, and thorough reviews of infrastructure investment options. Those states and local governments that claimed needs analysis generally provided the NIAC study team with a wish list or a list of assumed infrastructure desires aggregated by department. Only a handful of jurisdictions made even a passing attempt to define priorities among infrastructure projects. Even fewer were able to reflect in their submittals opportunity costing equations or analyses. That is, few states ask "what if" questions concerning infrastructure investment options or generate comparisons between the benefits and costs of varied infrastructure investments and/or between infrastructure investments and other public investment priorities.

Absence of appropriate or strategic state and local government background studies bothered many members of NIAC. They asked, "How could states and cities seek federal funds," or even more relevant, "How could states and cities spend their own funds for infrastructure without knowing more than most did about needs?" However, state and local government incapacity, while surprising, was understandable in light of several institutional and methodological problems.

ABSENCE OF CLEAR-CUT AGREEMENT
ON INFRASTRUCTURE NEED ASSESSMENTS

Only a few states and localities had initiated infrastructure needs analyses. These jurisdictions, and the others then considering needs assessments, rarely agreed on what infrastructure categories should be subject to analysis. Most states and localities that were studying their infrastructure needs limited their analysis to "basic" infrastructure— highways and bridges, and water and sewer systems. Relatively few states included public buildings, transit facilities, public and quasi- public utilities. Only a handful encompassed solid waste disposal.

The variation among states and localities emanated from differences in public sector responsibilities and in the age of developed infrastructure. Generally, if the infrastructure function was administered by a quasi-public or private sector entity or if it was not under the direct confines of the state and locality, it was not covered or was covered only partially in state and local infrastructure assessments. Similarly, older infrastructure was less likely to be included in state or local inventories or analyses. In this context, some jurisdictions "didn't know where the infrastructure was."

State and local jurisdictions rarely agreed on how to define needs or what factors generate needs. Most illustrated needs related to anticipated growth; some talked about needs generated by an area's changing economic and demographic characteristics. Only a handful accom- modated needs related to depreciation and/or replacement. Maintenance-related needs were not uniformly treated in state and local government analyses and/or budgets. Finally, as noted in the NIAC report, researchers were not always able to distinguish "backlog," "recurring," and "growth-oriented" needs. Often a needs assessment would focus on existing facilities that currently fall below standards (backlog needs). The amount specified for investment, however, would be to not simply restore the facility, but to expand, modify, or replace it to meet projected and uncertain levels of demand.

Other problems include needs assessments that focus on backlog needs and fail to take into account that other facilities will fall into the substandard category sometime in the future, if not worked on in the interim. In these instances, estimates of need are understated.[2] In other cases, however, it is likely that needs estimates are overstated. For example, a state may have prepared a capital needs assessment covering a 10-year period. Often these assessments include a substantial amount to bring existing facilities up to standard. Ideally, the investment required to cope with this backlog would be subtracted before extrapolating the 10-year investment to the longer timeframe required in this study. Often, however, the backlog portion of the needs estimate is not separately identified so that it is not possible to make the desired adjustment (Kaplan et al., 1984: 18).

ABSENCE OF CLEAR-CUT
RESPONSIBILITIES FOR ANALYSIS

Very few states and localities assigned their budget offices substantive responsibility for evaluating, amending, and/or prioritizing departmental capital budget requests. Coordinated capital budget processes, let alone capital budgets, were often a causality of time, staff, and political constraints.

The governor's/mayor's/city manager's control over capital investment often was muted by responsibilities assigned to independent commissions or independent districts. It was also frustrated by legislative earmarking of funds for infrastructure, federal funding formulae as well as federal mandates regarding infrastructure development.

No state was able to reconcile easily and/or provide a coordinated analysis of state and local government requests. Paucity of or uneven data and analysis at the state level was matched by similar or worse situations at the local government and/or special district level. Most local entities found themselves "running fast to merely stay even" with what they perceived to be crisis generated infrastructure needs. Capital improvement programs and budgets, where they existed, were generally aggregations of departmental desires. Lack of interjurisdictional relationships and lack of sufficient staff resources generally frustrated development of a "comprehensive" picture of infrastructure conditions, needs, and likely available revenues.

ABSENCE OF CONSENSUS
REGARDING VALUES

Estimates of needs were often premised on the values of the analyst. For example, tradeoffs exist over absolute (or as close to absolute) bridge safety versus other design variables. Similar tradeoffs exist with other cost loading factors associated with the design of water, sewer, and transportation systems. Dominance of the value setters by producer and professional groups, almost to the exclusion of the consumer and/or other public interest groups, generated skewed assessments. Clearly, values concerning infrastructure development might not be the same if producers and consumers, professionals and users were at the table. It is difficult to balance capital needs with social service needs if the values of both advocates and related professionals are never approximated in one place.

ABSENCE OF
AGREED UPON STANDARDS

Professional values regarding safety or amenity generally were converted into infrastructure standards in every area of the nation. Because the conversion process, again, often involved only a limited number of viewpoints—primarily producers and professionals—infrastructure standards often lacked relevance to a state or community's economic constraints or to noninfrastructure concerns. Would we design our bridges for maximum safety or absolute minimal risk if we knew that by doing so we could not repair key roads . . . or develop needed hospitals, and so on? Often times, the last ounce of safety or protection will raise the costs exorbitantly. Thus a public review process with wide participation, not just of engineers, but also of consumers, is necessary to discuss and understand tradeoffs between safety and other public priorities.

Even where infrastructure standards appeared responsible and consistent with perceived public interest or community objectives, their relationship to agreed upon or desired service levels seemed often tenuous. Enough information about community service preferences and/or community service patterns and infrastructure design simply does not exist to make the approximation of need more than solid guesswork.

ABSENCE OF ATTENTION
TO PRICE SENSITIVITY

Existing standards generally assume that infrastructure costs or prices will remain static. Infrastructure needs likely will change dramatically, if costs change and/or if government limits or eliminates various cost driven subsidies. Users of infrastructure, if they act rationally, "determine how much they want . . . only after they know the price and can calculate how much of alternative goods and services they have to forego" (Kaplan et al., 1984: 17). Clearly, water use and the consequent demand for water system development would change if farmers or ranchers were required to pay the full costs of extracting and distributing the water they consume. Similarly, the use of rapid transit systems would likely decline if riders were required to pay the full costs of construction, maintenance, and operations. How many airports would the nation need if airlines or private planes paid the full cost of service? Will Americans want bridges that are 100% safe or will they settle for something less, if the cost of the better bridge makes it inaccessible regarding household budgets?

INADEQUATE GROWTH
OR GROWTH-RELATED DATA

Projections of infrastructure need and condition are premised, in part, on projections of use and related population and economic growth trends. Nevertheless, our technical skills in making demographic and economic projections are limited. Thus it is often difficult to secure "hard" or reliable data concerning the number of future infrastructure users and the relevant characteristics associated with the intensity of their use patterns.

Similarly, it is difficult to gain a handle on infrastructure revenues and likely investments. Since infrastructure maintenance and construction levels are sensitive to available public sector monies (in turn sensitive to unpredictable or uncontrollable economic and political events), it is sometimes tough to estimate short- or long-term revenues. Revenue forecasting is difficult given the potential for economic, political, social, and legal changes.

INABILITY TO RECONCILE ISSUES RELATED TO PUBLIC PURPOSE AND PUBLIC RESPONSIBILITY

State and local governments and the private sector have used innovative means to finance infrastructure. For example, builders have increasingly front-loaded the costs of residential developments onto new home buyers with impact fees (See Nelson, this volume). While ingenuity regarding financing by public and private sectors is to be commended, a concern is that it has blurred the demarcation between heretofore public and private sector goods and responsibilities.

Equity as well as efficiency questions must be responded to in light of the expanded adoption of user fees and/or other revenue sources directly related to the ostensible beneficiaries of infrastructure. Is it fair to shift a once general household burden regarding financing of infrastructure to select groups? Can/should we control or limit use of infrastructure to beneficiaries and/or to people or groups who can or will pay for use? Can we control the incidence of benefits and/or costs? How do we handle the poor? If they can't pay the toll or tariff, should they be able to use freeways . . . parks, and the like? Until these public policy issues are resolved, formal estimates of infrastructure needs and revenues must remain open-ended and conjectural.

FUTURE DIRECTIONS

Despite the institutional and methodological problems involved, intensive public and, indeed, private sector involvement in refining infrastructure need assessments is essential. The infrastructure bill is and will remain an expensive one. Failure to begin making at least partial payments in a planned manner will condemn us to significant quality of life and productivity difficulties. Failure to define infrastructure needs, strategically, will condemn us to inefficient and unfair expenditures and revenue patterns. It is crucial that future national infrastructure initiatives be matched by state and local government efforts to put their own analytical houses in order. Development of mature state and local capital budgeting processes—processes that reflect refined analyses of infrastructure needs and available revenues and that measure infrastructure needs in the context of other public needs—should command priority attention.

NOTES

1. Media accounts were premised on anecdotes from various states. No firm handle existed on the total costs to respond to national need. NIAC's numbers included only basic infrastructure. An analysis that included schools, hospitals, and so on might generate a larger figure. However, an analysis that was premised on accepted opportunity costing techniques and revised standards would likely produce countervailing or downward pressure on need estimates.

2. I am indebted to the work of my colleague, Dr. Peggy Cuciti. Her thinking concerning methodological problems provided the background and catalyst to much of my own analyses. I commend the Ford Foundation supported handbook titled *Planning for Infrastructure: A Handbook for State and Local Officials*, which Ms. Cuciti developed for state and local government (University of Colorado, Center for Public/Private Sector Cooperation, 1985).

REFERENCES

KAPLAN, M., P. CUCITI, F. CESARIO, D. DONALD, et al. (1984) "Hard choices, a report on the increasing gap between America's infrastructure needs and our ability to pay for them." Study for the Subcommittee on Economic Goals and Intergovernmental Policy of the Joint Economic Committee of the Congress of the United States. Washington, DC: Government Printing Office.

NELSON, A. C. (1988) "Using development impact fees to finance growth," in J. M. Stein (ed.) Public Infrastructure Planning and Management. Newbury Park, CA: Sage.

3

Measuring Infrastructure Needs: Focus on Highways

DOUGLASS B. LEE

WHENEVER LISTS OF infrastructure "needs" are given, they always include highways, streets, bridges, or roads, and often several of these. "Crumbling infrastructure" typically means pavement and bridges. A large share of the anecdotal evidence offered in the popular press pertains to highway facilities, such as collapses of bridges, potholes, and schoolchildren having to walk across bridges too weak to carry them and their school bus at the same time.

Currently, expenditures on highways amount to about $45 billion per year, for all purposes by all levels of government. To replace the existing capital stock would require something in the range of one to three trillion dollars.[1] The system is an essential part of the nation's productive capacity, so underinvestment in highway infrastructure is of major direct and indirect economic significance. If the system is deteriorating, we should pay attention.

Much has been written recently about highway infrastructure needs, but different sources are inconsistent. Newspaper and magazine accounts suggest a high degree of urgency about the problem, but the evidence is largely circumstantial and the prescriptions are vague. More systematic surveys show a good deal of deterioration in selected categories (particularly bridges), but the magnitudes are not remarkable. At the other end of the spectrum, the Federal Highway Administration (FHWA) estimates, in its 1983 and 1985 needs reports to Congress, that current capital expenditures are sufficient to maintain existing performance and gradually improve pavement quality. Hence some reconciliation is needed that accounts for these differences.

POPULAR MYTHS

Numerous myths surround the topic of infrastructure deterioration and financing, but only two will be singled out for attention:

Deterioration increases costs. Poor pavement quality and capacity limitations do create costs, in the form of vehicle wear and delay, but these are not the only costs that should be considered. Not all of the existing highway infrastructure is worth rebuilding, because the user cost savings that would result from the investment are less than the costs of the reconstruction. With a high enough traffic volume, the net effect of rebuilding is to lower costs, but for low-volume segments the net result is increased costs. It is necessary to be selective in which highways are rebuilt.

Local governments cannot afford the expenditures. For some kinds of public services (e.g., schools), the tax base (real property) commonly used is not distributed coincidentally with the costs (schoolchildren), so equity urges that there be some tax base sharing from "rich" to "poor" communities. Thus the federal (or at least higher) level of government should undertake the financing. For highways, these arguments do not apply: Highways can and should be financed by users, and users are at least no worse off than the average taxpayer and probably better off. Local governments may prefer that some other level of government raise the necessary revenues, but local governments can levy user charges as well as the federal government. To claim that they can't afford to do so is to say that users are unwilling to pay for their highways.

DEFINITION OF "NEED"

Many analysts gag at the notion of "need" and the implication that needs are somehow inherent and exist independently of costs or other alternatives. The word, however, has stuck, and the only option left is to define need in a technical manner that avoids the value-laden connotations of the vernacular term. Such a definition, useful for purposes of assessing highway infrastructure needs and already accepted by many analysts, is this: An infrastructure need is any capital project for which the benefits exceed the costs.[2] Both benefits and costs are construed broadly, so as to include all impacts (positive and negative) of value, whether quantifiable in dollar terms or not, and the social or opportunity costs of all resources consumed whether their value is reflected in market prices or not. This definition provides a framework within which the need for greater or lesser levels of investment can be evaluated.

By and large, highway capital programming decisions have not been guided explicitly by benefit-cost criteria, and highway needs assessments also have used other methods. During the decades after World War II, when the highway system was expanding and a large share of the expenditures went for constructing new highways and paving dirt roads, needs were based on engineering design standards and long-range plans. It would be fair to describe tabulations of needs during this period as "wish lists." As the capacity and quality of the system improved, the marginal benefits of further new construction declined while costs rose. Toward the end of the 1960s the momentum slowed, due entirely to a political reaction against further new construction rather than any technical analysis indicating that the major needs had been met. In the last ten to fifteen years, highway needs assessments at the state and federal levels have become progressively more sophisticated and less biased, but they still do not apply a benefit-cost test. Thus an attempt to judge the various claims regarding highway capital needs requires at least some degree of independent analysis.

PREVIOUS HIGHWAY NEEDS ESTIMATES

Interest in infrastructure "needs" passes through peaks and valleys, so that although many studies have been done, there is little continuity or cumulative knowledge. The exception is FHWA's biennial highway needs report to Congress, and it is the only study worth serious consideration for original assessment of highway needs. The others either do no more than pass on second-hand information from somewhere else, or they collect a few local data and perform tabulations that are suggestive but incomplete, or they perform a superficial analysis for self-serving purposes. Most of these studies seek to call attention to infrastructure problems in general, and include highways as only one, albeit prominent, example, without attempting additional analysis. A few of the studies are conceptually sound, but offer no new empirical information on highways.

Regarding highways, the thrust of these studies tends to follow several themes. One is the observation that the physical quality of the existing system is deteriorating faster than it is being restored. Another is the observation that capital expenditures in real terms have declined from their mid-1960s peak. In general, the more strident is the study in its alarms, the less substance it contains.

FHWA's studies are authoritative and informative, based as they are on an extensive data reporting and modeling system. From the standpoint of confronting the true needs for investment in the nation's highways, however, the studies suffer from two defects. One is the absence of a benefit-cost framework for guiding the analysis. Instead, an evolutionary form of sufficiency ratings is used in a simulation model to forecast the likely patterns of highway improvements over a twenty-year period, under various budgetary restrictions. The basic question of how much investment *should* be undertaken cannot be addressed in this framework. The second defect is an emphasis on those portions of the highway system of interest at the national level, largely ignoring the bulk of the total mileage that lies in the collector and local systems. This does not mean their needs estimates are incorrect, but that the studies do not tackle directly the issue of existing segments that are not worth improving because of low traffic volumes.

INDEPENDENT NEEDS ESTIMATES

Several strategies might be followed, separately or in combination, for constructing an estimate of national highway investment needs:

(1) Use aggregate secondary data and make assumptions to derive several ballpark estimates that provide a sense of the approximate magnitude of needs.
(2) Assess the degree to which the engineering standards and minimum tolerable conditions (MTCs) used for highway programming and needs analysis yield results consistent with benefit-cost evaluation.
(3) Construct subsystem estimates, based on prototypical segments and conditions, that can be expanded to represent the entire system.
(4) Evaluate all candidate highway investment projects at the applicable level of government, using benefit-cost analysis, and sum the results for all projects generating positive net benefits.

The last approach (4) is preferred, but is not feasible until all highway departments adopt a benefit-cost standard and use the same overall methods. A prototype analysis (3) could readily be accomplished using FHWA's data base, and would be the next step in the evolution of their methodology, but has not yet been done. Analysis of bias in the

standards (2) could be used to develop shortcut rule-of-thumb procedures for evaluating highway improvement projects, without doing a
full benefit-cost analysis for each project. But, the analysis needed to
determine whether existing standards yield efficient projects would be
approximately the same as carrying out the third approach. There was a
time when it was easy to say that the application of volume-to-capacity,
pavement quality, geometric, and safety standards created a bias toward
overdesigned and underutilized highways, but these standards have
evolved (at least for needs analysis) to the point where the bias, if it
exists, is not obvious. Thus, in the short term, the "circumstantial
evidence" strategy (1) is the only feasible option, incorporating some of
(3) as well.

The ideal investment level. Optimizing the capital stock requires the
ability to accomplish two types of decisions: select the right total
amount to invest, and choose the best projects within that total.
Obviously, the first depends at least in part upon the second. If a
benefit-cost criterion was followed for each project, then (in principle)
the set of all feasible projects could be arrayed on a scale from most
worthwhile to least. A graph of cumulative costs and benefits would
then look like the diagram in Figure 3.1, with the level of total
investment along the horizontal axis and benefits or costs on the
vertical. The ideal level is where the difference between total benefits and
total costs is the greatest, which happens when the slopes of the two
curves are equal, that is, marginal benefit equals marginal cost.
Additional investment still increases total benefits, but at a rate slower
than it increases total costs.

This is the *efficient* (ideal, or optimum) level of investment. The
hypothesis asserted here is that actual investment in the highway system
as a whole has proceeded well beyond the efficient level, and that simply
maintaining and replacing all of the existing highway system when it
wears out is not worthwhile. The optimum system is *less* than what
currently exists, and any assessment of highway investment needs
should incorporate the pruning of excess mileage.

The question of what is the efficient level cannot be answered directly,
but aspects of the question can be viewed from several perspectives. The
condition of the system can be checked for deterioration. The process
for evaluating individual projects can be assessed to see how far it
deviates from a benefit-cost test. Levels of utilization or congestion can
be reviewed to determine the relative productivity of the various
subsystems. Finally, a simple performance standard—long-run cost per

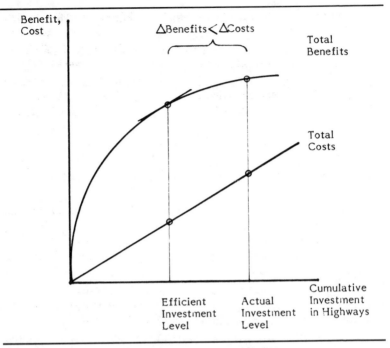

Figure 3.1 Determination of the Optimum Investment Level

vehicle mile—can be used to flag those portions of the system that do not seem to be generating the amount of traffic that warrants retention in the system.

Project-level evaluation. Figure 3.2 shows a simplified model of the investment decision process as it applies to a single highway segment. Until a decision must be made on a given link, the segment can be ignored. If the segment is worth retaining as part of the network, investment can range from resurfacing, at one end, to upgrading to expressway standards at the other. Resurfacing restores the surface and protects the pavement and base. Reconstruction eventually may be necessary, and also provides the opportunity for safety and geometric improvements.

Congestion and heavy truck traffic do not, by themselves, warrant capacity or strength increases. The gap between user charges and either short- or long-run marginal cost is greatest for vehicles operating in congested times and places, and for heavy trucks. Hence there is no evidence that the benefits of the incremental usage, demonstrated by

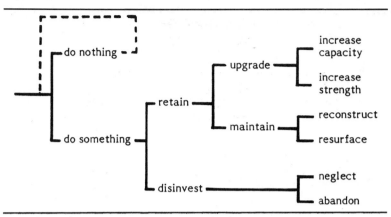

Figure 3.2 Decision Tree for Investment in Highway Segment

willingness to pay, are greater than the costs of providing the volume and weight capacity. Some urban expansion may be justified, and some kind of heavy truck network would probably be worthwhile, but until such users pay a larger share of their costs, the consumer demand evidence for investment is weak.[3]

Investment in capital improvements enhances the performance of the highways, resulting in benefits to users and thence to society. Better surface quality increases travel speeds and reduces vehicle wear and operating costs. Increased capacity reduces congestion and associated delay and user costs. Guardrails, medians, better sight lines, and better geometrics may reduce accidents and perhaps travel time.

Interactions among the various impacts complicates the analysis of benefits. Most improvements have some effect on all three benefit categories, often indirectly. Capacity improvements that allow speeds to increase above about 45 miles per hour may increase the number of fatalities, even while reducing the number of accidents. Travel speeds affect running costs. When impacts move in opposite directions (e.g., increased speed is offset by higher running costs and fatalities), the net effect is especially hard to assess.

Figure 3.3 and Table 3.1 focus on the particular relationships that are relevant to estimating benefits of road improvements. At the project level, these relationships can be incorporated into a benefit-cost analysis, although the quantitative precision on many of them is not high. At the program level or aggregate needs level, the information base is inadequate to support benefit-cost evaluation of this type.

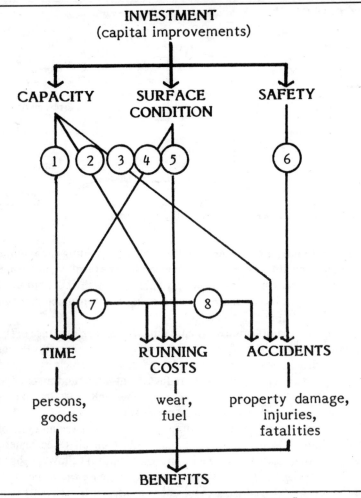

Figure 3.3 Relationships Between Highway Investment and Benefits

Conditions and performance. The components of the highway system vary widely with respect to their capacity, condition, and the demands placed on them. Segments of urban interstate highways yet to be completed cost as much as $100 million per mile (even ignoring New York's proposed Westway and Boston's Central Artery) and can be expected to carry as much as 200,000 vehicles per day, while a major

TABLE 3.1

Impacts of Highway Investment on User Costs

(Refer to Figure 3)

(1) Capacity improvements reduce the volume-capacity ratio and reduce congestion, thus reducing travel times. Traffic engineering analysis provides a reasonably strong understanding of these relationships.

(2) Reduced congestion reduces speed change cycles and hence lowers running costs, even for the same average speed.

(3) Reduced congestion is generally believed to reduce the number of accidents, although the empirical documentation is weak.

(4) Improved surface condition reduces travel times by providing a smoother running surface.

(5) Surface quality also affects running costs, through increased tire and vehicle wear, and less wasted energy absorbed in sway and vibration.

(6) Better safety structures and geometric design have an effect on accidents, but the quantitative relationship has not been satisfactorily established. Safety improvements may also affect speed, either increasing it or decreasing it.

(7) Increase speed above about 30 miles per hour increases running costs, in fuel consumption, tire wear, oil consumption, and other components.

(8) Speed increases the severity of accidents, which may partially offset travel time savings through increased fatalities.

portion of total road mileage remains unpaved and carries fewer than fifty vehicles per day.

Thus it is necessary to divide the system into categories that permit the differences between road type and usage to be recognized. The categories best suited for this purpose are called functional classes. Although several categorizations have been developed, by different agencies at different times, all classifications distinguish urban from rural and they all gradate from Interstate at one end to local roads at the other. Using such a set of functional classes, shares of road mileage and travel can be compared as in Figure 3.4. One obvious pattern is that travel per mile of road is higher (the ratio of the second bar to the first) on urban and on higher capacity roads than on rural collectors and locals.

With slow but steady growth in total travel volumes, congestion is increasing in selected urban and suburban areas. All functional systems have some congested mileage, but all systems also have a significant amount of lightly traveled segments, including the Interstates. Pavement quality has remained about constant overall, but much of the Interstate system has reached the end of its pavement life and needs restoration. At the lowest absolute level of pavement quality are the collector and local

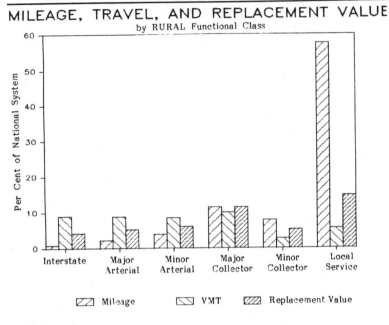

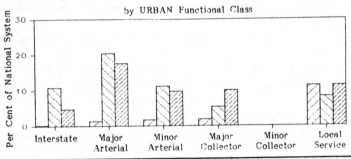

Figure 3.4 Percentage Shares of System Mileage, VMT, and Replacement Value, by Functional Class

systems, which have lost out —due to their typically low volumes—in the competition for scarce road funds.

Net systemwide investment. One starting point for making an aggregate needs estimate is to assume the existing system will be maintained indefinitely, with only marginal changes in extent and performance. Applying a prototypical cost per mile for resurfacing pavement and shoulders to the mileage of each of the functional classes, the entire system could be resurfaced once every twenty years for about $28 billion per year in 1985 dollars. This ignores bridges, interstate completion, backlogs, and any substantial upgrading or rearrangement of the system. It also ignores any need for reconstruction.

Such a bare-bones figure would not be expected to be sufficient to keep the existing system in a stable condition. Yet it is more than FHWA's estimate for maintaining current performance with traffic growth at 2.8% per year, if local roads are deleted from the resurfacing estimate. Even on the Federal-Aid system, then, FHWA's needs estimate is less than enough to resurface the pavement on the existing system.

Another perspective comes from comparing gross capital investment with actual capital consumption. No estimates of depreciation of the highway capital stock have been generated, but a simplified one can be based on the per-mile reconstruction cost of prototypical segments of each functional class. The result is $98 billion per year to rebuild each segment once every twenty years. No interest or land costs are included in this figure. Although bridges and major upgrading also are not included, the figure probably constitutes an upper bound on the annual capital expenditures that would be necessary to retain the existing system in its current state. Nonetheless, it is clear that current capital expenditures are not enough to retain the entire system in a stable condition.

Costs on the existing system could be reduced by disinvestment and eventual abandonment of some portions, especially the low-volume rural local system. Although the costs per mile are not high, the extent is enormous. Undoubtedly, in addition, there are many segments in the higher functional classes that also will not be able to pass a benefit-cost test when the time comes to resurface or reconstruct them. "Neglected" roads become effectively unpaved, low-speed roads for light use, while abandonment is desirable when there is an alternative, more productive use for the land. Abandonment may require a sufficient time delay to amortize previous investment, divert traffic to other routes, and provide access to abutting property. Giving or selling the land to adjacent owners is the most common method.

Although the more extreme claims regarding highway capital needs are unsupported or erroneous, FHWA's needs estimates fall well short of what is necessary to retain all of the existing highway system in its current state, for several reasons.[4] First, FHWA ignores the local road system, which is financed primarily by city and county property taxpayers. State road tax distributions are insufficient to maintain local roads, and local jurisdictions do not collect much revenue from road users. Second, FHWA's estimates are adequate only if the Federal-Aid system itself is significantly pruned. Because of "relaxed" engineering standards and the simulation modeling process, FHWA implicitly applies triage to low-volume and (nationally) unimportant roads by letting them deteriorate (in the model) indefinitely.

This unstated policy of abandonment at the national level is not necessarily paralleled by actual removal of highway mileage at the state and local levels. Lower units of government are proceeding on the apparent assumption that all highway links, along with their associated bridges and other facilities, will be kept in service indefinitely. As a result, highway user revenues are spread too thinly, rather than being concentrated on the portions of the system that warrant being preserved or upgraded. Because the highway program is not required or expected to be fully self-financing, the incentives to invest only where demand justifies the expenditures are largely absent. Most state and local governments are hoping that a higher level of government will increase road fund revenues and distribute them back to the lower units.

Prototype analysis. For any given improvement to a segment, there is some level of traffic on that segment that will justify the cost of the improvement. Perhaps there are improvements costing so little that almost any traffic at all is sufficient, or improvements costing so much that the necessary volume exceeds the capacity of the facility, but, more typically, high utilization levels will justify suitable improvements. Thus if travel benefits could be calculated, they would turn primarily on the volume of travel. Different persons, vehicle types, trip purposes, locations, and so on, will have different values per mile of travel, and this will affect total benefits, but the dominant factor is the volume of vehicle trips. There will be some threshold volume above which it pays to improve a particular segment, and below which it does not.

One representative improvement type will be considered here, namely, reconstruction of the pavement and shoulders. Assuming a segment reaches the end of its life, the evaluation consists of determining whether the benefits of restoring the road to its original condition are worth the reconstruction costs. If not, the road continues to deteriorate and its speed and capacity are reduced. Benefits take the form of time and cost savings, primarily user cost savings, and can be estimated for any given project. Without knowledge of the alternatives (e.g., substitute routes), the absolute magnitude of the benefits cannot be estimated, but

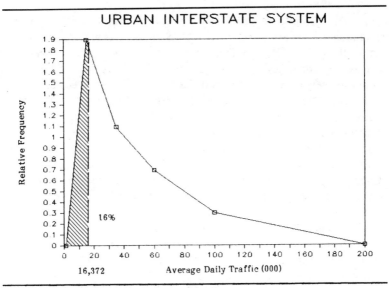

Figure 3.5   ADT Distribution for Urban Interstate Highways

relative thresholds can be tested against distributions of travel volumes.

A simplified needs study using published FHWA data on unit costs and usage, by functional system, can be performed with a modest effort. Frequency distributions made up of straight line segments can be fitted to data on average daily traffic (ADT) for twelve functional classes, with an example of the results shown in Figure 3.5. Each functional class can be represented by a prototypical road section (number of lanes, width, terrain, adjacent land use), for which costs can be estimated, for any improvement type. The nature of the benefit-cost evaluation is whether the volume of travel warrants the cost of the improvement.

Although the correct threshold is not known, it is possible to determine the volume required to keep the average cost per vehicle mile at a given level. If this is the maximum amount that users would be willing to pay to use the facility, then segments carrying less traffic than this threshold volume do not warrant reconstruction. The threshold is

$$\frac{(ROW\$/mi)(DR) + (RECON\$/mi)(CRF)}{\text{Maximum acceptable cost}/VMT} = \text{Min. required annual volume}$$

where ROW\$/mile = right-of-way cost for the road type in dollars per road mile, DR = discount rate, RECON\$/mile = reconstruction cost per road mile, and CRF = capital recovery factor, using a lifetime of 20 years. The value represents the average rate at which use of the highways should be generating benefits in order to cover long-run costs.

Excess system mileage. Choosing a cost/VMT is mostly a matter of taste, at this point, but patterns could be developed from well-documented project case studies. The current charge is roughly \$.02/mile for cars, but the average long-run cost is about \$.13 per mile. A figure of \$.20 would appear to be very high, but if all segments that failed to meet this threshold—that is, had lower volumes than would be sufficient to keep average long-run cost below \$.20—were eliminated from their respective functional systems, capital replacement costs would be cut in half.

For a constant cost/VMT parameter, the threshold volume varies a great deal by functional class. Only 11% of rural interstate highways fall below the volume needed to keep per-VMT cost below \$.20, but 85% of rural local service roads and 82% of rural minor collectors fail the criterion. Urban highways range from 14% for interstates to 60% for urban local streets. Volume thresholds for urban facilities are higher than for rural, because urban facilities are more costly to build, and this comes close to offsetting the higher utilization of urban facilities. Results are shown in Table 3.2.

One puzzle is why a cost standard that is much higher than the average can eliminate half of all reconstruction needs. Two factors are involved. First, the distribution of ADTs for each functional class is highly skewed, with the result that the mean (average of the distribution) is well to one side (above, in this case) of the median (which splits the distribution in half). Larger amounts of road mileage lie below the average than above, because the above-average volumes are farther from the mean. Second, the high-cost (low-utilization) mileage tends to be on the more extensive functional systems, though the least expensive per road mile. The net effect of this second factor is that cutting 10% from the local or collector systems saves more than cutting 10% from the interstate system. It is also evident that the urban systems are less overbuilt than the rural systems.

Removing large amounts of mileage would, of course, have effects on the rest of the system. In principle, segments would be deleted from the least productive end of the list, and the traffic redistributed over the remaining network. In this process, some previously underutilized links

TABLE 3:2
Excess Highway Mileage by Function System
(at Average Cost/VMT exceeds $.20)

	Rural	Urban	Total
Interstate			
System reconstruction cost[1]	$ 3,832	$ 4,662	$ 8,494
Threshold volume (at $.20/VMT)	4.280	16,372	
Excess mileage (%)	14.0%	16.4%	
Adjusted needs (millions annually)	$ 3,295	$ 3,897	$ 7,193
Major Arterial			
System reconstruction cost	$ 3,554	$16,372	$19,927
Threshold volume	2,018	11,240	
Excess mileage (%)	26.0%	38.1%	
Adjusted needs (millions annually)	$ 2,630	$10,130	$12,769
Minor Arterial			
System reconstruction cost	$ 6,212	$ 9,124	$15,335
Threshold volume	1,395	4,828	
Excess mileage (%)	38.5%	40.1%	
Adjusted needs (millions annually)	$ 3,822	$ 5,467	$ 9,289
Major Collector			
System reconstruction cost	$12,600	$ 9,571	$22,171
Threshold volume	910	2,942	
Excess mileage (%)	67.8%	60.3%	
Adjusted needs (millions annually)	$ 4,058	$ 3,797	$ 7,854
Minor Collector			
System reconstruction cost	$ 6,114		$ 6,114
Threshold volume	615		
Excess milage (%)	84.0%		
Adjusted needs (millions annually)	$ 978		$ 978
Local			
System reconstruction cost	$15,722	$10,281	$26,003
Threshold volume	232	849	
Excess mileage (%)	86.2%	61.9%	
Adjusted needs (millions annually)	$ 2,174	$ 3,916	$ 6,090
Total			
System reconstruction cost	$48,034	$50,010	$98,044
Adjusted needs (millions annually)	$16,957	$27,217	$44,173

1. Pavement reconstruction cost per year for functional system, in $1985 (millions).

would acquire enough traffic to pass the threshold. Hence the percentages of excess mileage greatly overstate the share that would fail the threshold if links were removed sequentially. At the same time, however, it should be recognized that raising user charges sufficiently to cover long-run costs would substantially reduce the total volume of traffic. In short, efficient pricing and investment would result in a distinctly smaller road network.

USER CHARGES

Omission of even the mention of user charges in infrastructure discussions is so pervasive as to suggest conscious intent. Perhaps infrastructure proponents consist only of special interests that would be adversely affected if demand for highways was dampened by higher prices to users, and liberals who believe that the regressivity of user charge financing outweighs any possible efficiency gains. Whatever the reasons, the omission is misleading.

Revenue impacts. Current revenues from user taxes are $36 billion, enough to support existing capital expenditures but well short of the $52 billion in expenditures for all purposes other than interest and debt service. Allowing generously for price elasticity, a penny-per-gallon fuel tax will bring in $1 billion annually and a penny-per-vehicle-mile user charge increase will add $15 billion annually.

Although raising user charge revenues to the degree necessary to cover expenditures implies a significant percentage increase in user taxes, the amounts are small relative to the cost of travel. At roughly $.30-.40 per vehicle mile for the long-run average cost of automobile travel (FHWA cost estimates), a 10% increase in this price would mean an almost 200% increase in highway revenues.

Demand effects. Even assuming a travel demand elasticity of -1.0, the aggregate travel effects of raising user charge revenues by $15-30 billion would be small. Depending upon how they were levied, however, the influences on some segments would be large. Given that a large share of the total mileage is already being used at a rate that probably does not warrant capital replacement, increases in user charges would amplify the need to consolidate and prune the system.

At the present time, there are no incentives to eliminate gradually segments that are inefficient, and many obstacles to doing so. The Iowa DOT recently recommended the elimination of 10,000 miles of rural county roads—a drastic action yet a drop in the bucket—but progress toward that goal is painfully slow.

Opportunity costs. All of the needs estimates discussed above ignore the opportunity cost of land and capital. In effect, they assume that the interest rate is zero. If an analogy is made between the highway enterprise and a typical business enterprise, these opportunity costs are real; revenues from a given investment must pay borrowing costs as well as earn a rate of return at least as great as is available in other sectors. If not, investment will shift to those sectors.

Replacing the existing highway system would cost something like $2.9 trillion. If it is assumed to be 50% depreciated, the net worth of the system is about $1.5 trillion. For this system to be earning revenues of $36 billion amounts to a return on investment of only 2.4%. Even if it is insisted that benefits greatly exceed user charges, it is virtually impossible that the present system is earning a social rate of return anything like what it ought to.

As has been suggested above, the functional classes vary considerably in their relative earning capacity. Users of both urban and rural interstates could pay a modest 6 cents per mile and cover capital replacement, interest on the undepreciated capital (the "remaining balance"), and "rent" on the land in right-of-way. Prices on the other functional systems would have to be as much as 40 cents per mile to achieve the same self-sufficiency. Needless to say, such user charges would have a severe impact on traffic, further exacerbating the revenue shortfall. Obviously, the solution for these systems is to remove the inefficient links and consolidate traffic on the viable ones.

CONCLUSIONS

The results of the previous discussion can be summarized using Figure 3.6. Total expenditures on highways, and the share obtained from user revenues, are shown in the first bar. FHWA's estimate of annual capital needs, for the Federal-Aid system, is shown as the second bar. Current capital expenditures, and the share applied to the Federal-Aid system, make up the third bar, while annual resurfacing costs for these same categories make up the fourth bar. From these it can be seen that actual expenditures are about the same as FHWA needs, and resurfacing-only costs.

The second bar from the right shows the annual expenditures needed to reconstruct the entire system once every twenty years, with pay-as-you-go financing. Finally, the last bar shows annual costs if interest on capital expenditures and opportunity cost on land in right-of-way are also included (the bottom portion is ROW). Only the left-hand bar includes operating expenditures; the others pertain only to capital costs.

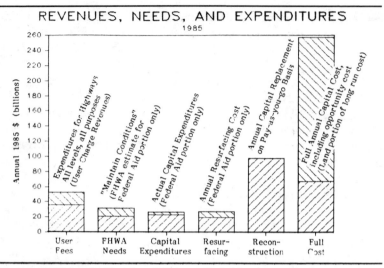

Figure 3.6 **Alternative Measures of Highway Capital Investment Needs**

Only the middle four bars are directly comparable, in that they consist of capital expenditures without borrowing or other opportunity costs.

Two interpretations might be suggested. One is that the level of expenditures needed to maintain and replace the existing capital stock probably lies between the fourth (resurfacing) and fifth (reconstruction) bars. The second is that user charges ought to be at least as high as the right-hand bar in order to demonstrate that user benefits justify the costs of providing the present highway system. Both interpretations—hardly more than hypotheses without more thorough supporting studies—help give credence to several conclusions:

(1) Although the national highway system is not running down at anything like an alarming rate, current maintenance and rehabilitation efforts are not enough to keep the entire system in a stable condition indefinitely.

(2) Current user fees are much too low on either efficiency or equity grounds, and both direct and indirect support from the general taxpayer is too high.

(3) The mileage in the existing system is too large and needs to be pruned and consolidated. All functional classes have underutilized segments, for which the benefits do not justify the capital rehabilitation costs, but excess miles (and bridges) are especially prevalent on the rural collector and local systems.

(4) State and local governments should be given the responsibility and the means to finance the system entirely from user charges. This will serve the dual purposes of imposing fees on the vehicles that create the costs and stimulating highway agencies to invest only in those segments that warrant the investment. If this were done efficiently, capital investment needs could be cut in half by deleting 75% of the road mileage (mostly rural/local) while affecting (i.e., diverting) only 15% of the traffic.

At present, the highway system is managed according to political rather than economic criteria. Worse, the assignment of functional responsibilities to the numerous agencies that make up the highway enterprise is so ambiguous as to severely obstruct progress toward rational pricing of and investment in the system. Continuation of these policies will ensure that financing the highway system becomes even more of a fiscal drag than it is now, and will leave management of the system vulnerable to scares about "crumbling infrastructure" that divert attention from the real problems that need to be attended.

NOTES

1. Total highway expenditures for all levels of government comes from FHWA's *Highway Satistics* (1985). As shown in CBO (1985), highway capital expenditures (about $20 billion) equal those for rail, water supply, wastewater, transit, aviation, and water resources combined. The replacement value estimate is mentioned in GAO (1982) without citation, so presumably it is their own. A replacement cost estimate of $2.9 trillion is constructed in the study from which this chapter is drawn (Lee, 1987), and a further explanation of data and methods used throughout this chapter can be found there.

2. The benefit-cost standard is widely accepted as applicable to public works in general, and has also been recommended for highways, for example, in Gomez-Ibanez and Lee (1982), NCPWI (1986), Vaughan (1983), and Wohl and Hendrickson (1984).

3. All vehicle classes underpay, but some by much larger amounts than others. Documentation of this assertion requires more space than can be devoted here, but much of the research is summarized in the 1982 Federal Highway Cost Allocation Study (FHWA, 1982, Appendix E). Even according to the narrow "pay-as-you-go" accounting standard used by FHWA, users as a whole cover only about 70% of direct expenditures.

4. FHWA presents two tiers of estimates, one for "Full Needs" and one for "Maintain Conditions," and it is always the latter that is referred to here.

REFERENCES

CHOATE, P. and S. WALTER (1983) America in Ruins: The Decaying Infrastructure. Durham, NC: Duke.
Congressional Budget Office (1982) Financial Options for the Highway Trust Fund. Washington, DC: Government Printing Office.
Congressional Budget Office (1982) The Interstate Highway System: Issues and Options. Washington, DC: Government Printing Office.

Congressional Budget Office (1983) Public Works Infrastructure: Policy Considerations for the 1980s. Washington, DC: Government Printing Office.

Congressional Budget Office (1985) The Federal Budget for Public Works Infrastructure. Washington, DC: Government Printing Office.

Congressional Budget Office (1987) Reducing the Deficit: Spending and Revenue Options. Washington, DC: Government Printing Office.

Federal Highway Administration (1978) Performance-Investment Analysis Process. Washington, DC: Government Printing Office.

Federal Highway Administration (1980-1985) Highway Statistics. Washington, DC: Government Printing Office. Federal Highway Administration (1981) The Status of the Nation's Highways: Conditions and Performance. Washington, DC: Government Printing Office.

Federal Highway Administration (1982) Final Report on the Federal Highway Cost Allocation Study. Washington, DC: Government Printing Office.

Federal Highway Administration (1982) Third Annual Report to Congress on the Bridge Replacement and Rehabilitation Program. Washington, DC: Government Printing Office.

Federal Highway Administration (1983) Status of the Nation's Highways: Conditions and Performance. Washington, DC: Government Printing Office.

Federal Highway Administration (1985) Status of the Nation's Highways: Conditions and Performance. Washington, DC: Government Printing Office.

GAKENHEIMER, R. (forthcoming) "Infrastructure shortfall: the institutional problem." J. of the Amer. Planning Assn.

General Accounting Office (1981) Deteriorating Highways and Lagging Revenues: A Need to Reassess the Federal Highway Program. Washington, DC: Comptroller General of the U.S.

General Accounting Office (1982) Transportation: Evolving Issues for Analysis. Washington, DC: Government Printing Office.

GITAJN, A. (1984) Creating and Financing Public Enterprises. Washington, DC: Government Finance Officers Association.

GOMEZ-IBANEZ, J. A. and D. B. LEE (1982) Benefit-Cost Evaluation of Highway Investment Needs. Staff Study, prepared for FHWA. Cambridge, MA: US DOT/TSC.

GOMEZ-IBANEZ, J. A. and M. M. O'KEEFFE (1985) The Benefits from Improved Investment Rules: A Case Study of the Interstate Highway System. Cambridge, MA: Harvard University.

HAMLETT, C. A., G. PAUTSCH, S. B. MILLER, and C. P. BAUMEL (1987) The Economics of Reducing the Size of the Local Rural Road System. Ames: Iowa State University, Dept. of Economics.

Kidder, Peabody & Co. (1984) Infrastructure Finance. Author.

LEE, D. B. (1982) "Monitoring and evaluation of state highway systems." Transportation Research Record 891: 24-28.

LEE, D. B. (1987) Highway Infrastructure Needs. Cambridge, MA: US DOT, Transportation Systems Center.

POLENSKE, K. et al. (1984) "Massachusetts," appendix 10 in Joint Economic Committee of the U.S. Congress, Hard Choices: A Report on the Increasing Gap Between America's Needs and Our Ability to Pay for Them. Washington, DC: Government Printing Office.

VAUGHAN, R. J. (1983) Rebuilding America: Financing Public Works in the 1980s, Vols. 1 and 2. Washington, DC: Council of State Planning Agencies.

WOHL, M. and C. HENDRICKSON (1984) Transportation Investment and Pricing Principles. New York: John Wiley.

4

The Death of the City
and the Urban Fiscal Crisis

KENNETH NEWTON

THE PURPOSE OF THIS CHAPTER is to trace the effects of the decline of cities on the public finances of urban authorities and, in particular, to examine the impact of decay on the finances of the larger and older industrial cities in the West. In contrast to the generally accepted claim that the urban fiscal crisis is the inevitable result of the city's loss of function in the postindustrial era—a decline that both causes physical decay and reduces the tax base of the authorities that are charged with the maintenance of the urban infrastructure, the chapter argues that cities are not so much losing their economic functions, as changing them. Moreover, cities of the Western world retain not only the need for their urban infrastructure, but also retain the means, in large part at least, to refurbish and develop it.

The theory that links the urban fiscal crisis with the decline of cities is well known and needs only brief outlining here. It runs as follows: The economic conditions that made cities in general, and industrial cities in particular, essential to the advanced urban-industrial economy are rapidly disappearing in the postindustrial era. The requirements of the nineteenth-century mass production system required a massed and therefore an urban work force. Factories thus had to be accessible to the work force and major transportation routes as well as energy courses (van den Berg et al., 1982: 24-29). In the postindustrial economy, however, industry and labor are largely released from the constraints of location: energy can be piped or wired almost anywhere; mass and rapid transit systems enable the working population to commute over large distances; and modern communications technology allows the most complex messages to be transmitted cheaply and instantaneously.

Consequently, industry and its workers are now footloose—free to locate where they will, and no longer tied to the dirty, expensive, dangerous and out-moded cities (Williams, 1971; Klaasen and Scimemi, 1981; Brotchie et al., 1985: 1-14). The city, and particularly the large industrial city, is fast becoming an anachronism that is doomed to inevitable decay and eventual extinction. The ample body of statistical material on deindustrialization, industrial deconcentration, and counter-urbanization verifies this rather startling claim. This evidence shows a marked tendency for heavy industry to be replaced by light and high-technology engineering, and for both businesses and populations to forsake the cities, especially the larger of the central cities for the suburbs and the small towns and villages (Berry, 1976; Berry, 1981; Hall and Hay, 1980; Castells, 1985; Bradbury et al., 1982).

The impact on urban public finances is direct and sometimes dire. Cities lose population, but must continue to run and maintain essentially the same public service infrastructure. Although some infrastructural costs can be reduced, most tend to be fixed, and hence per capita costs rise. At the same time, the infrastructure of the older cities is wearing out, or becoming outdated, or both, and although it is expensive to run, it is no less costly to replace. As a consequence of rising per capita costs, the cities are under great pressure to increase their tax rates. However, this may simply encourage a vicious spiral in which the more affluent businesses and individuals leave the city to escape high and rising taxes, causing a further cycle of decline. Direct attempts by public authorities to attract businesses and populations back to the city, especially the inner city, are usually expensive and contribute to further financial problems (Friedland, 1982; Molotch, 1976; Mollenkopf, 1983; Kennedy, 1984).

At the same time, a deteriorating public infrastructure, in turn, encourages a further exodus of people and jobs. Evidence from several OECD countries shows that a poor environment and infrastructure are a major cause of migration from the city (OECD, 1983: 65; see also van den Berg and Klaasen, 1979).

DIFFERENT NATIONAL PATTERNS
OF URBAN GROWTH AND DECAY

Even when stated in such a brief and crude form, the theory has an obvious power and appeal, and is supported by a fair weight of empirical evidence (Norton, 1979; Baumol, 1972; Kennedy, 1984; Gordon, 1978; Solomon, 1980; Howell and Stamm, 1979; Friedland, 1982: 183-188). Moreover, the theory has an impressive generality, especially in its postulating the decline of cities after no less than two millennia of sustained urban growth and development. Before we consign all cities to the graveyard of urban history, however, we should pause a while to examine the theory more carefully.[1]

First, the links between urban change and financial crisis are not direct, but mediated by the special features of each nation's local government and political system (Pickvance, 1986). A city with boundaries drawn widely enough to incorporate its suburbs and the rural periphery will not be adversely affected by suburbanization and counterurbanization as a central city that is neatly severed from its suburbs. Cities that rely on their own revenue raising capacities will be more adversely affected than those that receive grants from higher levels of government. Cities with a wide range of expensive service responsibilities will be harder hit than those with more modest functions.

Nor is the scale of infrastructural decay the same in different nations, or different regions in the same nation. Great Britain, the first urban-industrial nation, has some acute problems. In many of its cities, sewers, bridges, roads, public buildings, and water pipes, built in early Victorian times, are now near or past the end of their natural life. The problem is compounded by the effects of wartime bomb damage. In the Manchester and Liverpool areas, for example, it is estimated that 15% of sewers are more than one hundred years old, and that a large proportion are either decrepit, inadequate, or in the wrong place for modern requirements (Lloyd, 1980: 523). As a consequence, each day now registers an average of two sewer collapses, forty blockages, and twenty-five water main bursts (*The Times,* January 12, 1980). Manchester's City Engineer foresees the day when collapsing pipes will create holes in the road big enough to swallow up double-decker buses (*The Times*, November 24, 1979). It is estimated that the water pipes of Britain are now so old that a third of the water supply seeps away before delivery. A similar tale can be told of old and inadequate school buildings and housing stock (Newton and Karran, 1985: 58-59).

A worn out and out-dated urban infrastructure is a severe problem in large parts of Britain, northern France, Belgium, the Netherlands, and the Ruhr, as well as in the northeastern megalopolis of the United States. It is much less of a concern, however, in Scandinavia and parts of southern Europe that urbanized later, and in those cities largely rebuilt after World War II. Nevertheless, there is also considerable variation within nations, even in the ones with widespread urban decline, some cities are growing and booming (Weinstein and Firestine, 1978; Fothergill and Gudgin, 1982; Sawers and Tabb, 1984). Here the need is not to replace infrastructure, but to add facilities to accommodate the rapid growth.

Apart from these national and historical differences, there are also social, economic, and political variations that cause different patterns of urban growth and decline in different regions and nation states. A good deal of the writing on urban decline and decay originates in the United States where the processes have gone further and faster than in almost any other industrial society of the Western world. Even where there are general points of comparison, as there are between the United States and Britain, the temptation to generalize from the American literature should be resisted (Pahl, 1975: 146). Britain shows a similar tendency for counterurbanization, but it is less marked than America's, and has resulted in less inner-city decay. Outside Glasgow, Liverpool, and parts of London, there is little in Britain to compare with the desolation of block after block in Boston, Philadelphia, Detroit, or Washington. A variety of rather special social, economic, and political factors in the United States have created a problem that is rather special, though not unique (Hill, 1980; Marcuse, 1981).

Other nations in Europe do not repeat the Anglo-Saxon pattern of counterurbanization, and urban and industrial deconcentration. Some of the large cities in France, Spain, and Portugal are continuing to expand and to attract businesses and middle-class residents—although the growth rate has been slowing down (Hall and Hay, 1980). The same is true of some cities in eastern Europe (Szelenyi, 1983). Nor is there any necessary connection between the urban fiscal crisis and counterurbanization. In Denmark, Norway, and Sweden, where cities show traces of the Anglo-Saxon trend of counterurbanization, there are *relatively* few financial problems, and certainly nothing approaching the scale of New York, Atlanta, Liverpool, or Liege (Hansen, 1981; Kjellberg, 1981; Brunn and Skovsgaard, 1981; Sharpe, 1981).

URBAN DECAY OR URBAN CHANGE?

In many ways, then, the theory that spells out the "death of the city" in the postindustrial era ignores the experience of some cities in Britain and the United States, and of many cities in other Western nations. Even within Britain and the United States, the theory ignores the important development of growth in services, industries, and commercial activity. Western cities may have lost their supreme importance as centers of industry and production, but they have gained as centers of industrial and commercial coordination and control. Cities are not dying so much as changing. The focus of economic activities is shifting from the actual manufacturing of goods to the organization and coordination of the processes of producing and distributing goods and services (Kasarda, 1980; Pred, 1977; Hawley, 1950, 1971). The more these processes are decentralized, the more a branch plant economy develops in both manufacturing and retailing. Thus the urban office economy increasingly plays the new role of integrating and controlling these decentralized operations (Goddard, 1979; Dawson, 1982; Kantor, 1985; Goddard and Marshall, 1983).

Cities are also becoming more important as centers of consumption—not the routine consumption of the weekly shopping trip, which can easily be decentralized to the suburbs, but the more specialized and usually more expensive purchases of the downtown department store and the specialty shops. The latter sell everything from art and books to xylophones and zoological specimens. Downtown consumption also includes the leisure and entertainment business—from ballet and opera to sporting events and night clubs.

What this suggests is not the death of the city in the postindustrial era, or the decay of the public and private infrastructure, but a profound change: the office block replaces the factory; service industry replaces manufacturing; the needs of senior and middle management replace those of the factory worker and engineer; the multistory parking garage replaces the railway shunting yard; and computer software consultants replace machine tools salesmen (Fainstein and Fainstein, 1982: 161-162; Stanback, 1985). Because the nature of the urban economy is changing, so also are the demands made upon the authorities that provide and service its public infrastructure.

THE CHANGING URBAN ECONOMY:
BRITAIN AS A TEST CASE

This rather abstract and general theory needs bringing down to earth, and Britain is as good a test case as any for four main reasons. First, as previously discussed, Britain shows a clear trend toward industrial deconcentration and counterurbanization. Second, the processes of deindustrialization and industrial decay—not the same things—have proceeded further and faster in Britain than almost any other Western nation (Hall, 1985; Dicken and Lloyd, 1979; Massey, 1983; Fothergill and Gudgin, 1982). Third, the link between infrastructural decay and the urban fiscal crisis is stronger in Britain because local authorities derive all their local revenues from a property tax, and are heavily dependent upon industrial property as a tax base (Newton, 1980: 138-139).[2] Finally, a good many writers have attributed the urban fiscal crisis in Britain to deindustrialization and urban deconcentration (Eversley, 1972, 1973; Cameron, 1980: 8-10; Kirwan, 1980: 76-77; Jackson et al., 1982; Young and Mills, 1982: 77-92; Young and Mills, 1983; Dunford et al., 1981; Hamnet, 1976).

The trends toward deindustrialization and industrial deconcentration in Britain over the past quarter century or so are beyond question. One study reports that London lost almost 38% of its manufacturing jobs between 1959 and 1975, and that the major conurbations lost 16% in the same period (Dicken, 1982: 179). At the same time, there was a marked and consistent shift from urban to rural locations (McCallum, 1980: 26-34; Keeble, 1980). Between the censuses of 1961 and 1971 the percentage of the work force engaged in manufacturing in the six largest conurbations in the United Kingdom outside London fell by almost 13%, whereas the figure increased by almost 10% in the rest of the country, albeit on a smaller base figure (McCallum, 1980: 33).

The flight of industry from the city is particularly important for urban authorities, because Britain's local governments alone of all the Western industrialized states, have one and only one source of local revenues—the property tax. Known as the rates, property tax is levied primarily on domestic, industrial, and commercial property. A high proportion of local revenues are derived from industrial and commercial property, partly because they are more valuable than domestic property, and partly because they are taxed at a higher level. In the period 1974-1975, for example, nondomestic property provided 63% of local authority rate income, domestic property providing the remaining 37% (Layfield Committee, 1976: 386).[3] Since there has been intense political pressure to minimize tax increases on individual householders, the tendency has been for local authorities to increase taxes on business property rather sharply.

The strong reliance of urban authorities in the United Kingdom on

TABLE 4.1

Percentage of Ratable Values Made up by Commercial and
Industrial Property, by County Boroughs and County Councils
(1964, 1972) and by Metropolitan and Nonmetropolitan Counties,
England and Wales (1977, 1982)

	1964	1972	Net Change
County boroughs (n = 79)	39.6	38.4	−1.2
County councils	28.0	27.2	−0.8
	1977	1982	Net Change
Metropolitan counties and GLC (n = 7)	41.7	41.9	+0.2
Nonmetropolitan	30.0	30.6	+0.6

SOURCES: Rates and Ratable Values in England and Wales (London: DOE, 1965, 1974). *Local Government Financial Statistics, England and Wales, 1981/2* (London: DOE and Wales Office, HMSO, 1983).

business property taxes, is shown in Table 4.1. In the old system of local government almost 40% of the total ratable value of the county boroughs was made up by industrial and commercial property, whereas in the more rural counties the equivalent figure was just over 25%.[4] In the newer system of local government, the metropolitan counties and the Greater London Council (GLC) show a similar reliance upon commercial and industrial property that makes up over 40% of their tax base, compared with less than a third in the more rural nonmetropolitan counties.

Moreover, the urban authorities include a disproportionate share of the nation's total business property. In 1981, for example, the metropolitan counties and the GLC contained 36.6% of the population of England and Wales, but well over half the national commercial and industrial ratable value (Table 4.2). In short, a disproportionate amount of business property is found in the urban authorities, and they derive a disproportionate amount of their local revenues from this source. Therefore, if the local fiscal crisis is indeed a consequence of the economic decline of cities, particularly of industrial cities, we would expect a clear decline in the size of the urban tax base formed by business property.

Yet the data do not show this. On the contrary, the cities are rather well endowed so far as their property tax base is concerned; with rather more than a third of the population, the metropolitan counties and the

TABLE 4.2

Percentage of National Industrial and Commercial Ratable Value
Located in County Boroughs and Councils (1964, 1972)
Metropolitan and Nonmetropolitan Counties,
England and Wales (1977, 1982)

	1964	1972	Net Change
County boroughs (n = 79)	39.8	45.6	+5.8
County councils	60.2	54.4	−5.8
	1977	1982	Net Change
Metropolitan counties and GLC (n = 7)	55.7	54.6	−1.1
Nonmetropolitan counties	44.3	45.4	+1.1

SOURCES: Rates and Ratable Values in England and Wales (London: DOE, 1965, 1974). *Local Government Financial Statistics, England and Wales, 1981/2* (London: DOE and Wales Office, HMSO, 1983).

GLC contained 45.2% of total national ratable value in 1981, including nearly 40% of domestic ratable value.

Whatever causes financial problems for urban authorities in Britain, it is not, apparently, a poor tax base. Nor is it a decline in this tax base, for the figures in Tables 4.1 and 4.2 show that the cities have more than held their own in this respect. In spite of industrial decline and dispersion, the old county boroughs increased their share of national industrial and commercial ratable value between 1964 and 1972. Since the national total increased in absolute terms, this represents both an increased proportion of the national pie, and a substantial increase in absolute terms. The metropolitan counties and the GLC of the new system show a slight decline of 1.1 percentage points between 1977 and 1982 (Table 4.2). Even this, however, represents an absolute increase, since ratable values tend to drift upwards by an average of around 2% per year, even without revaluation (Newton and Karran, 1985: 149).

How can this be reconciled with what we know about industrial decay and decline, in Britain of all places, and with what we know of the reliance of urban authorities on business property for raising local taxes? There are two main answers. First, one city's industrial loss may well be another's industrial gain. The process of industrial relocation within the nation generally involves movement from the inner areas of the largest cities to either the metropolitan periphery or the smaller free-standing towns and cities that are growing. As a result, urban authorities such as Wallasey, Solihull, West Bromwich, Birkenhead,

TABLE 4.3

Ratable Value of Metropolitan and Nonmetropolitan Authorities
by Property Type, 1977, 1982, England and Wales

	Metropolitan Counties and the G.L.C.			Nonmetropolitan Counties		
	1977	1982	Net Change	1977	1982	Net Change
Domestic	43.2	42.9	−0.3	54.3	53.9	−0.4
Commercial	31.3	32.8	+1.5	18.5	19.4	+0.9
Industrial	10.4	9.2	−1.2	11.5	11.2	−0.3
Other	15.1	15.1	0.0	15.7	15.5	−0.2

SOURCE: DOE and Welsh Office, *Local Government Financial Statistics, England and Wales,* London, HMSO, 1977, 1982.

Dewsbury, Barnsley, Rotherham, and Leicester increased their business tax bases faster than the national average during the 1960s and 1970s. Other cities declined, both absolutely and relative to the national average. But it must also be noted that contrasting patterns of growth and decline also characterize the rural authorities. Between 1964 and 1972, Hertfordshire, Lancashire, and Cheshire grew, whereas Essex, Surrey, and Kent declined. Thus it is not a matter of the decline of cities, but a decline of some cities and the growth of others, and the decline of some rural areas and the growth of others. Regional variations are as large as urban-rural variations (McCallum, 1980: 50).

The second reason for the growth of the business tax base in the cities concerns the other side of the coin of deindustrialization and urban deconcentration—the growth in commerce and service activities. Table 4.3 shows the composition of ratable values by property type in urban and rural authorities. Domestic, as well as industrial, have declined in both urban and rural areas—though faster in the conurbations than outside them. In contrast, the contribution of commercial property (mainly shops and offices) has increased in both places—though faster in the conurbations than outside them. Thus the increase in taxable value of offices and shops in the largest urban areas has more than offset losses caused by the decline and dispersion of industry.

The point is made more clearly in Table 4.4, which presents figures for per capita ratable values of business property in urban and rural authorities. Per capita values increased in both the urban and the rural authorities of the old system, but they grew rather faster in the former. The same is true of the new system. In general, the larger urban areas lost population, but the increase in commercial property values allowed the

TABLE 4.4
Per Capita Industrial and Commercial Ratable Values
in County Boroughs and Councils (1964, 1972),

	1964	1972	Net Change
County boroughs (n = 79)	15.96	18.61	+2.65
County councils	9.68	11.14	+1.46
	1975	1983	Net Change
Metropolitan counties	40.50	45.00	+4.50
Nonmetropolitan	36.40	40.12	+3.72

SOURCES: DOE, *Rates and Ratable Values in England and Wales* (London: HMSO, 1976). CIPFA, *Financial and General Statistics, 1983/4* (London: CIPFA, 1983).

local tax base to maintain its strength. The result is that the per capita tax values of the larger urban areas rose faster than those of the smaller urban and rural authorities. In 1964, county values were 60.7% of the county borough figure, but by 1972 they had drifted down slightly to 59.9%. In 1975 the nonmetropolitan value was 90% of the metropolitan county figure; by 1983 it was 89.2%. The change is not large by any means, but it is certainly not consistent with the claim that the cities have suffered from economic decline.

In fact, some of the largest urban areas, including those that have lost most from industrial decay and industrial relocation, seem to have gained most from the growth of commerce and the service sector—cities such as Birmingham, Manchester, Liverpool, Sheffield, Leeds, Bristol, Nottingham, and Leicester (Table 4.5). The gains are small, but they are gains both in absolute terms and relative to other cities. The inclusion of Liverpool in the list is significant because it is probably the best single example of urban and industrial decay of any city in Britain (Parkinson, 1985). Yet between 1964 and 1972 it increased its share of national commercial and industrial ratable value from 1.80% to 1.83%. The rural county councils also grew in this period, but not as fast as the cities. Nevertheless, the phenomenon under consideration is not one of urban decline, but of urban growth and decline—and of rural growth and decline.

The growth of the urban tax base explains why research has failed to find evidence of a worsening financial crisis in the cities, or, at least, of a crisis that is worsening more rapidly in the cities than the countryside. Kirwan, for example, found no evidence of a tax base loss between 1965 and 1977 that was worse in the metropolitan than other areas. But he draws the wrong conclusion that tax losses must not have outstripped population losses. The actual picture seems to be one in which tax gains

TABLE 4.5
Percentage of Total National Commercial and Industrial
Ratable Value of England and Wales, Located in
Selected Large Cities, 1964, 1972

	1964	1972
Birmingham	4.14	4.26
Manchester	2.17	2.21
Liverpool	1.80	1.83
Sheffield	1.69	1.91
Leeds	1.37	1.57
Bristol	1.35	1.48
Nottingham	1.10	1.15
Leicester	1.04	1.25

SOURCE: DOE, *Rates and Ratable Values 1964-65, 1972-73* (London, HMSO 1965 and 1973).

contrast with population loss in the big cities. Nor does Kirwan find any evidence for any large increases in metropolitan debt ratios, a reasonably good indicator of financial stress. He therefore concludes that "despite the well-founded fears of many observers, it appears that metropolitan decline in Britain has not so far been accompanied by a significant deterioration in the fiscal situation of the major cities" (Kirwan, 1980; 85-89; see also Bailey, 1980). The actual picture is not one of general metropolitan decline, but of industrial and population decline offset by commercial and service sector growth.

Similarly, Jackson et al. (1982) point out that big city debts have not increased inordinately, and that cities in the United Kingdom continue to be good credit risks. This is confirmed, paradoxically, by the recent experience of Liverpool similar to the experience of Cleveland in the United States. Liverpool was brought to the brink of bankruptcy not by economic factors, but by the political confrontation of the city council and the central government. Liverpool was then saved by loans on the international money market.

SUMMARY AND CONCLUSION

Paradoxically, the financial problems of British local government in general, and of big cities in particular, are caused as much by political and governmental factors, as by financial and economic ones (see also Hoggart, 1986). Mrs. Thatcher's government has made it most difficult for the big cities that have the financial means to solve at least some of their problems. Two policies, in particular, have had deleterious effects. First, a cap has been placed on the rates, which effectively sets an upper limit on local tax levels. Second, the metropolitan tier of local government in the form of the GLC and the metropolitan counties has been abolished. The result is a more fragmented system of metropolitan government that is likely to increase the financial problems of the central cities.

These two measures have been implemented on the grounds that local tax levels have discouraged economic growth, particularly in the cities. There is, however, no evidence from either Britain or the United States to show that above average local taxes have a damaging effect on local economies, or any significant impact on the location of jobs (Crawford et al., 1985; Wasylenko, 1981). There is good evidence, however, from Britain and elsewhere that the provision of infrastructure makes a contribution to economic development, and that its absence increases migration. It would seem, therefore, that the government's policy is likely to have the reverse of its avowed effect: By preventing city governments from using their expanding commercial tax base to finance investment in the urban infrastructure, the policy will result in economic decline and infrastructural decay.

NOTES

1. Scenarios for the urban future vary between those who foresee a continued decline of all cities as modern technology, particularly communications technology, removes the remaining constraints of location, those who foresee a future for commercial cities that undertake nonroutine economic functions, and those who foresee reurbanization as a consequence of recent economic decline.

2. For a recent account of the financial circumstances of local government in Britain see Pickvance, 1986.

3. Unfortunately, a more current figure is not available. The total yield of the nondomestic rates cannot be calculated from the figures that are available. However, it is known that the nondomestic rate has increased far more rapidly than the domestic, and its contribution to the total local tax take is likely to have increased in rough proportion.

4. In the old system of local government in England and Wales, the larger urban areas were run by county borough councils, although the county boroughs included a few of the smaller cities, such as Canterbury. The predominantly rural areas were run by county councils, although the counties included some fairly urban and industrial areas such as Lancashire. Reforms were implemented in 1974, which placed the six largest urban conurbations outside London under the control of metropolitan counties (total population twelve million) and the rest of the country—including some fairly large cities, such as Bristol, and some fairly urban and industrial areas—under nonmetropolitan counties. Although not strictly accurate, it is reasonable to treat the county boroughs and the metropolitan counties as the urban authorities, and the counties and the nonmetropolitan

counties as rural ones. London is run by the Greater London Council (population over six million) that was created in 1965 by greatly expanding the London County Council. Mrs. Thatcher's Conservative government has now abolished the metropolitan counties and the GLC, leaving them to be run by thirty-six metropolitan districts and thirty-two London boroughs, respectively.

REFERENCES

BAILEY, S. (1980) Central City Decline and the Provision of Local Authority Services—A Case Study of the City of Glasgow. Glasgow: University of Glasgow, Centre for Urban and Regional Research.

BAUMOL, W. J. (1972) "The dynamics of urban problems and its policy implications," pp. 123-131 in B. Corry and M. Peston (eds.) Essays in Honour of Lord Robbins. London: Weidenfeld & Nicholson.

BERRY, B.J.L. [ed.] (1976) Urbanization and Counter-Urbanization. Newbury Park, CA: Sage.

BERRY, B.J.L. (1981) Comparative Urbanization: Divergent Paths in the Twentieth Century. London: Macmillan.

BRADBURY, K. L., A. DOWNS, and K. A. SMALL (1982) Urban Decline and the Future of American Cities. Washington: Brookings Institute.

BROTCHIE, J., P. NEWTON, P. HALL & P. NIJKAMP (1985) "Introduction," pp. 1-14 in J. Brotchie (ed.) The Future of Urban Form. London: Croom Helm.

BRUUN, F. and C. J. SKOVSGAARD (1981) "Local determinants and central control of municipal finance: the affluent local authorities of Denmark," pp. 29-61 in L. J. Sharpe (ed.) The Local Fiscal Crisis in Western Europe: Myths and Realities. London: Sage.

CAMERON, G. (1980) "Introduction," pp. 1-13 in G. Cameron (ed.) The Future of the British Conurbations. London: Longman.

CASTELLS, M. [ed.] (1985) High Technology, Space and Society. Newbury Park, CA: Sage.

JACKSON, P. et al. (1982) "Urban fiscal decay in United Kingdom cities." Local Government Studies 8: 23-43.

KANTOR, P. (1985) "The dependent city: the changing political economy of urban economic development in the United States." Presented to the annual meeting of the American Political Science Association, New Orleans.

KASARDA, J. D. (1980) "The implications of contemporary redistribution trends for national urban policy." Social Sci. Q. 61: 373-400.

KEEBLE, D. E. (1980) "Industrial decline, regional policy and the urban-rural manufacturing shift in the United Kingdom." Environment and Planning A 12: 945-962.

KENNEDY, M. D. (1984) "The fiscal crisis of the city," pp. 91-110 in M. P. Smith (ed.) Cities in Transformation: Class, Capital and the State. Newbury Park, CA: Sage.

KIRWAN, R. M. (1980) "The fiscal context," pp. 72-100 in G. Cameron (ed.) The Future of the British Conurbations. London: Longman.

KJELLBERG, F. (1981) "The expansion and standardization of local finance in Norway," pp. 125-173 in L. J. Sharpe (ed.) The Local Fiscal Crisis in Western Europe: Myths and Realities. London: Sage.

KLAASEN, L. H. and G. SCIMEMI (1981) "Theoretical issues in urban dynamics," pp. 8-28 in L. H. Klaasen et al. (eds.) Dynamics of Urban Development. Aldershot, Hants: Gower.

Layfield Committee (1976) Report of the Committee of Inquiry into Local Government Finance. London: H.M.S.O. (Cmnd 6453).

LLOYD, J. G. (1980) "Underground dereliction in the North West." Water Services 84: 104-523.

MARCUSE, P. (1981) "The targeted crisis: on the ideology of the urban fiscal crisis and its uses," Int. J. of Urban and Regional Research 5: 330-355.

MASSEY, D. (1983) "Industrial restructuring as class restructuring: production decentralization and local uniqueness." Regional Studies 17: 73-90.

McCALLUM, J. D. (1980) "Statistical trends of the British conurbations," pp. 14-53 in G. Cameron (ed.) The Future of the British Conurbations. London: Longman.

MOLLENKOPF, J. (1983) The Contested City. Princeton: Princeton Univ. Press.

MOLOTCH, H. (1976) "The city as growth machine: towards a political economy of place." Amer. J. of Sociology 82: 309-332.

NEWTON, K. (1980) Balancing the Books: Financial Problems of Local Government in West Europe. London: Sage.

NEWTON, K. and T. J. KARRAN (1985) The Politics of Local Expenditure. London: Macmillan.

NORTON, R. D. (1979) City Life-Cycles and American Urban Policy. New York: Academic Press.

OECD (1983) Managing Urban Change: Vol. 1, Policies and Finance. Paris: author.

PAHL, R. E. (1975) Whose City? Harmondsworth: Penguin.

PARKINSON, M. (1985) Liverpool on the Brink. Hermitage, Berks: Policy Journals.

PICKVANCE, C. G. (1986) "The crisis of local government in Great Britain: an Interpretation," in M. Gottdiener (ed.) Cities in Stress: A New Look at the Urban Crisis. Newbury Park, CA: Sage.

PRED, A. (1977) City Systems in Advanced Economies. London: Hutchinson.

SAWERS, L. and W. K. TABB [eds.] (1984) Sunbelt/Snowbelt: Urban Development and Regional Restructuring. New York: Oxford Univ. Press.

SHARPE, L. J. (1981) "Is there a fiscal crisis in western European local government: a first appraisal," pp. 5-27 in L. J. Sharpe (ed.) The Local Fiscal Crisis in Western Europe: Myths and Realities. London: Sage.

SOLOMON, A. P. [ed.] (1980) The Prospective City. Cambridge: MIT Press.

STANBACK, T. M. (1985) "The changing fortunes of metropolitan economies," pp. 122-142 in M. Castells (ed.) High Technology, Space and Society. Newbury Park, CA: Sage.

SZELENYI, I. (1983) Urban Inequalities under State Socialism. Oxford: Oxford Univ. Press.

VAN DEN BERG, L. and L. H. KLAASEN (1979) "Municipal capital and urban development." Rotterdam: Netherlands Economic Institute.

VAN DEN BERG, L. et al. (1982) Urban Europe: A Study of Growth and Decline. Oxford: Pergamon.

WASYLENKO, M. (1981) "The location of firms: the role of taxes and fiscal incentives," pp. 155-190 in R. Bahl (ed.) Urban Government Finance: Emerging Trends. Newbury Park, CA: Sage.

WEINSTEIN, B. L. and R. FIRESTINE (1978) Regional Growth and Decline in the United States. New York: Praeger.

WILLIAMS, O. P. (1971) Metropolitan Political Analysis. New York: Free Press.

YOUNG, K. and L. MILLS (1982) "The decline of urban economies," in R. Rose and E. Page (eds.) Fiscal Stress in Cities. Cambridge: Cambridge Univ. Press.

YOUNG, K. and L. MILLS (1983) Managing the Post-Industrial City. London: Heinemann.

Part III

Planning and Financing
Public Infrastructure

5

Planning Infrastructure
for Urban Development

ANTHONY JAMES CATANESE

FROM AN OVERALL VIEWPOINT of community and regional development, infrastructure provides the basic framework for growth. This framework should be planned for both in the short term (3-5 years) and in the long term (6-10 years). Planning infrastructure can be an effective tool for guiding and controlling the timing, direction, and magnitude of urban development. Such planning would allow for viable public/private partnerships to be formed in order to improve the quality of urban development.

THE PLANNING AND
INFRASTRUCTURE MISMATCH

While the basic principle of planning for infrastructure as a key to staging urban development is well-known, the recent experience is less than convincing. The traditional tool for planning infrastructure has been the *Capital Improvements Plan* (CIP). The CIP was seen as a vital component of local and regional comprehensive plans as early as the 1920s. During the 1960s and early 1970s, the CIP was required by the Federal Government as part of the *workable program* needed to qualify for categorical grants-in-aid. However, as a result of revenue sharing and block grants replacing categorical grants-in-aid, the recent decline in federal funding for infrastructure, and the Gramm-Rudman-Hollings Deficit Reduction Law, there are no longer federal requirements for a CIP.

Most cities, nevertheless, undertake some form of planning for infrastructure. A recent survey, for example, indicates that the plans tend to cover general goals and objectives, rather than specific or quantitative analyses (Jenne, 1985). Moreover, for most local and state governments, economic development goals are the major consideration for specific infrastructure improvements (Bamberger et al., 1985). An unfortunate result of this economic development orientation is that infrastructure planning has become more short range than long range. That is, it is not generally seen as part of the comprehensive planning process in the sense of being used as a tool to shape long-range growth patterns.

This has raised several questions in recent years. There is a concern in high-growth areas that the fiscal capacity of local and state government is being strained (Stein, 1988). There is also a realization that the lopsided growth that favors suburban and exurban land over central city sites creates an imbalance. In other words, much infrastructure in central cities is underutilized while suburban infrastructure is near or above capacity. Consequently, it often occurs that infrastructure quality declines in central cities since the revenue base is diminished while social needs escalate.

There is a major need to improve the current state of infrastructure planning. While it may not be possible to return to the process of CIP requirements in comprehensive plans, there are improvements that seem plausible. At the very least, state and local governments should instill a process that allows coordination for infrastructure and development. To allow the infrastructure and development mismatch that occurs without planning is irrational and too expensive for government. Even the short-term gains made by developers who build on cheap suburban land and then demand public infrastructure are not great enough to offset the public costs.

COORDINATION OF PLANNING

A typical infrastructure planning process would go something like this, at least in a growing area. A developer will propose a major project, let us say in a suburban area, that would probably require rezoning of the land use classification and master plan changes. The planning department would refer the proposal to the various functional departments dealing with infrastructure. Comments would be returned to the planning department within some set time period. The planning department would consider these comments along with its own analysis of land use patterns. The developer, knowing this process, usually would provide his or her own analyses of infrastructure needs and costs, attempting to show that the benefits, in terms of jobs, tax revenues, and multiplier effects, outweigh the costs. In some places, the developer would participate in negotiations with the planning and functional departments during the review process, but that only occurs in sophisticated governments and for large-scale projects. The planning department will then make a recommendation to the planning commission—usually a small group of political appointees representing political, community, economic, and social interests of the polity. These citizen-commissioners will have to make highly technical decisions, within a politicized environment, as to the scope and nature of the proposed development. Their decisions are passed on to the elected governing body that considers all that has transpired and makes the final decision based on what is best for the community. More and more, this is becoming tied to economic growth and development in the near term, rather than long-term plans and visions. Too frequently, this orientation takes on an aura of opportunism without strategic thinking.

What is wrong with this approach, which, at the least, can be fostered for its simplicity? The inherent problem is that public planning tends to be reactive to private initiatives. Thus planners and functional agency specialists must react quickly to opportunities posed by a new plant, shopping center, or office park. Infrastructure becomes requisite for approval of such developments rather than the instrument for implementing public policy. Transportation facilities, water systems, and sewerage, for example, are required in most new developments. In the usual process, in a growing region, this infrastructure is an adjunct to the private proposal rather than a guide for development.

Is this premise defensible? Can infrastructure effectively guide development? There seems to be an overwhelming amount of evidence to prove the premise (Hanson, 1984). The history of urban development in this country has been dependent upon the availability of publicly provided infrastructure (Dunn, 1980). Furthermore, it is clear that infrastructure has played the major role in shaping urban development even as technology has changed urban structure (Tarr, 1984).

A significant problem for the coordination of planning in order to achieve the benefits of infrastructure as a guide to development is that different levels of government are responsible for various facilities. In transportation, for example, regional authorities often provide mass transit; states build freeways and arterial roads; counties construct arterial and collector roads; and cities provide collector and local streets. To further complicate coordination, federal funding from the Highway Trust Fund is a significant portion of financing for interstate and national highways. Coordination for highway planning is attempted through metropolitan planning organizations that are designated by the governor of each state for every metropolitan area. This allows for some coordination of mass transit and highway infrastructure, but it is not necessarily related to water quality, sewer systems, open space, and other infrastructure. Furthermore, this approach is the most sophisticated in effect, so coordination for other infrastructure is far from adequate. The problem of coordination among different levels of government exacerbates the potential for planning. Examples of such problems are seen in moratoria and other emergency measures imposed by state and county governments upon local areas when their development outpaces infrastructure.

In a recent survey of coordination of infrastructure planning in the growing Southeast, it was found that most local governments could barely keep up with infrastructure needs created by new development (Landis, 1985). Only a few local governments in that survey indicated that they were able to coordinate infrastructure with comprehensive planning, but those that did were able to report excellent results in managing growth. On the other hand, a recent analysis of older, industrial cities in the Northeast and Midwest indicated that where infrastructure is adequate and underutilized it is possible to form a coordinated planning process among government, business, and cities to affect rebuilding (Porter and Sweet, 1984). This can be described as a win-win strategy. Perhaps it is an indication that public planners, business people, and neighbors are more likely to cooperate when their community is threatened by stagnation and decline.

THE POLITICS OF INFRASTRUCTURE

In a recent case in the Atlanta region, a national developer proposed a huge mixed-use development containing office, retail, and residential space. The project was in a rapidly growing area that had overrun the highway, water, and sewerage infrastructure. After considerable political pressure from state and regional officials, neighborhood groups, and other developers, the county commissioners refused the request for rezoning and infrastructure. They based their decision on infrastructure problems rather than zoning matters. The dejected developer, whose land was in an unincorporated area, approached a nearby small city and proposed that it annex the area and grant him the rezoning that the county had denied. He persuaded the local politicians that the benefits of the development would be great when measured in terms of property tax revenues, *ad valorem* inventory taxes, sales taxes, jobs, and economic multipliers and spinoff effects. The costs would be relatively small since the expensive infrastructure required, namely, highways, sewers, and water facilities, were to be provided by the county and state. Despite vehement political protests from the state and county, the area was annexed to the city, rezoning was granted, and requests for the infrastructure were formally made by the city. In that curious panoply of Sunbelt politics, the project is under construction and the infrastructure will be provided. While there are many political scars from this episode, the city, county, state, and developer have come to an agreement on cost-sharing for the infrastructure. The rationale proffered is that such growth is intrinsically good, so politics can be accommodating.

This case study may or may not reflect Sunbelt political dogma, but it does portray some inherent political values for growth. The paramount value is that growth is good, and political actions are required to nurture, encourage, and facilitate growth. Infrastructure is regarded as a supporting mechanism for economic development (Bamberger et al., 1985). While there is very little left of the Slow Growth or No Growth Movement in the Sunbelt, opposition to new development frequently arises from neighborhood groups. People belonging to such groups are often frustrated by the rapid change in their surroundings and the belief that the quality of their lifestyle and environment is threatened when development outpaces infrastructure as well as educational and social services. Oftentimes, planners side with these neighborhood opponents as natural allies for demanding that development follows patterns established by zoning and infrastructure.

At the risk of overgeneralization, the neighborhoods, and sometimes planners, tend to lose in the political arena. In a sense, the deck is stacked against both of them. Except in areas where overdevelopment has reached a crisis stage, which are, in fact, few and far between, the political values favor growth and development. Given the choice of cutting the ribbon on a multimillion dollar construction site or affirming the planning department's recommendations, politicians inevitably side with growth. Unfortunately, neighbors and planners are cast in the role of naysayers and too often seen as obstacles to growth and change. It is becoming more and more clear that growth-oriented politicians do not consider infrastructure a problem but a potential for development. The major political issue is who will pay for what and how much is required.

With the decreasing federal role in determining criteria for funding eligibility, state and local politics can be expected to play a larger role in infrastructure planning. This requires that planners must be effective politically. That means that planning for infrastructure must form a bridge between the ideal, long-range vision and the short-term political expediency (Catanese, 1984). Planning for infrastructure must recognize that there is a balance between public and private goals as well as public and special interests. To ignore such balance is to ensure that the political process will override rational planning. In order to achieve this balance, planners must understand what developers, politicians, and citizens desire for the quality of growth in their area.

The politics of infrastructure planning in an age of lessened federal guidelines means that planners must develop and employ new skills. The sophistication of the planning profession is now such that many planners understand their role in the political process. They have a range of roles to perform that vary from technical to activist, but most planners find a version of skilled professional with political astuteness and sensitivity to be acceptable.

There are new techniques to help planners in solving political problems of infrastructure. Especially promising is the area of conflict resolution (Elliott, 1988). Conflict resolution techniques include sophisticated approaches that lead to negotiating and mediation by essentially providing a set of ground rules. It establishes a framework for resolving conflicts within an open political forum that requires the consent and will of elected leaders. Such an approach affords negotiated settlements that attempt to attain win-win outcomes. It also allows for the resolution of disputes without resort to litigation. Many planners are now studying the utility of conflict resolution techniques for settling disputes and negotiating infrastructure for development.

The politics of infrastructure have not responded well to the pleas for intervention in the crisis (Choate and Walters, 1981). Rather than seeing our infrastructure as an indication of urban ruin, politicians have been concerned with financing (Melman, 1983). The predominant political attitude is that our infrastructure problems can be solved through technology, engineering, and public works—the political issues revolve around how to pay for it (Peterson, 1981).

PUBLIC/PRIVATE PARTNERSHIPS
IN AN AGE OF AUSTERITY

Major changes have been occurring that relate to the roles of government and business in providing infrastructure in recent years. With the decreased role of the federal government in financing infrastructure, state and local governments have sought alternative methods of paying for infrastructure. This has meant that the private sector will play more of a role in the planning and provision of infrastructure. In essence, rather than infrastructure being a public monopoly, it is becoming a public/private partnership (Catanese, 1984).

The major growth of the U.S. economy, coupled with deficit reduction legislation and stable taxation, allow the private sector to implement public plans through construction. Major private development cannot occur without public infrastructure, and government is no longer willing to simply provide infrastructure to meet all demands. Business and government are partners in urban development in the true sense of sharing risks and rewards. Throughout the country, state and local governments are finding new and creative mechanisms for partnerships. These range from incentives and inducements to exactions and profit-sharing.

Typical examples of public/private partnership mechanisms can be classified in the following way.

Incentives and inducements. These are used by government to encourage developers to locate projects at sizes and scales deemed appropriate in areas planned for infrastructure expansion or in areas already well-served. For example, the following techniques are common:

Capital grants: These are given to businesses in order to facilitate project development according to plans.

Tax abatements/exemptions: Projects that locate in desired areas are forgiven part or all of various state and local taxes for various time periods.

Land writedowns/assemblages: Governmental powers are used to aggregate land parcels, sometimes through eminent domain, and are often made available to developers at discounted prices.

Zoning bonuses: special privileges, such as greater density and floor areas, are allowed.

Public/private deals: These are special arrangements that enable government and business to plan and develop projects jointly and share both the risk capital and profits.

All of these techniques can be augmented to enable the public and private partners to pay for required infrastructure. In large-scale, complex developments, all of these techniques may be used. For example, in New York City, it is common in large projects to find government making capital grants, tax abatements, land writedowns, and zoning bonuses to developers who will provide infrastructure and public amenities. In Los Angeles, some large projects have been negotiated to enable the redevelopment authority to share profits in order to pay for infrastructure and provide public amenities. In San Francisco, all of these techniques have been used and extended to include social needs such as child care and low-income housing.

Contributions and exactions. Public/private partnerships work best when they are mutually desired. Since government is still required to provide infrastructure, however, there are times when contributions and exactions are required from the private partner. Many state and local governments are establishing formal rules and requirements for public/private partnerships that specify the nature of contributions and conditions for exactions in order to create fairness and equity. Contributions and exactions can be classified in this typical manner.

> *Cost-sharing*: General rules are developed that specify the proportion of infrastructure costs that are to be borne by the developer's contributions.
>
> *Impact fees*: These are similar, but they are based on formal specifications based upon the size of project, such as number of housing units, square footage, and density.
>
> *Negotiations*: Some local governments have a negotiation process that determines developer contributions and exactions for infrastructure on a case-by-case basis.
>
> *Voluntary contributions*: Developers are often prone to pay voluntarily for some of the infrastructure costs in order to secure approvals and speed-up the permit process even though there may not be any requirements.
>
> *Private provision*: There are a few local governments that will not provide infrastructure outside of planned areas and require developers to bear all such costs and even operate facilities.
>
> *Social services supplements*: Local governments sometimes require developers to go beyond infrastructure and provide social services and facilities, such as, schools, recreation, fire safety, and security.

All of these techniques and others have occurred in recent years. There are still many ethical, political, and legal questions that surround these contributions and exactions. Yet there seems to be a consensus that changing societal attitudes and behavior require such new approaches. The political process seems to be adjusting to allow such changes to occur.

This should not be misconstrued as to signify that government is getting out of the infrastructure business. Quite to the contrary, for the foreseeable future, government will provide most of the infrastructure required for growth and development—and the public will pay for most of it. General funds, general obligation bonds, revenue bonds, and user fees and charges will remain the major sources for government financing of infrastructure. Yet this will become problematic in the near term since there is growing concern about debt levels of state and local governments and possibly federal curtailment of private purpose tax-exempt bonds. Furthermore, some growing areas are experiencing problems relating to default, near default, and solvency for mistakes made by government and business in locating new development. As these problems worsen, as they will, there will be increased efforts for public/private partnerships. When this is not possible, infrastructure quality will deteriorate, and the seeds of destruction will be sown within rapid growth. None of these dire consequences will occur if sound planning and effective implementation are taken seriously by government and business.

SOUND PLANNING AND EFFECTIVE IMPLEMENTATION

There is a great need in this country to undertake sound planning that provides the basis for effective implementation of infrastructure. The reason that this has not occurred is that there is a gap between day-to-day managers and long-range planners. While somewhat contrived, the nature of this gap is such that managers believe planners to be less than practical and planners consider managers to be shortsighted.

Recent thinking on this problem has centered on approaches to fill the long-range and short-term gap for infrastructure (Brevard, 1985). The approach that is obvious is to work in the middle range and build a bridge—a concept that has been discussed in planning circles for over 30 years (Meyerson, 1956). The way this concept would work is that planners would form the long-run strategies and then work with infrastructure managers to devise the tactics for implementation. This means that plans would have to be programmed into time periods and chunks of growth. Such tactics would allow for the practical, short-run information that managers have argued was missing. Working together, this new CIP would enable planning to be implemented by a team approach among planners, managers, and developers.

A more novel approach to infrastructure planning has been initiated by the state of Florida in 1985 (Chapters 85-55 and 85-57). This new law requires that a hierarchy of plans establish the framework for infrastructure improvements. Specifically, the state develops a plan that serves as the guide for regional plans that themselves guide local government plans. Local governments are required to have plans adopted that are consistent with state and regional plans in order to provide a basis for local development controls and infrastructure. The state reviews and certifies these plans, and it can intervene if a local government refuses or cannot comply with the law. The local comprehensive plan must contain a capital improvements element that sets forth the need for and location of infrastructure. The capital improvements element must show specifically how infrastructure will be used to implement the comprehensive plan, and it must be programmed into 5-year segments. The financing for such infrastructure must be detailed in the 5-year segments. The capital improvements element must be reviewed annually and updated as necessary. Interestingly, any changes to this element and the entire comprehensive plan are limited to two times a year.

As rigorous and formal as this hierarchical process appears to be, it offers clear benefits and is strongly supported by the major actors involved—government, business, and neighborhoods. The reason for their acceptance is that the rules of the game are now explicit for all to understand. If developers want to build in areas not served by infrastructure, they will have a difficult time in securing approvals, and, even if they can prevail, they will have to absorb most of the costs of unplanned infrastructure. On the other hand, if developers follow the plans, they will be assured of fair and equitable treatment as they seek approvals for new projects. Florida's local governments make extensive use of impact fees and user charges, so developers can be assured further that they will not be coerced unfairly into paying for infrastructure that was planned already by government. This new process warrants continuing evaluation and, perhaps, emulation.

Elsewhere, state and local governments are examining their planning and infrastructure processes to seek improved ways of coordination. The key to success is to develop a mechanism to ensure that planning, whether a middle-range bridge, long-range, or statewide hierarchy, is

consistent with infrastructure construction, maintenance, and improvement. Several mechanisms are possible.

Referral. The basic mechanism in most local governments is one in which the
planners refer proposals to infrastructure managers to assess the reason-
ableness and propriety of the project. The planners assemble the opinions
and make an overall evaluation, which they then refer to decision makers
on planning boards and councils. These referral mechanisms range from
the highly structured and well-defined to the casual. In some places,
referral mechanisms are proscribed by area of review, time periods, and
proof of opinion. In other places, it may not involve much more than a
phone call to the city engineer.

Interagency councils. Another mechanism takes the referral process to a
higher plane through the use of interagency councils to review formally all
new developments for their infrastructure needs. This can even include
voluntary or mandatory inclusion and referral to other levels of
government. Where these councils exist, there is much evidence that
referrals are more thorough. Problems sometimes develop when the
process takes too long, but such councils have an intrinsic potential to
reduce delays for permits by providing a "one-stop" service.

Public/private councils. A mechanism to include private interests is a further
elaboration of the interagency council. These councils may or may not
provide binding recommendations—usually they are advisory. The major
advantage is that they allow for the private perspective to be considered
along with the public viewpoint. They also can provide a longer-range
view of planning for infrastructure since new information on growth can
be incorporated from developers.

Developer councils. Special groups that represent developers' interests are
becoming ubiquitous. These councils arise because developers often feel
that they are not adequately affecting infrastructure decisions. They seek
to form an interest group consensus that can be used with considerable
leverage. Sometimes these developer councils are related directly or
indirectly to political action committees or individual political contributions. When they are related in such a way, they may be more effective, but
they are more controversial.

What is clear from all of this is that it is essential for those who plan
infrastructure to enter into a new communications process with
developers and other private sector users. This is needed since it is no
longer rational or affordable simply to provide infrastructure upon
demand. The strength of the economy has fueled development, but the
public revenues and user fees have not kept pace with the costs of

infrastructure. Hence those who demand infrastructure must interrelate more closely with those who plan infrastructure.

CONCLUSION

There is much evidence to show that America's infrastructure needs can be met if it is planned. Governments in growth areas are beginning to understand how to plan for infrastructure and how to work with the private sector. The same thing is occurring in older, industrial areas, with the only difference being that government is in more of an inducement mode. In general, it appears that the mismatch among planning for infrastructure and the timing, direction, and magnitude of development is no longer to be tolerated. State and local governments are seeking ways to ensure that development is consistent with planned infrastructure.

These efforts require innovation and creativity. The decreasing role of the federal government in terms of funding and policy means that there will be little in the way of national standards. That may be acceptable, since the diversity of problems among the regions of this country requires diverse solutions. It is clear, however, that the tenor of the nation is prodevelopment, and much of infrastructure politics is seen as being supportive of development. That offers a unique opportunity for planners. Planners can now show how highways, transit, open space, parks, water facilities, and sewer systems, along with other infrastructure, can provide the framework and context for growth, development, and redevelopment. This opportunity enables new potentials to shape the structure of urban regions. What is needed most is vision, new thinking, and commitment.

All of this kind of planning takes place within the political process. Planners, developers, and neighborhoods must work within the political process to form coalitions based upon compromise, mutual adjustment, and fair play. Political leaders must work closely with planners to understand how individual decisions are related to the growth and development of the region. They must rely more fully on the professional judgment of planners, yet planners themselves must relate technical matters to pragmatism.

Will it play in Peoria? Will politicians, planners, and developers really be able to negotiate plans that will satisfy the best interests of the public? There is little in the history of infrastructure to prove that, so we must view this more in normative terms of "what ought to be." It is certain, however, that the past, replete with pork barrel projects, corruption, scandal, and special interests, is no longer acceptable to the public. With that as a given, politicians, planners, and developers have no choice but to work together for planning infrastructure for urban development.

REFERENCES

BAMBERGER, R., W. BLAZAR, and G. PETERSON (1985) Infrastructure Support for Economic Development. Chicago: American Planning Association.

BREVARD, J. H. (1985) Capital Facilities Planning. Chicago: American Planning Association.

CATANESE, A. J. (1984) The Politics of Planning and Development. Newbury Park, CA: Sage.

CATANESE, A. J. and J. C. SNYDER [eds.] (1988) Urban Planning. New York: McGraw-Hill.

CHOATE, P. and S. WALTERS (1981) America in Ruins. Washington: Council of State Planning Agencies.

DUNN, E. S. (1980) The Development of the U.S. Urban System. Baltimore: Johns Hopkins Univ. Press.

ELLIOTT, M. (1988) In A. J. Catanese and J. C. Snyder (eds.) Urban Planning. New York: McGraw-Hill.

HANSON, R. [ed.] (1984) Perspectives on Urban Infrastructure. Washington, DC: National Academy Press.

JENNE, K. (1985) "The use of formal programming in capital improvement planning." Planning 51, 11: 22-24.

LANDIS, J. (1985) "Infrastructure planning practices in the southeast." Georgia Planning Association Annual Conference, Savannah, October 30.

MELMAN, S. (1983) Profits Without Production. New York: Knopf.

MEYERSON, M. (1956) "Building the middle-range bridge for comprehensive planning." J. of the Amer. Institute of Planners 22 (May): 329-340.

PETERSON, G. (1981) Financing Options for Urban Infrastructure. Washington, DC: Urban Institute.

PORTER, P. R. and D. C. SWEET [eds.] (1984) Rebuilding America's Cities: Roads to Recovery. New Brunswick: Center for Urban Policy Research.

STEIN, J. (1988) In A. J. Catanese and J. C. Snyder (eds.) Urban Planning. New York: McGraw-Hill.

TARR, J. A. (1984) In R. Hanson (ed.) Perspectives on Urban Infrastructure. Washington, DC: National Academy Press.

TOUCHE, ROSS & CO. (1985) Funding Infrastructure in America. Chicago: author.

6

Infrastructure Financing: Examining the Record and Considering the Options

JOHN E. PETERSEN

THE PAST FEW YEARS have seen much discussion about the present or pending "crisis" in public infrastructure. In a nutshell, the complaint is that much of the nation's stock of capital goods has deteriorated badly and needs replacement. In growing areas new development is handicapped by a lack of adequate facilities. In declining areas, the dilapidated condition of public facilities is an impediment to restoring economic vigor. Overcrowded jails, congested highways, polluted waterways, and leaky water mains are all taken as manifestations of the crisis. Identifying the physical dimensions of the needs for public capital spending is not devoid of controversy. But it is only a first step in doing something about the situation. The larger and much more difficult chores are to figure out how the needed improvements are to be financed and who, ultimately, will pay for them.

WHAT IS PUBLIC INFRASTRUCTURE?

Defining what public infrastructure is and how to measure its condition present difficult technical problems. However, at the risk of oversimplifying, a sensible measure of the aggregate investment in domestic infrastructure is found in the total outlays made for state and local government-owned capital facilities. A good working definition is found in the National Income Account's measurement of spending on government equipment and structures, which it calls fixed capital investment.[1] Others have taken a more limited view that considers only such public works as transportation—and water-related public facilities (see U.S. Congressional Budget Office, 1983). But the public utility and economic character of such items as jails, schools, and solid waste facilities would argue for the more inclusive definition in most applications.

Focusing on states and localities in the definition creates problems as regards comprehensiveness, since the federal government and the private sector also make outlays that contribute to—or substitute for—meeting the public's infrastructure needs. But, in our economic system, their roles as providers of capital services used by the general public are relatively minor, at least for the present. Other definitional and data problems emerge regarding what is included as capital spending (for example, governments include land acquisition, but the National Income Accounts do not) and the more esoteric points surrounding the measurement of capital's condition, the benefits of the role of maintenance spending, appropriate depreciation techniques, and the like. While these issues are of interest in many applications, our concerns lie mainly in broad contours of financing of state and local capital spending.

State and local governments are big spenders on capital goods (gross fixed investment was an estimated $65 billion in current dollar terms in 1985), but probably not as big as they should be or would like to be. Examining capital outlays in any one year is unsatisfactory from a normative standpoint, since it fails to account for the fact that an investment made in any one year provides its services over time to changing cadres of users. Since capital improvements last several years and one is typically interested in the "bricks and mortar" that are put in place each year to serve each citizen, it is desirable to adjust for growth in population, changing prices, and the accumulation of capital into a stock that physically depreciates over time and, ultimately, is retired from service (see Petersen and Gitajn, 1985).

First, let us examine the annual expenditures on gross fixed investment between 1950 and 1985. Figure 6.1 illustrates that, in real per capita terms, state and local government investment peaked in 1968 and has been in a more or less constant decline up until the last year. Until the late 1970s the level of annual investment, nonetheless, was sufficient to offset the depreciation and retirement of facilities and added to the total capital stock per person. By 1979, however, the real per capita amount of publicly owned capital stock began to decline, as is displayed

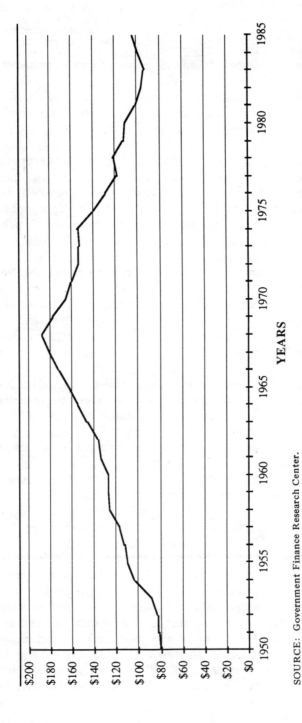

SOURCE: Government Finance Research Center.

Figure 6.1 Gross Fixed Capital Formation Per Capita 1950-1985 (in 1972 constant dollars)

96

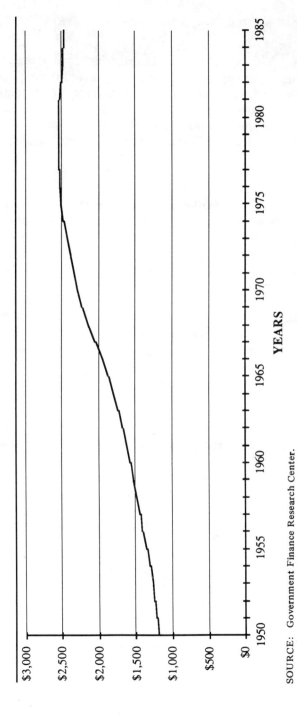

SOURCE: Government Finance Research Center.

Figure 6.2 Net Stock Per Capita 1950-1985 (in 1972 constant dollars)

in Figure 6.2. The measurement of the real value of public capital stock is admittedly crude and declines in certain areas or for some purposes are not necessarily bad. However, to see the aggregate figure continue to fade has constituted a reason for worry. Moreover, most observers contend that, at present levels, the amount of capital stock is far below that which is needed, as is discussed below (see Petersen and Forbes, 1985: Ch. 1).

The aggregate spending and stock figures mentioned above mask over the capital spending patterns for the individual functional categories of capital. In Table 6.1 another perspective is given on capital spending patterns of state and local governments, this time focusing on the growth rates of real aggregate (not per capita) spending by function. Cyclical patterns that reflect both the changing demography and fiscal circumstances of state and local governments are evident. Throughout the 1950s, for example, highway spending (largely propelled by federal grants for the interstate system) grew rapidly. In the early 1960s, conservation and water supply were the favored categories, followed by other buildings and hospitals in the latter part of that decade. By the 1970s, real spending on all types of structures began to decline, with the exception of sewers (assisted mightily by federal construction grants). The malaise spread to virtually all forms of capital spending in the late 1970s as fiscal stringency, high rates of inflation, and taxpayer resistance all took their toll on capital spending levels. So far in the 1980s, only highway spending (spurred by the unique passage of the federal highway tax in 1982 and increased state fuel taxes) has staged much of a comeback.[2]

The above discussion makes a prima facie case that capital spending needs are not being met. But tallying up the needs for public capital spending is highly judgmental, as is specifying the pace at which needs should be fulfilled. One set of needs' figures, developed by the Government Finance Research Center, reflects the magnitude of the effort to reverse the recent trend: It estimated that annual state and local government capital spending would need to be doubled over the remainder of the decade of the 1980s simply to return to the 1978 per capita real level of capital stock (see Petersen and Gitajn, 1985: 19-22).

SOURCES OF FUNDS

What to do about increasing investment in publicly owned infrastructure opens up the intertwined questions of which levels of government

TABLE 6.1

Growth Rates of State-Local Capital Outlays by Functional Category, 1950-1984
(in constant 1972 dollars) (in percentages)

	Five-Year Annual Averages						
	1950-1954	1955-1959	1960-1964	1965-1969	1970-1974	1975-1979	1980-1984
Structures[1]	8.4	4.7	6.4	2.9	-1.4	-5.1	-1.8
Education buildings	12.3	-0.9	6.7	3.0	-1.9	-11.0	-8.8
Hospitals	-7.5	3.9	0.7	9.0	2.2	-13.2	-1.4
Other buildings	4.3	2.3	6.0	13.6	6.1	-6.8	1.9
Highways	10.6	6.7	5.0	0.3	-6.5	-7.6	5.5
Conservation and Development	0.0	6.1	17.4	-0.7	-10.3	-4.8	-5.5
Sewers	5.6	7.8	8.2	0.0	12.3	2.2	-5.3
Water supply	6.0	-2.4	11.8	-1.2	-3.6	0.1	-5.6
Equipment	7.6	-8.1	7.5	13.3	7.6	-3.2	6.3
All structure and equipment	8.3	3.6	6.4	4.0	0.0	-4.8	11.5

SOURCE: Advisory Commission on Intergovernmental Relations, Bureau of Economic Analysis, and author's estimates.
1. Including structures not separately classified.

are responsible and have the resources to support increased spending. Before examining those issues, however, it is useful to review briefly from what sources state and local infrastructure spending has been financed in the past.

When the sector is viewed as a whole, state and local government capital outlays can be financed from three sources:

- borrowing in the credit markets
- current revenues from a government's own sources, and
- federal government aid

Based on estimates developed by the Government Finance Research Center, these alternative sources of funds seems to have fluctuated greatly in importance over the past 30 years (Petersen and Gitajn, 1985: Appendix F). Table 6.2 provides annual estimates of the dollar amounts for the period 1955 through 1985, and Figure 6.3 shows the relative importance of these sources as percentages of funds used in financing capital spending.

In the 1950s, before the dramatic growth in the state and local sector, capital spending by these governments was largely financed by long-term bond sales. During the 1960s, federal aid for public construction grew, as did contributions from current revenues, and the importance of borrowed funds diminished. The 1970s first saw a dramatic rise in the importance of federal aid as a source of capital funds—followed later by a sharp decline in contributions from current revenues, as this source of funds came under the pressure of taxpayer revolts and recessionary conditions. In the 1980s, the trend has been one of diminished federal aid and a growing reliance on debt financing, once again. It appears that financing from current revenue sources is at historic lows, accounting for only a little over 10% of capital spending.

For reasons that are well-known, it is evident that the dollar value of federal grants is unlikely to grow with any vigor, and there will likely be a decline in real, per capita terms. Financing from current revenues will be difficult to expand rapidly, if at all, in the near future, although certain "nondebt" methods of financing may present interesting, if limited, alternative sources of funds. Last, the debt financing option appears the most promising option, although it is one that has many uncertainties attached to it. In the following sections, each of these will be discussed.

TABLE 6.2
Sources of Funds for State and Local Government Fixed Capital Formation

Year	Fixed Capital Formation (Aggregate Amounts in Billions)	Federal Grants	Debt Financed	Current Receipts	Federal Grants (As a Percentage of Fixed Capital Formation) (in percentages)	Debt Financed (in percentages)	Current Receipts (in percentages)
1955	10.3	0.8	5.3	4.2	7.8	51.5	40.8
1956	11.6	1.3	5.3	5.0	11.2	45.7	43.1
1957	12.9	1.8	5.3	5.8	14.0	41.1	45.0
1958	13.9	2.3	5.8	5.8	16.5	41.7	41.7
1959	14.3	2.8	6.5	4.9	19.7	45.7	34.6
1960	14.3	3.3	6.7	4.3	23.1	46.9	30.1
1961	15.5	3.7	6.9	5.0	23.7	44.3	32.0
1962	16.3	4.0	7.0	5.3	24.5	42.9	32.5
1963	18.0	4.3	7.8	5.9	23.9	43.3	32.8
1964	19.5	4.7	8.6	6.2	24.1	44.1	31.8
1965	21.4	5.0	9.5	6.9	23.4	44.4	32.2
1966	23.8	5.4	9.9	8.5	22.7	41.6	35.7
1967	26.0	5.8	11.2	9.0	22.3	43.1	34.6
1968	28.5	6.2	12.6	9.7	21.8	44.2	34.0
1969	29.2	6.6	13.3	9.3	22.6	45.5	31.8
1970	29.8	7.0	14.3	8.5	23.5	48.0	28.5
1971	31.5	7.8	17.1	6.7	24.7	54.2	21.1
1972	32.2	8.5	19.2	4.4	26.5	59.7	13.8
1973	34.7	9.3	19.3	6.1	26.8	55.6	17.6
1974	41.2	10.1	18.2	12.9	24.5	44.2	31.3
1975	42.5	10.9	19.4	12.2	25.6	45.6	28.7
1976	40.4	13.5	19.3	7.6	33.4	47.8	18.8
1977	39.6	16.1	20.5	3.0	40.7	51.8	7.6
1978	46.6	18.3	21.5	6.8	39.3	46.1	14.6
1979	49.4	20.0	22.0	7.3	40.5	44.6	14.9
1980	54.9	22.5	21.2	11.2	41.0	38.6	20.4
1981	53.0	22.1	19.9	11.0	41.7	37.5	20.8
1982	51.5	20.5	25.6	5.5	39.8	49.6	10.6
1983	51.5	20.5	27.2	3.8	39.8	52.8	7.4
1984	59.4	22.7	30.2	6.5	38.2	49.2	12.6
1985	64.0	24.8	33.2	6.0	38.8	51.9	9.4
1986	76.0	26.2	38.2	11.6	34.5	50.3	15.3

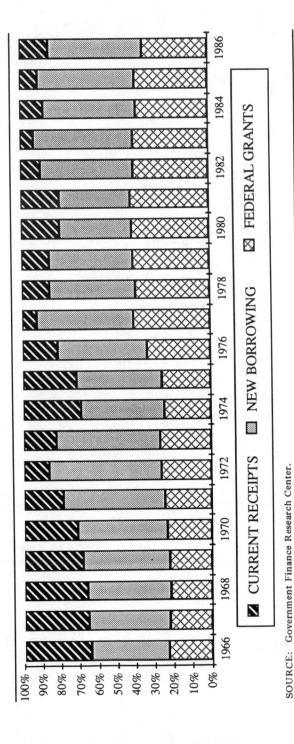

SOURCE: Government Finance Research Center.

Figure 6.3 Sources of Funds for State and Local Government Fixed Capital Formation 1966-1986 (as a percentage of fixed capital expenditures)

FEDERAL AID FOR
CAPITAL SPENDING

As was depicted in Figure 6.3, federal assistance has been of major importance in financing state and local capital spending. The importance, of course, has varied by functional category. For example, federal assistance has been of greatest direct importance in the areas of highways, wastewater treatment, transit, and community development.

There is little question that federal assistance has had a pervasive effect both on what types of capital spending state and local governments have undertaken and the way in which it has been financed. For the recipient governments, the often generous matching grants have spelled greatly lowered capital costs that have tended to skew state and local budgets toward those project areas where federal assistance was available (see U.S. Congressional Budget Office, 1985: 7-8). Also, the federal funds have substituted for funds that in many cases might have been raised by the states and localities themselves (see U.S. Congressional Budget Office, 1986: 80-86). A particularly graphic example of this substitution phenomenon is present in the case of federal wastewater facility construction grants. As seen in Figure 6.4, the real spending by the recipient governments dropped dramatically in response to the rapid uptick in federal assistance in the early 1970s. Partially in recognition of the diseconomies and distortions built into the original Clean Water Act, the federal matching percentages and funds available to municipal wastewater treatment have declined dramatically, and program emphasis is shifting toward the use of loans rather than grants (Petersen, 1985a).

As has been already noted, federal aid in general, including that for capital assistance, has slowed down markedly and, by all indications, will continue to decline in significance. Based on federal budget estimates as of fiscal year 1987, current dollar expenditures will be out paced by the growth in price levels, leading to declines in real dollar assistance (see Petersen and Gitajn, 1985: 8-9).

Of course, all bets are off as regards to what will happen to the federal budget in view of the continuing saga of the federal deficit. General revenue sharing, an important source of local capital spending money in smaller communities, was an early casualty in the budget crunch. However, the adopted legislated cure, the Gramm-Rudman-Hollings Act, which would have been draconian in its impacts on domestic spending, apparently has been rendered toothless (Ross, 1986). Nonethe-

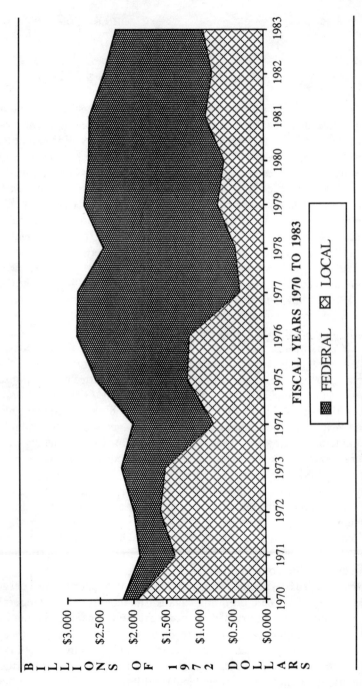

Figure 6.4 Substituting State and Local Funding with Federal Dollars

less, were it ever to become effective, all federal grants to states and localities would face large reductions. Contemporary estimates were that total federal assistance to state and local government (along with other nonprotected domestic programs) would be reduced from current levels by approximately 20% in current dollar terms, which would have meant a $5 billion reduction in federal capital assistance, with continuing rounds of cuts in succeeding years.[3]

FINANCING FROM
CURRENT REVENUES

As was displayed in Figure 6.3, current revenues from state and local governments' own sources once contributed approximately 50% of all funds to capital spending. By our estimates, this source of funds has receded in importance fairly steadily over the years, although it can be of major importance in particular functional areas and at certain levels of government. A leading example has been in the area of highways, streets, and roads, where fuel tax revenues are often used directly by states or passed on to localities for capital spending. Local governments often use current revenues, some of which are earmarked for such purposes, to pay for their recurring and smaller capital outlays. Recent studies by the U.S. Joint Economic Committee have documented that cities of all sizes on average financed about 40% of their general government capital spending from current revenue sources, either currently collected or accumulated in carry-over balances from previous fiscal years (Petersen and Matz, 1985: 12-13).

A problem in the use of current revenues is that, except for very large units, the amounts available in any given year are relatively meager. Furthermore, attempts to accumulate funds in a "savings account" in the form of growing fund balances not only postpones the receipt of the benefits of the desired expenditure, but requires a political discipline that can seldom be sustained. Last, the literature, both academic and applied, is replete with arguments, both sophisticated and prosaic, that justify borrowing as the preferred method for aligning over time benefits and costs in the case of capital facilities (Gordon and Slemrod, 1986).

In considering the broader question of obtaining capital services through the use of current revenues, it should be borne in mind that many financing techniques have been developed for governments to procure the services of capital goods without purchasing the facilities outright or resorting to what is legally defined as borrowing. Leading alternatives are the leasing (or the installment purchasing) of facilities from other governmental units or the private sector, or entering into service contracts whereby an entire service (as opposed to simply the use of facilities) is procured (Petersen, 1986). These techniques can be complicated, but the basic idea is that there are ways that a government can enjoy capital services without actually taking ownership of property or borrowing for purposes of state law. Because of these devices, the underlying capital spending and, often, the de facto borrowing do not show up as governmental fixed investment but rather as a current operating expenditure. The extent of this behavior is unknown, but it probably amounts to several billion in outlays each year (Petersen, 1986: 1-12).

Last, it is worthwhile mentioning that large, but unknown, amounts of capital facilities are not bought outright but rather are "given" to governments through dedications made by private developers. Such exactions are frequently required as a condition for many types of planned development; and the nature, location, and amount of facilities to be dedicated to use by the general public are part of the negotiations surrounding rezonings and the approval of site plans. Projects of this nature may in fact be financed by special districts through the sale of private-purpose tax-exempt bonds; but the security provided often is the credit of the developer and the payment of principal and interest is reflected in higher sales prices and rental rates, rather than in governmentally collected tax receipts and user charges. While such techniques have been heavily employed in many areas, they are best suited to rapidly growing areas, and have been tightly constrained as a result of the new Tax Act (Petersen, 1986: 1-12).

DEBT FINANCING AND
RELATED TECHNIQUES

Going into debt to finance capital outlays has historically been the means to raise the large amounts typically needed to finance major capital expenditures. It has also been one of the most circumscribed of governmental activities since the ability of one legislature to bind the actions of future generations is a potent power and one that can be abused. Nonetheless, in an age where large-scale financing is common-place and the act of going into debt has lost its opprobrium, it is not surprising that governments, directly or indirectly, for themselves or on behalf of others, have become active participants in the credit markets.[4]

The prospects for increased debt financing of public works are bright from the perspective of the needs and the lack of alternatives, but on what terms and conditions governments will be able to borrow remains very much in doubt. The last five years or so have been turbulent and confusing for both the issuers and buyers of governmental debt, as a result of widely fluctuating financial markets and the equally unpredictable twists and turns in federal tax policy. The latter aspect, while important to all forms of capital financing, is especially so in the case of state and local obligations, the vast majority of which pay interest income that is exempt from federal income taxes (and usually also exempt from the taxes in the state where they are issued). While tax exemption has been of great importance in saving state and local governmental borrowers money over the years, that feature has also cost the U.S. Treasury foregone tax revenues.[5]

The appropriate starting point is to calculate how much financing in the credit markets has been done to support public infrastructure spending. As has been widely observed, only a minority of tax-exempt long-term borrowing over the past few years has been targeted for this purpose. Figure 6.5 sets forth the trends in tax-exempt borrowing for selected years since 1970, making the distinction between that borrowing done to support publicly owned facilities (traditional borrowing) and that done to finance various private-purpose (nontraditional) uses, such as business facilities or residences that are owned and operated by nongovernmental private parties. Figure 6.5 also shows the distinction between that borrowing done to raise new capital and that which represents refundings of outstanding debt, a topic we will discuss later. According to the figure, by 1985 (the most recent year with complete figures), the traditional purposes constituted only 37% of the total borrowing for new capital.[6]

The dividing line between public and private purposes is hazy and controversial, but the distinction is important in appreciating the role of borrowing in supporting state and local capital facility financing. The large quantity of borrowing for nongovernmental purposes has been an added source of demand on the tax-exempt securities market and has driven up the cost of borrowing under most market conditions (Office of State and Local Finance, 1985: 298-301). Thus although capital spending for public facilities has represented a minority use of the funds raised in the tax-exempt securities market, as revealed in Figure 6.3, that

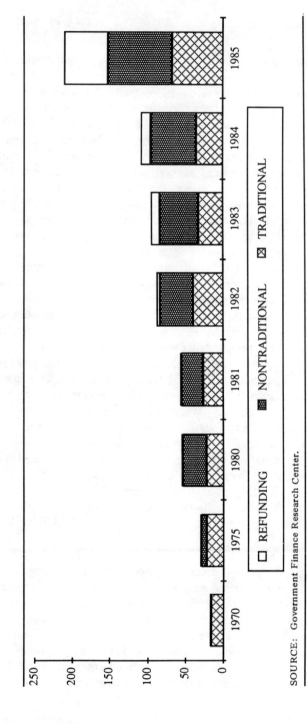

SOURCE: Government Finance Research Center.

Figure 6.5 Volume of New Long-Term Tax-Exempt Bonds by Traditional and Nontraditional Purposes 1970-1985 (in billions of dollars)

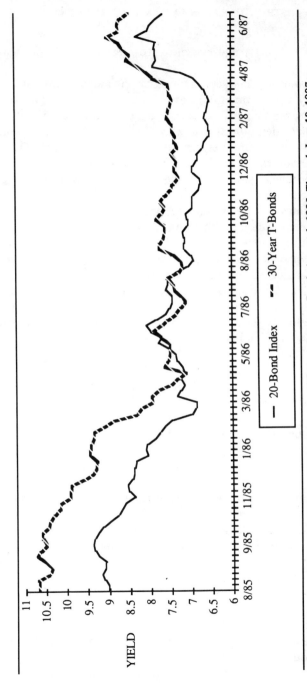

Figure 6.6 Average Yields: Bond Buyer 20-Bond Index and 30-Year Treasury Bonds August 1, 1985, Through June 18, 1987

source is of greater and evidently growing importance in financing spending.

The tax-exempt market has found itself in a state of turmoil over the past two years, as wave after wave of tax reform proposals have led to confusion as to what can be issued (because of uncertain effective dates and slippery definitions) and what tax-exemption will be worth to investors in the future (Petersen, 1985c; Morgan Economic Quarterly, 1986). To add to the confusion, the credit markets have witnessed a general decline in interest rates, despite the presence of a large federal government deficit. As Figure 6.6 illustrates, the level of tax-exempt interest rates has fallen with the general decline in rates, but has fluctuated compared to those on taxable securities, such as long-term U.S. Treasury bonds. At the time of the Tax Reform debate, tax-exempt rates rose in relationship to those on taxable securities, greatly reducing the cost-saving advantages of tax exemption to governmental borrowers. In addition to the threatening tax changes, another factor in the poor performance was the large supply of bonds seeking to slip into the market before the effective dates of the tax revisions and the refinancing of outstanding high-interest debt issued in earlier years.[7]

AFTER THE TAX
ACT: A NEW ERA

Those provisions of the 1986 Tax Reform Act that will affect the tax-exempt bond market are reasonably clear (see Petersen, 1987: Appendix A). Of critical importance is the changes regarding for what purposes and how much tax-exempt borrowing can be done. There has been a tightening of the definitions as regards what purposes bonds can be sold on a tax-exempt basis, the major distinction being that drawn between governmental and private-activity bonds. Furthermore, where they can continue to be sold on a tax-exempt basis, new and tighter ceilings are placed on the issuance of private-activity bonds. Because the law is complicated and its ramifications diverse, the final impacts are yet to be appreciated. Nonetheless, it is clear that the financing of infrastructure through borrowing will be affected, though not as materially or as negatively as was once feared.

Figure 6.7 depicts, based on 1984 bond volumes, the impact of the Tax Act on the volume of tax-exempt bond sales caused by the changes in classification. Under the Tax Act definitions, almost half of the year's

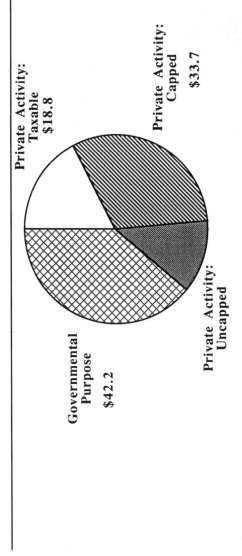

Private Activity:
Taxable
$18.8

Private Activity:
Capped
$33.7

Governmental
Purpose
$42.2

Private Activity:
Uncapped
$13.9

SOURCE: Government Finance Research Center.

Figure 6.7 Impact of the Tax Act on the Status and Volume of Municipal Bonds: Based upon 1984 Volume (billions of dollars)

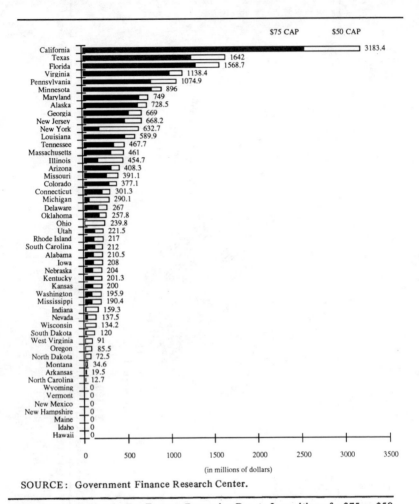

SOURCE: Government Finance Research Center.

Figure 6.8   Reduction in Tax-Exempt Borrowing Due to Imposition of a $75 or $50
Per Capita Cap on Private Activity Bonds, Based upon 1984 Borrowing
Volumes (in millions of dollars)

market would have been either subject to volume caps or no longer
saleable on a tax-exempt basis. Of the $33.7 billion in 1984 borrowings
subject to caps, examination on a state-by-state basis shows that the
maximum allowable under the cap would be $21 billion in 1987 and
$13.7 billion in 1988, as the per-resident cap is lowered from $75 to $50.
Figure 6.8 illustrates, again using the 1984 volumes, the impact on a

state-by-state basis in terms of the dollar reductions that would be required as the cap becomes effective. As may be seen, the largest dollar reductions caused by the caps will occur in California, Texas, and Florida (using 1984 as the base year).

The good news is that the new restrictions on private-activity bonds will mean that the total dollar volume of tax-exempt security issuances will be smaller, thus presenting less competition for governmental purpose bonds in attracting investible funds. However, these changes (along with other revisions in the tax code) will have an adverse impact on those types of financing arrangements that involve the private sector and that sometimes are conveniently grouped under the heading of privatization. For certain types of activity where joint private-public financings have been undertaken (such as water supply, wastewater treatment, solid waste disposal), the new provisions may have a substantial impact on infrastructure spending. However, for most infrastructure outlays where the government is the owner and operator of the facility, the impact should be minimal (Petersen, 1987: 2.1-2.5).

Of greater consequence to governmental borrowers issuing bonds for traditional purposes will be the limitations that are placed on certain issuance procedures and the investment of bond proceeds. As noted, state and local governments, recently faced with rapidly declining interest rates, have heavily engaged in the refinancing of their outstanding debt through a practice called advanced refunding. This practice, which enables issuers to reduce interest rates but adds to the total volume of outstanding tax-exempt debt, will be substantially curbed (Petersen, 1987: 1-10). This means it will be more difficult for governments to refinance debt in order to lower their interest costs. Another financing technique that borrowers have employed, that of arbitrage, which involves governments earning higher interest income on their invested bond proceeds than the interest costs they must pay on their borrowings, will be largely curtailed under the new tax act (Petersen, 1987: 1-11). Loss of arbitrage profits will probably require governments to borrow both more and more frequently.

More serious in the eyes of many observers is the impact of the tax changes on the investors in tax-exempt securities and, hence, on the interest rates that state and local governments may have to pay in order to borrow. Here, the final outcomes present mixed scenarios. The lowering of corporate and individual marginal tax rates might ordinarily be expected to lessen the demand for tax-exempt securities were it not that the host of other tax shelters once found in the tax code have disappeared. As a result, the likely outcome will be that tax-exempt securities will retain (and maybe find enhanced) their relative attractiveness to individual investors when compared to taxable securities (Petersen, 1987: Ch. 3).

On the other hand, three provisions of the new tax code may spell difficulties for the demand for tax-exempts coming from institutional investors. First, banks will lose their unique ability to write off 80% of the interest costs they pay for purposes of investing in tax-exempt securities. A special exception is granted to bank holdings of obligations of governments that issue less than $10 million a year. The upshot of this would be to lessen bank demand for tax-exempt securities, except for those small governmental issues. Second, the new tax law contains provisions that subject corporate and personal incomes that are currently untaxed to an alternative minimum income tax. Although the applications are complicated, the outcome will tend to discourage certain financial institutions from owning tax-exempt securities, especially those of a private-purpose character. In the case of individual investors, the exclusion of public-purpose tax-exempt bond interest income from the alternative tax base may actually enhance demand from that source. Third, property and casualty insurance companies are subject to reducing deductions for loss reserves by 15% of their tax-exempt interest income. This works out to a 5.1% tax on tax-exempt income. However, a return to profitability and the fact that other income is subject to higher rates of taxation may stimulate demand from these investors.

How significant a reduction in institutional demand will be when weighed against the reduced supply of tax-exempt securities remains a matter of conjecture (Petersen, 1987: 3-10). On balance, because of a better matching of supply with demand, the interest rates on tax-exempt securities should drop relative to those on taxable securities. It appears certain, however, that governments will find it necessary to begin thinking about different, taxable-bond markets, if they are going to pursue many of their economic development and housing-related borrowing activities (Hawthorne, 1986).

CONCLUSIONS

The question of how future state and local government capital spending will be financed is unresolved. The federal government, for both philosophical and practical reasons, can no longer be looked to as a growing source of funds. Strenuous effort will be needed to keep the nominal dollar value of federal assistance to state and local capital projects at current levels. As federal aid diminishes in importance, growth in capital spending will need to be picked up by the states and localities themselves or shifted to the private sector. Furthermore, the retreat in federal assistance in noncapital areas will place pressure on governments to divert current revenues to the competing areas of operating expenditures and transfer payments. In view of the less than robust financial condition of many states and not a few localities, it is unlikely that substantial diversions of current revenues to capital spending will occur.

Furthermore, rhetoric aside, steps toward private ownership and operation of capital facilities have been slowed by the recent tax act, which has curbed many of the economic incentives. Private involvement in providing infrastructure will continue, of course. But, where possible, it will be channeled into legal forms where governments will necessarily exercise some controls and responsibility, such as special taxing districts and assessments that meet the new government purpose tests for bond sales.

The remaining choice open to states and localities in financing their capital spending needs is to borrow in the credit markets, a traditional method of raising funds for large-scale, long-lived improvements. Despite the many uncertainties preceding the recent passage of the Tax Reform Act, the credit markets are alive and well. Thus the choice of borrowing is likely to be both affordable and popular.

NOTES

1. Government equipment and structures are physical assets that, were they owned by the private business sector, would be counted in fixed business capital, plus equipment and facilities that have no counterpart in the business sector. See Musgrave (1980).

2. The Surface Transportation Act of 1982 increased federal motor fuel taxes by five cents a gallon (four cents going to highway uses and one cent being devoted to transit assistance), which increased funds available to highway spending by about $5 billion annually.

3. With 1987 fiscal year capital assistance spending at approximately $25.5 billion, a 20% reduction to meet the needed spending reduction in domestic spending would amount to $5.1 billion in reductions for fiscal year 1988.

4. The tax-exempt bond market has been a hotbed of innovation, as well as the scene of rapid growth and sudden decline in volume of new issue activity during this period. See Petersen (1985b) and Petersen and Forbes (1985).

5. The tradeoffs between tax exemption as a means of reducing borrowing costs for states and localities versus the federal taxes foregone is an old and ongoing controversy. For recent review, undertaken from the federal government's viewpoint, see Office of State and Local Finance (1985, Ch. IX).

6. Nontraditional debt-financing functions are defined to include housing, industrial development, pollution control, hospitals, and student loans, most of which entail the state and local government acting as a conduit to access the tax-exempt market on behalf of nongovernmental users or borrowers.

7. Approximately 45% of $48 billion in long-term tax-exempt borrowing done in the first half of 1986 was for purposes of refinancing outstanding debt. See The Daily Bond Buyer (July 7, 1986: 3).

REFERENCES

The Daily Bond Buyer (1986) "A decade of municipal finance." (July 7).

GORDON, R. and J. SLEMROD (1986) "An empirical examination of municipal financial policy," in H. S. Rosen (ed.) Studies in State and Local Public Finance. New York: National Bureau of Economic Research.

HAWTHORNE, F. (1986), "Public finances: tilling new ground." Institutional Investor.

Morgan Economic Quarterly (1986) "Turmoil in tax-exempts: impact on issuers and investors." (March).

MUSGRAVE, J. C. (1980), "Government-owned fixed capital in the United States, 1925-79." Survey of Current Business (March).

Office of State and Local Finance (1985) U.S. Department of the Treasury, Federal-State-Local Fiscal Relations. Washington, DC: Government Printing Office.

PETERSEN, J. E. (1985a) Financing Clean Water. New York: First Boston Corporation.

PETERSEN, J. E. (1985b) Recent Developments in the Tax-Exempt Bond Market. Washington, DC: Government Finance Research Center.

PETERSEN, J. E. (1985c) "The impact on local government capital financing," in J. Petersen and W. Davis (eds.) Tax Reform and Local Government: An Assessment of Reagan's Plan. Washington, DC: National League of Cities.

PETERSEN, J. E. et al. (1986) Non-debt Financing of Public Works. Washington, DC: Government Finance Research Center.

PETERSEN, J. E. (1987) Tax-Exempts and Tax Reform: Assessing the Consequences of Tax Reform Act of 1986 on the Municipal Bond Market. Chicago, IL: Government Finance Officers Association.

PETERSEN, J. E. and R. FORBES (1985) Innovative Capital Finance. Chicago, IL: American Planning Association.

PETERSEN, J. E. and A. GITAJN (1985) Projections of State-Local Capital Stock Requirements. Washington, DC: Government Finance Research Center.

PETERSEN, J. E. and D. MATZ (1985) Trends in the Fiscal Condition of Cities: 1983-1985. Washington, DC: Joint Economic Committee.

ROSS, T. (1986) "Gramm-Rudman-Hollings: Fiscal Armageddon for state and local governments." Washington, DC: Public Sector Review.

U.S. Congressional Budget Office (1983) Public Works Infrastructure: Policy Considerations for the 1980s. Washington, DC: Government Printing Office.

U.S. Congressional Budget Office (1985) The Federal Budget for Public Works Infrastructure. Washington, DC: Government Printing Office.

U.S. Congressional Budget Office (1986) Federal Policies for Infrastructure Management. Washington, DC: Government Printing Office.

7

Financing New Infrastructure
with Development Impact Fees

ARTHUR C. NELSON

THE FINANCING OF COMMUNITY infrastructure to support growth is not inexpensive. The cost to support 1,000 new residents in Irvine, California, for example, was estimated to range up to $23,800 per house in the early 1980s (California Office of Planning and Research, 1982: 2). Infrastructure needed to support growth include schools, streets, parks, water and sewer systems, drainage systems, libraries, and police and fire facilities, to name a few.

To pay for these facilities, communities have traditionally relied upon general funds, federal support, and tax-exempt general obligation bond issues. In recent years, however, communities in the United States and Canada have used development impact fees to shift the burden of paying for new infrastructure on to development and new residents.

This chapter first considers the historical and political context of development impact fees. Remaining sections review the legal rationale for impact fees, impact fee calculation, affordable housing and equity considerations of impact fees, strategies for mitigating the adverse effects of impact fee systems, and the future of development impact fees as a way to pay for growth.

THE HISTORICAL AND POLITICAL
CONTEXT OF DEVELOPMENT IMPACT FEES

Impact fees are the latest step in the evolution of local government infrastructure finance. Prior to the 1920s, communities readily extended infrastructure to undeveloped tracts of land in order to accommodate demand and induce economic development. It was not uncommon to find speculators subdividing vast tracts of land considerable distances away from cities in anticipation that purchasers of lots would demand, and eventually receive, city services (Schultz and Kelley, 1985: 8).

By the end of the 1920s, many communities became unwilling to install water, sewer, and street services within the boundaries of development. The reason was fundamentally cost. Many communities found they could shoulder the cost of building central treatment and delivery facilities, but they could not afford the cost of extending service to every house and along every street within subdivisions. By the 1940s, it was common practice for communities to require developers to install most of the on-site infrastructure. A kind of partnership thus emerged, especially in rapidly growing communities: The community would provide central facilities, main lines, and roads to an area, while the developer would extend those services to each lot or home in the development at his cost.

But many communities also discovered that development requires new parks and schools. During the 1940s, and especially after World War II, therefore, many states enabled communities to require new subdivisions to dedicate land for parks and school sites. If land could not be dedicated, then an appropriate fee in lieu of the mandatory dedication would be charged. These fees were the first attempt at forcing development to account for some of its impact on communities (Nelson, 1987: 23).

Still, until about a decade ago, most residential subdivisions and other kinds of developments were usually provided government-subsidized infrastructure, such as streets and water and sewer systems, funded at least in part from abundant federal funds, locally issued double-tax-exempt obligation bonds, and general funds. The prevailing attitude was that incremental development supported by expanding community infrastructure would so broaden the fiscal base that the average cost to households would decline. All citizens, both new and existing, would benefit from growth as the quality of community life would improve.

Challenges to the growth ethic emerged in the late 1960s, however, as some citizens observed that unbridled growth caused pollution, congestion of streets, overuse of other community services, increasing crime, and generally a lowering of the quality of life. Even more disturbing was the realization that rapid growth actually caused per capita tax expenditures for infrastructure and services to rise. Instead of depending on growth to improve the quality of life, many communities found growth to be inimical to the reasons people had for choosing to live in those communities (see, generally, Scott et al., 1975). There thus emerged an antigrowth sentiment in many rapidly growing areas, especially in those having unique scenic resources and higher than average proportions of affluent and well-educated households (Connerly and Frank, 1986: 572; Dowall, 1980: 425).

In addition to the antigrowth sentiment has been the decline in government funds spent on infrastructure in recent years. Since the mid-1960s, federal, state, and local government capital spending has not kept pace with inflation or population growth. Total government capital spending, for example, declined from 3.4% of gross national product in 1965 to 1.3% in 1984. While nominal dollar expenditures increased from $20.6 billion in 1965 to $50.7 billion in 1984, inflation-adjusted spending actually fell from $31.3 billion to $20.5 billion (in 1972 dollars). Even more dramatic has been the decrease in real per capita infrastructure investment from $161 in 1965 to less than $87 in 1984 (Duncan et al., 1986). The decline in government support for infrastructure, partly explained by the "taxpayer revolt," has meant that many communities have become unwilling to subsidize the cost of new community infrastructure required by growth (Weschler et al., 1987: Ch. 2).

In recent years, many rapidly growing communities have sought to shift the burden of paying for new infrastructure from the community at-large to newcomers. Some of these communities justify exacting from developers money and other concessions in return for the privilege to build. Many communities have become adept at exacting various forms of concessions from developers in order to build off-site infrastructure (Frank and Rhodes, 1986). Many developers and public officials dislike negotiated exactions, however, since the exactions are unpredictable, can result in protracted project review, and discriminate against similar projects (Porter, 1987: 12).

In response to the pitfalls of negotiated exactions, many communities have adopted development impact fees. Impact fees are predictable, scheduled charges levied by a local government on a new development in order to generate revenue for specific off-site facilities substantially benefiting that development (Jurgensmeyer, 1985: 24). Strictly speaking, impact fees do not include negotiated exactions, mandatory dedications, or in-lieu-of fees (though some communities assess these against some developments in addition to impact fees). Thus they have the advantage of protecting both developers and communities against the uncertainty of negotiated exactions (Porter, 1987: 3). Impact fees are usually collected at the permit stage so that funds become available close to the time when project impacts occur. Impact fees are also assessed on projects that do not involve subdivision of land, such as condominiums and apartments, which have escaped mandatory dedications and in-lieu fees in the past. They are the latest and most rational step in the evolution of local government infrastructure finance (Snyder and Stegman, 1986: 5-6). Since their initial use in California and Florida, development impact fees have become an increasingly popular method of financing new infrastructure, especially in rapidly growing communities (Frank and Downing, 1987: 5-6).

Development impact fees have gained political popularity in many rapidly growing communities for five reasons (Frank and Downing, 1986: 11-12). First, they protect existing residents and taxpayers from the additional costs of new development. Fees thus answer current residents' concerns that (a) their tax burden is already too high, (b) they have already paid for their infrastructure and do not want to pay for newcomers' infrastructure, and (c) newcomers should pay for their own infrastructure.

Second, communities use impact fees to synchronize development with the installation of new infrastructure. This approach seeks to avoid the chronic congestion of facilities resulting from development approvals issued without regard to the availability of service capacity. Local government officials thus prohibit new development unless sufficient facility capacity exists.

Third, impact fees are used to impose price discipline on development by forcing development to internalize infrastructure costs in finished development prices. Developers will respond by investing only when projects are economically prudent and not before as when they are induced by community-subsidized infrastructure. Local government officials can thus defend development approvals on the grounds that developments not only pay their own way, but development occurs only when it is economically justified.

Fourth, impact fees may be used to enhance the quality of life within communities since communities with deficient facilities can, to some extent, assess new development to make-up some of those deficiencies. Forcing development to improve facilities that benefit all residents is common practice in California as impact mitigation. In most states, courts have allowed existing residents to benefit incidentally from impact fees assessed against new residents.

Finally, impact fees can mollify local anti- or slow-growth sentiments. This is perhaps the main reason why developers are willing to pay impact fees. They see the fees as essential to overcoming the objections of some residents (Porter, 1987: 11).

A variety of impact fees are currently being levied. Although initially collected for road and park improvements in both Florida and California during the mid-1970s, the menu now includes fire and police facilities, water and sewer systems, drainage systems, school facilities, libraries and cultural facilities, museums, day care, and administrative facilities. Impact fees, however, cannot be used to finance operation and maintenance of facilities.

What is also becoming difficult to ascertain is the number of municipalities and special service districts that assess impact fees. Downing and Frank (1982) and Downing et al. (1985a, 1985b) surveyed all jurisdictions with more than 15,000 persons and found that 219 employed recreation impact fees in 1982, 21 assessed fire facility impact fees in 1985, and 190 levied sewer impact fees in 1985. These numbers are certainly higher today. Their research suggests that growth states, such as California, Colorado, and Florida, Texas, and Washington, and growth islands within other states, such as in Illinois and Oregon, lead the nation in the use of impact fees. Every state and province in North America has at least one example of a development impact fee.

LEGAL DEFENSE OF
DEVELOPMENT IMPACT FEES

Courts have been concerned that impact fees may be a form of taxation without either adequate statutory authority or electoral approval. Such is the case if fees are not clearly used for specific improvements that directly benefit contributing development, or if the amount of fees collected exceed that needed to pay for those improvements. Communities prefer to avoid having their impact fees viewed as a tax since this would usually require voter approval, which is often difficult to obtain. In California, for example, approval requires a two-thirds majority vote.

Impact fees are defended as appropriate expressions of community police power. They are used to maintain or promote the health, safety, and general welfare of the community in the face of growth. As expressions of police power, impact fees paid by contributing development must be related to the benefit or service being purchased, and be uniquely attributable to the development (Callies and Freilich, 1986: 380, 385). These judicial objectives are achieved when impact fee systems meet the "rational nexus test" (Bosselman and Stroud, 1985: 545-546).

Courts review impact fee policies in terms of up to five factors making up the rational nexus test (Stroud, 1987). First, development must clearly benefit from facilities financed from the impact fees it pays. Second, fees should be earmarked to finance only those facilities that benefit contributing development. Third, the fees should be expended within a reasonable period of time. This is usually satisfied by adopting a capital improvements plan that clearly shows when projects financed by the fees will be built. Fourth, to further ensure that fees collected will benefit the contributing development, fees should be expended within a zone or district where development is located. Finally, to avoid double taxation, contributing development must receive credit for other tax payments it makes, such as excise, property, and sales taxes, that are used to pay for the same facilities financed by the fees (National Association of Home Builders, 1984). Otherwise the courts can find a portion of the fee to be an unauthorized tax that must be refunded.

CALCULATING DEVELOPMENT IMPACT FEES

Two different kinds of formulas can be used to calculate impact fees. A fixed assessment formula calculates impact fees on a per unit basis (for example, per dwelling unit, bedroom, or square foot). The second, and less common method, involves an algorithm in which the assessment depends on the location of the development and the variable cost of adding new or expanding existing facilities. Although more complicated, the second approach has the advantage of distributing impact fee burdens based on more precise cost estimates of different projects.

To show how a fixed assessment formula works, consider a community of 50,000 residents living in 20,000 dwelling units. The community has adopted a standard of five acres of park per 1,000 residents. Suppose it has 250 acres of park and therefore meets this standard currently.[1] Suppose further that within ten years the city is projected to double, to 100,000 residents living in 40,000 dwelling units. It therefore needs to add 250 more acres of park over the next decade. If the present cost of providing new parks is $30,000 per acre, the community needs to raise $7.5 million in current dollars over the next ten years. The capital improvement plan might specify that 25 acres of park land should be added each year for the next ten years. The community raises these funds by assessing impact fees of $150 per new resident (in current dollars). Since it is impractical to assess new residents directly, the community can reasonably assess new dwelling units instead. At an average of 2.5 persons per residence, the fee would average $375 per new unit. However, the fee might be adjusted to reflect the size and the probable average number of residents occupying different housing types. Detached single-family dwellings, which are determined to average three persons per unit, would be assessed $450. Each half of duplex buildings, which average 2.5 residents, would be assessed $375. Each unit in high-rise buildings, which average 1.8 persons, would be assessed $270.

In contrast to the fixed assessment schedule is, for example, the Traffic Review and Impact Planning Systems (TRIPS) used by Broward County, Florida. Instead of determining average impacts in the manner described above, TRIPS matches the fee assessed to the actual impact of a specific development on the county's roads.

TRIPS involves four steps (Frank, 1984). First, the travel impact of each development is estimated. This entails an initial estimate of the number of vehicle trips a proposed development will generate. A gravity model is then used to distribute trip purposes between traffic destination zones throughout the county. Trips are assigned to those paths that constitute the minimum travel-time routes to each traffic zone. The assignment procedure accounts for home-based shopping trips, home-based work trips, home-based school trips, recreation trips, other miscellaneous trips, and non-home-based trips. A "tuning factor" is built into the model to ensure that predictions of travel behavior reasonably relate to the predictions made by the county's transportation planners.

The second step involves evaluating the capacity of each road segment used by trips generated by the development. It does this by comparing average daily travel capacity at the preferred level of service, to the sum of: (1) existing traffic volume, (2) assigned volume for previously evaluated projects that have not been completed, and (3) the traffic volume generated by the development. No impact fee will be assessed against developments for any road segment where the service level is not exceeded by traffic generated by the development. One problem with this particular approach, however, is that earlier developments can "soak up" capacity without being assessed an impact fee. Variable impact fee systems can be designed to avoid this problem.

For congested road segments that the county identifies, the model estimates the cost of those improvements plus the average daily travel capacity gained by improvements. Lastly, the model computes the development impact fee to be assessed based on the proportion of the improved capacity that can be assigned to the traffic generated by a development.

Once a plat or plan has been approved and an impact fee collected, the TRIPS model functions like a trust fund accounting device. It keeps track of the fees paid by each development, monitors the accumulation of contributions to each scheduled road improvement, and notes the status of each improvement in the capital improvements program.

TRIPS depends on two sets of data. One is a road network file containing a link-node description of both the existing network and the network programmed for improvement. Associated with each of the segments are descriptions of its current average daily travel, its average daily travel capacity at congestion, its desired level of average daily travel, and cost of improvements that are programmed, among other factors.

The second data file contains information on existing land uses within traffic zones. Each traffic zone is linked to one or more connecting roads. All trips originating or terminating in the traffic zone are assumed to connect onto the road network through these links.

AFFORDABLE HOUSING AND EQUITY CONSIDERATIONS OF IMPACT FEES

While development impact fees can help communities finance the cost of development, they may have detrimental effects on housing costs and availability, as well as social equity.

Tax incidence theory generally supports the view that developers do not bear the full impact fee burden, especially in the long run (Schechter, 1976). In competitive housing markets, housing prices are market determined. Since home builders are not normally price setters, they cannot simply factor development impact fees into their production process and charge higher prices for new homes (Ellickson, 1982: 153-154; Snyder and Stegman, 1986: 100).

In markets where housing demand is relatively price inelastic, as in communities with environmental features and amenities that make them attractive places to live, a large portion of impact fees and associated builder mark-ups are probably passed solely along to home buyers. Landis's (1986) study of San Jose, for example, showed that builders responded to high impact fees by changing their market orientation to more affluent households. Buyers priced out of the San Jose market sought housing in other nearby communities having lower or no fees. In markets where housing demand is somewhat more price elastic, developers may not increase finished house prices or reduce production, but instead downgrade lot or dwelling unit size, quality, and amenities.

Why would not landowners internalize fees in lower land sale prices? In markets where buyers are not very price sensitive, developers can upscale their product, thereby passing the fee forward to buyers instead of backward to landowners (Snyder and Stegman, 1986). In markets where buyers are more price sensitive, landowners may not be as competitively oriented as economic theory would suggest. Many landowners do not have a sense of their opportunity costs and will not sell unless their asking price is met (Dowall, 1984: 111). The supply of buildable land is therefore constrained by landowner idiosyncrasies.

Where development impact fees cause new home prices to increase, the price of comparable existing housing will also increase and thereby confer on those owners a windfall (Snyder and Stegman, 1986: 97). Furthermore, if impact fees improve the quality of life for the entire community, then all property becomes more desirable and values receive yet another windfall.

When impact fees raise housing prices, the income and social mix of communities change. Developers in Orlando, Florida, for example, indicated that they upgraded their product line to the $60,000-$80,000 range because development impact fees were too significant a cost element in the $40,000-$50,000 range (Snyder and Stegman, 1986: 98). Naturally, only households with incomes that could justify higher-priced housing could afford to live in Orlando. Such reorientation of the residential mix of communities is a nearly unavoidable effect of impact fees (Dowall, 1984: 141). The income and social mix of the community is also affected by the regressive nature of impact fees as fees are not assessed on an ability to pay basis.[2]

In effect, impact fees may act as an "entrance fee" households pay to "join" certain communities (Beatley, 1987). Such "clubby" communities are exclusionary (Blewett, 1983: 3). Just as large lot zoning can preclude from some communities all but affluent households, so might high development impact fees allow entry to only the "right" households. Unfortunately, the courts have not considered the exclusionary tendency of fees since fees are reviewed under "benefit" standards and not exclusionary standards (Schell and Ramis, 1987: 11).

This has implications for the distribution of regional fair-share housing. If a community charges substantially higher development impact fees than others, it will exclude lower-income households unless it specifically provides for their needs. Development impact fees may thus maldistribute the distribution of lower-income households within the region.

Another concern is that not only new but also existing residents may pay impact fees. This is the case when existing residents move up from lower-valued homes or from rental units to new housing. They are not "new" residents, but they must pay the same impact fees that the community intended new residents to pay. Those existing residents have not only paid for older infrastructure, but now must pay for new infrastructure. However, residents who sell their older home and buy a new one are compensated to the extent that their sales price captured the windfall generated by the impact fees assessed on new homes. This would not be the case among existing renters who purchase homes, however.

This leads to an intergenerational consideration. The infrastructure used by the current generation was probably subsidized by an earlier generation from abundant federal funds and tax exempt borrowing. By assessing impact fees on the new generation, the current generation is choosing not to extend the same advantages to the next generation.

WHAT CAN PUBLIC OFFICIALS DO TO MITIGATE THE NEGATIVE EFFECTS OF IMPACT FEES?

Public officials have not generally come to grips with the housing and equity effects of development impact fees. Although difficult to accomplish, there are at least eight tactics officials might employ to reduce the negative effects of impact fees (Weitz, 1984):

(1) Assure that long-range community plans adequately foresee future demand for developable land by providing that land with infrastructure,

and thereby keep the land market from internalizing supply shortages attributable solely to unserviced land.

(2) Give adequate notice to developers that development impact fees are being considered. This will allow them greater leverage in negotiating more favorable purchase agreements with landowners.

(3) Tailor impact fees to the effects that specific developments have on communities. Fixed assessment fee schedules that account for categorical variation impacts, and variable fees should be preferred.

(4) Attempt to assure a competitive land market. In a tight land market, where demand for land exceeds supply in the short term, officials might consider increasing the supply of buildable land by allowing for greater densities or adding to the supply of vacant buildable land.

(5) Assure consistent land use practices. In communities where landowners perceive that allowable land use intensities can be easily upgraded, developers may be forced to pay land prices that are only justified by much more intense development. This is not to say that regulations should be inflexible, just that they should be administered in a predictable way that sets reasonable limits on the manner in which the land market can operate.

(6) Full property tax assessments and rates should be levied on vacant land. Assessing vacant land at its full value for property tax purposes will prevent landowners from using preferential tax programs or underassessments to subsidize their holding costs. Preferential property tax programs should therefore not be extended to urbanizable land.

(7) Collect development impact fees as the home is sold, rather than at the platting or building permit stages. This saves developers from paying fees with money borrowed at commercial interest rates and having to mark-up prices to reflect the costs of administering the charge.

(8) Make greater use of long-term special assessment financing in lieu of development impact fees. This maintains the policy to shift the financing burden to new development, but allows that burden to be paid over time and at lower than commercial lending rates. Home prices are not as influenced by long-term special assessment encumbrances as they are by impact fees.

THE FUTURE OF
DEVELOPMENT IMPACT FEES

What is the future of impact fees? In light of declining federal, state, and local support for new infrastructure, more communities that are experiencing growth will turn to impact fees. More state legislatures should be expected to enable communities to assess impact fees, and more courts should become sympathetic to the rationale communities use to defend impact fees.

Developers will become increasingly willing to "pay to play" (Porter, 1987: 1). The development community actually prefers impact fees to negotiated exactions since the fees are generally viewed as more predictable and fair. Developers also have come to believe that impact fees will give them leverage to demand the public facilities that they need. There is thus a quid pro quo between communities and developers. Without fees, communities cannot readily accommodate development and builders cannot readily build (Snyder and Segman, 1986: 3).

There remains the critical concern that the adverse effects of impact fees will be ignored unless political and legal pressure is brought to bear on those communities insensitive to the effects. More research must be undertaken to determine the extent of those effects so that effective policy interventions can be made to mitigate them.

NOTES

1. If the community does not meet its own standard, it must show in its land use and capital improvements plans how the current deficiency will be overcome. Impact fees cannot be assessed on new development to overcome current deficiencies (Nelson, 1987: 23-24).

2. Some communities, such as Loveland, Colorado, address this problem by reducing or waiving the fee on lower-valued homes under certain conditions (Amborski et al., 1987: 14).

REFERENCES

AMBORSKI, D. P., J. H. LILLYDAHL, A. C. NELSON, T. V. RAMIS, A. RIVASPLATA, and S. R. SCHELL (1987) State and Provincial Approaches to Development Impact Fees. New Orleans: Univ. of New Orleans, School of Urban and Regional Studies.

BEATLEY, T. (1987) "Ethical issues in the use of impact fees to finance community growth." Presented to the 1987 Conference of the American Planning Association, Division of Urban and Environmental Planning, University of Virginia, Charlottesville.

BLEWETT, R. (1983) "Fiscal externalities and residential growth controls: a theory-of-clubs perspective." Public Finance Q. 11: 3-20.

BOSSELMAN, F. P. and N. E. STROUD (1985) "Pariah to paragon: developer exactions in Florida 1975-85." Stetson Law Rev. 14, 3: 527-563.

California Office of Planning and Research (1982) Paying the Piper: New Ways to Pay For Public Infrastructure in California. Sacramento: Office of Planning and Research.

CALLIES, D. L. and R. H. FREILICH (1986) Cases and Materials on Land Use Law. St. Paul, MN: West.

CONNERLY, C. E. and J. E. FRANK (1986) "Predicting support for local growth controls." Social Sci. Q. 3: 572-586.

DOWALL, D. E. (1980) "An examination of population-growth-managing communities." Policy Studies J. 9: 414-427.

DOWALL D. E. (1984) The Suburban Squeeze. Berkeley: Univ. of California Press.

DOWNING, P. B. and J. E. FRANK (1982) Recreational Impact Fees. Tallahassee: Florida State Univ., Policy Sciences Program.

DOWNING, P. B., J. E. FRANK, and E. R. LINES (1985a) Community Experience with Fire Impact Fees: A National Survey. Tallahassee: Florida State Univ., Policy Sciences Program.

DOWNING, P. B., J. E. FRANK, and E. R. LINES (1985b) Community Experience with Sewer Impact Fees: A National Survey. Tallahassee: Florida State Univ., Policy Sciences Program.

DUNCAN, J. B., T. D. MORGAN, and N. R. STANDERFER (1986) Simplifying and Understanding the Art and Science of Impact Fees. Austin: City of Austin Planning Department.

ELLICKSON, R. C. (1982) "The irony of exclusionary zoning," in M. B. Johnson (ed.) Resolving the Housing Crisis. Cambridge: Ballinger.

FRANK, J. E. (1984) "How road impact fees work in Broward County." Planning 50, 6: 24-27.

FRANK, J. E. and P. B. DOWNING (1986) "National experience with impact fees." Presented to the 1986 Conference of the Association of Collegiate Schools of Planning, Florida State University, Department of Urban and Regional Planning.

FRANK, J. E. and P. B. DOWNING (1987) "Patterns of impact fee usage." Presented to the 1987 Conference of the American Planning Association. Florida State University, Department of Urban and Regional Planning.

FRANK, J. E. and R. M. RHODES [eds.] (1987) Development exactions. Chicago: American Planning Association.

JURGENSMEYER, J. C. (1985) "Funding infrastructure: paying the costs of growth through impact fees and other land regulation charges," in J. C. Nicholas (ed.) The Changing Structure of Infrastructure Finance. Cambridge: Lincoln Institute of Land Policy.

LANDIS, J. D. (1986) "Land regulation, market structure, and housing price inflation: lessons from three California cities." J. of the Amer. Planning Assn. 52, 1: 9-21.

National Association of Home Builders (1984) Impact Fees: A Developer's Manual. Washington, DC: National Association of Home Builders.

NELSON, A. C. (1987) "Impact fees as an emerging method of infrastructure finance." Florida Policy Rev. 2, 2: 22-26.

PORTER, D. R. (1987) "Developers: will they pay to play?" Presented to the 1987 Conference of the American Planning Association, Urban Land Institute, Washington, DC.

SCHECTER, B. (1976) "Taxes on land development: an economic analysis," in P. R. Portney (ed.) Economic Issues in Metropolitan Growth. Baltimore: Johns Hopkins Univ. Press, Resources for the Future.

SCHELL, S. R. and T. V. RAMIS (1987) "Systems development charges in Oregon." Presented to the 1987 Conference of the American Planning Association, Portland, OR.

SCHULTZ, M. M. and R. KELLEY (1985) "Subdivision improvement requirements and guarantees: a primer." J. of Urban and Contemporary Law 28: 3-106.

SCOTT, R. W., D. J. BROWER, and D. D. MINER [eds.] (1975) Management and Control of Growth, Three Volumes. Washington, DC: Urban Land Institute.

SNYDER, T. P. and M. A. STEGMAN (1986) Financing the Public Costs of Growth. Washington, DC: Urban Land Institute.

STROUD, N. E. (1987) "The legality of development impact fees." Presented to the 1987 Conference of the American Planning Association.

WEITZ, S. (1984) "Funding infrastructure for growth: minimizing the impact of increased developer contributions on housing costs," in National Association of Home Builders (ed.) Impact Fees: A Developers Manual. Washington, DC: editor.

WESCHLER, L. P., A. H. MUSHKATEL, and J. E. FRANK (1987) "Politics and administration of development exactions," in J. E. Frank and R. M. Rhodes (eds.) Exactions: Issues and Impacts. Chicago: American Planning Association.

8

Planning Urban Park Systems:
The Charleston Experience

LEON S. EPLAN

Charleston has a landscape that encourages intimacy and partisanship. I have heard that an early inoculation to the sights and smells of the Caroline lowcountry is an almost irreversible antidote to the charms of other landscapes, other alien geographies. You can be moved profoundly by other vistas, by other oceans, by soaring mountain ranges, but you cannot be seduced. You can even forsake the lowcountry, renounce it for other climates, but you can never completely escape the sensuous, semitropical pull of Charleston and her marshes. It is one of those cities where childhood is a pleasure and memory a flow of honey; one of those cities that never lets go, that insinuates its precedence by the insistent delicacy of its beauty [Conroy, 1980].

This chapter is about Charleston, South Carolina, and the approach the city used to plan for its leisure services system. It is also about the way cities have begun to use their park systems as a means for realizing the larger goals for the growth, change, and revitalization of their communities.

AUTHOR'S NOTE: *The Charleston Parks and Leisure Services planning team was chaired by D. William Wallace, Director of the city's Department of Planning and Urban Development. Yvonne Fortenberry, Senior Planner, served as Project Director. An Atlanta, Georgia planning firm, ERLA Associates, headed by the author, was chosen as consultants to the city. They were assisted by The Research Group, a public management firm, also of Atlanta.*

THE CHANGING IDEA OF THE PARK

Parks, like so many of the people and living organisms they serve, tend to take on the coloration of the world around them. Urban parks have particularly reflected, both in design and function, the society of the time: prevailing values, attitudes of people toward one another, current social issues and trauma, along with ideals and idealism of the city and suburb.

As American cities have grown larger and more dense, their character and functions have also changed. Rapid urbanization and the industrial-ization that drew people into cities over a century ago increasingly created places that were unhealthy, unsafe, and barely habitable. The first urban parks—regarded as opportunities for leisure and pleasure—became an antidote to this environment. "Pleasure gardens" were established as places where the masses, unable to flee the overcrowding, disease, and foul air, could find near to their homes a bucolic, agrarian environment. The prototypical pleasure garden was Central Park in New York, designed by Frederick Law Olmstead and Calvert Vaus in 1857. It provided a forceful, healthy contrast to the increasingly oppressive urban conditions, a place of gentle rolling landscapes, a natural, almost casual, location of trees and open fields, and freely flowing watercourses and ponds. An escape, which Olmstead referred to as the "lungs of the city."

When new social forces appeared, the notion of the urban park changed to reflect the new order. With the advent of the late nineteenth-century reform movement, led by Jacob Riis, Lincoln Steffens, and other muckrakers, citizens organized to demand an end to election frauds, slum housing, dirty water and food, labor abuses, and other social ills. The idea of the urban park shifted from that of an agrarian pleasure garden to the carefully structured neighborhood park and the playground. Recreation needs in the minds of the Progressives were tied to the idea of social and urban reform. The "reform park," often placed in tenement districts, was oriented to the needs of the working class (Cranz, 1978: 15).

Under the reform movement, recreation needs were to be met in small, controlled spaces, suitable for children's play, and located near their homes. Both the neighborhood park and the playground were formal spaces, designed for organized play, using straight and rigid lines for fields, paths, and activity areas. Parks included fieldhouses, gymnasiums, and meeting rooms, often attached to the apartment houses, factories, and schools. Planted areas were to be observed, water was contained in pools, and grass and flowers were for definition and decoration. Clubs were formed, which met in facilities, and programs were organized for youth, women, and the elderly. Classes were set up for the training of professional play leaders.

During this period, which lasted until the Depression, many large cities established two types of public bodies to oversee leisure activities: recreation commissions, often composed of reformers and social workers, to administer recreation programs, supervise personnel, and maintain the parks; and park commissions, usually composed of businessmen and philanthropists, to oversee capital improvement programs and construction. One group emphasized activity participation, the other, passive recreation (Cranz, 1978: 13-15).

From the 1930s until recently, the idea of the park as an adjunct to social reform began to disappear. Active recreation became the true value of parks and facilities the common feature. Cities grew as did their park facilities. Stadiums, large fieldhouses, tennis complexes, swimming pools, and huge gymnasiums came to dominate the design and use of parks in cities. Management of these facilities increased in importance and park professionals began to be trained in colleges and business schools in working with the elderly, handicapped, children, and ethnic groups.

In the decades immediately preceding and following World War II, many park and recreation commissions became departments of city governments. This strengthened efforts to establish recreation as an accepted and essential municipal service. With full departmental status, parks and leisure services were henceforth in a stronger position to receive a greater share of the tax revenue base of cities and, during the next decades, to qualify for state and federal funds, increasingly a major source of capital. It also conferred on park systems important police powers, useful for improving, regulating, and managing the system (Shivers and Halper, 1981: 69-70).

Throughout the 1960s and 1970s, larger societal interests once again influenced how parks and open spaces could be provided and protected, and how they should be designed. Out of the growing attention to early child education and development, highlighted by the Head Start program, came a new understanding of the function of play, influencing the design of the playground and the materials, equipment, and forms occupying the play spaces. The aging of the American society helped influence efforts to create more passive parks areas and programs. Interest in protecting the environment, stated as national policy in the Environmental Policy Act of 1969 (Congress, 1970), now found its way into the urban communities through its support of those seeking to protect the streams, wooded areas and the natural terrain found in parks. During this decade, as health and exercise assumed greater importance, jogging trails, exercise courses, and hiking paths have gained entry into parks.

SHORTCOMINGS IN
TRADITIONAL PARK PLANNING

Recent efforts toward serving today's urban society with an appropriate level of leisure activities have been only marginally successful. Needs have far exceeded the supply, even when both private and public responses are combined. And the gap is widening because of increases in available leisure time, rising prosperity, ease of movement, and higher expectations.

Despite recent efforts to improve the nation's park systems, a wide chasm still exists between demand and supply in leisure services (U.S. Department of the Interior, 1978: 10-11). As a result, important changes are being made in the way cities and counties plan their recreation facilities and programs. Some communities have now begun to build a more complete recreation planning process, one that directs the available resources more comprehensively and continuously. These latest efforts are designed to overcome several important shortcomings in the planning for recreation in cities. Among the most important of these flaws are the following.

(1) Recreation has seldom been viewed as a system of leisure activities. The tendency is to view separate sites and programs and deal with each individually. The design of a single park, for example, is undertaken apart from the park's relationship to other parks. Parks are viewed in isolation, rather than as links in a total system. This separation may be a result of the absence of physical linkage, as is the situation with water and sewer and highway systems. Usually parks are not even programmatically integrated, as are school systems.

(2) Traditionally, the focus of recreation planning has been on facilities and programs rather than on the larger needs of a diverse society. Recreation planning has rarely been viewed as a means for addressing larger societal issues. Rather than beginning with how people spend their lives, park planning has increasingly sought to satisfy

the needs of specific groups: children, elderly, handicapped, softballers, joggers. Space is carved out for each group—separate demands of discrete interests are met, but the sum is rarely satisfactory for the total society.

(3) Urban recreation planning is given large responsibilities but sparse resources. Most cities place a low priority on parks and programs. In recent years, cities have had only limited means for maintaining their services and facilities. The unfortunate result has been to limit most recreation plans to those tasks that at best simply maintain ongoing recreation activities.

(4) Finally, recreation planning has been restricted by the little time that many administrators have to realize the value of such planning. While the quality of recreation leadership has risen steadily, the daily mundane chores of running a good park system make good planning difficult. Park systems are exceptionally labor intensive. They primarily employ people with low skill levels and little education, and the pay is commensurate. Characteristically, worker morale is low and turnover is high. Therefore, administrators usually focus on maintenance, personnel, and funds—immediate matters and politicized priorities—with little time left for thinking about the future.

NEW DIRECTIONS IN PARK PLANNING

Recent efforts by many cities have sought to broaden their approaches for meeting the leisure service needs of their citizens. These planning efforts have been characterized as "a blend of environmental design, social science, and public administration to provide leisure opportunities as part of a human service and environmental management system. Both public and private spaces and services are included in a system of opportunities integrated at the neighborhood and metropolitan scale" (Gold, 1980: 9).

Such comprehensive approaches in recreation planning have cast their net across a full range of urban behavior. Park systems are becoming a means for meeting the immediate and longer-term goals and aspirations of the society, not simply a way to provide space and facilities for the specific activities or for particular interests. In implementing the city's park plan, such space and activities may be provided, but these decisions are now being placed in a larger context of their ability to realize citywide goals. How parks, for example, may relate to human development, or to the transportation system.

Recreation, rather than being isolated from other efforts to create more livable cities, has become a chief means for improving urban quality. This larger focus requires, however, the abandonment of traditional ways of thinking. Such recreation planning begins with a view of the nature of the local society and proceeds to carve out a role of the place that recreation can play within that society. It requires also that this definition and role be made part of a design process, which would include, among others, consumers who utilize the city and its recreation system.

This broader approach to recreation planning emerged from the findings contained in the National Urban Recreation Study (U.S. Department of the Interior, 1978). As a result of the major deficiencies highlighted in that effort, Congress, in 1978, passed the Urban Park and Recreation Recovery Act (UPARR). It provided federal grants to economically hard-pressed communities to rehabilitate recreation areas and facilities, and to develop and improve recreation programs. It also sought to encourage and stimulate local governments to revitalize their park and recreation systems and to make long-term commitments to continuing maintenance of these systems (Urban Park and Recreation Recovery Act, 1978). But a broader approach was also sought, one that tied park system rehabilitation to the revitalization of the entire city, a theme that President Carter set forth in his National Urban Policy (U.S. Department of Housing and Urban Development, 1978).

Although the program was short lived (it did not survive the first month of Secretary of the Interior James Watt's tenure), it managed to encourage a number of cities to embark on a comprehensive assessment of their park systems, prioritize the major needs, and prepare plans and implementation strategies for carrying out their plans (U.S. Department of the Interior, 1979). The UPARR Act, despite its brief existence, thereby became the first national effort to induce local governments to undertake systemwide planning for their park systems and to make commitments to the plan.

Over a span of three years, the requirements and guidelines of the UPARR Act served a useful purpose for cities setting out to plan their park systems. Specifically, for a local government to receive grant monies under the Act, an Action Program had to be submitted documenting the community's recreation needs and how the park system would be revitalized and maintained. The rehabilitation effort had to be linked to described goals, priorities, and strategies for the system, as well as to the objectives, needs, plans, and institutional arrangements of the total community. Furthermore, the system's plans and programs had to be consistent with the community's overall long-range goals and plans as expressed in its comprehensive plans and other documents.

THE CHARLESTON EXPERIENCE

Charleston, South Carolina, was one of hundreds of cities that sought and received federal grants under the UPARR Act. As required, it prepared the extensive information, plans, and programs under the guidelines issued by the Heritage Conservation and Recreation Service. Its plan was adopted by the city council on May 21, 1981 (City of Charleston, 1980-1981).

SETTING THE STAGE
FOR THE PLANNING

Charleston was a particularly appropriate candidate for UPARR funds. Its population had not grown during the previous two decades, except in annexed areas. Families and the affluent were being replaced by single persons and the poor; in 1980, 21.8% of the residents had incomes below the poverty level, almost twice the national average. Large segments of the economy had stagnated or declined and the tax base had leveled off. Consequently, the quality of the public services— the schools, parks, and infrastructure—were being threatened.

The park system had especially suffered. Public spaces within this old and historic community had been in a serious deterioration for many years and several were being utilized only sparingly. The design of a number of parks was no longer appropriate for a new and different user. The inadequacy of maintenance and inappropriate designs, however, did not diminish the rapidly rising but unmet demand for organized recreational activities and programs, in part, due to demands placed on the system by a growing visitor and tourist population.

Parks are intimately tied to the design and special ambience of Charleston. Several were part of the city almost from its start: Rutledge Pond was included in the royal grant made in 1760; Citadel Square was shown in Purcell's Plan of 1789; and a racetrack existed in Hampton Park as early as 1792. Yet parks have not been considered among the city's highest priorities. Several recently completed surveys of historical buildings had largely passed over the historical contribution that parks had made to the city. By the mid-1970s, local government expenditures primarily supported functions considered to be more basic to the health, safety, and welfare of the community. Unfortunately, this did not include the park system.

Two events occurred that turned Charleston's attention to its park system. One was the 1976 election of Joseph P. Riley, Jr., as mayor. Riley brought with him a team of bright, young professional managers and immediately began to focus on the stagnant economy and ways to improve public services. The second event was the UPARR program. Charleston, a conservative community, had a long-standing antipathy toward the use of some federal programs, even shunning the use of urban renewal funds. The city had, however, made use of the less controversial Land and Water Conservation Fund and Community Development Block Grant monies, some of which had helped to maintain its park system. Riley saw benefits in infusing his bare-bones municipal treasury with new sources of revenue. And coming from an old Charleston family, he also was wedded to the revival of the old and beautiful parks and squares of the city. In the UPARR program he found a way to upgrade the system so as to improve the livability of many older neighborhoods on the historic Peninsula, and to increase the amount of park and open space in the growing fringe areas.

THE PLANNING PROCESS

A planning team was formed within city government to study the park system. The effort was designed to develop a plan that would meet the needs of the community and, at the same time, comply with the guidelines set forth in the UPARR Act. Two city departments became the key public agencies involved, the Department of Leisure Services and the Department of Planning and Urban Development. The City's Leisure Service Advisory Board and the citywide Neighborhood Council provided important citizen input into the planning process.

The city's park planning team made considerable use of the UPARR guidelines in structuring its planning process. These required that the city's Action Program be based on a clearly defined decision-making process in order to "demonstrate how the jurisdiction will allocate its park and recreation resources on a continuing basis" (U.S. Department of the Interior, 1979). The guidelines also suggested that the process address four questions:

(1) How will identified park and recreation needs be met in the future? UPARR indicated the importance of the Action Program identifying longer-term recreational needs, developing a comprehensive plan for realizing these needs, and placing immediate concerns within this planning context.

(2) How will citizens and public officials be involved in program decisions and the allocation of park and recreation resources? The UPARR guidelines wanted cities to involve citizens from the very start in its recreation-related decisions. Furthermore, the guidelines strongly encouraged the utilization of "existing processes of citizen participation, coordination and evaluation."

(3) What mechanisms will be employed to ensure coordination among park and recreation interests and other community revitalization efforts? The guidelines sought assurances that recreation needs would not be satisfied in isolation, separate from other ongoing efforts for restoring and rebuilding the urban area or from the ability jointly to meet recreation needs.

(4) How will the adopted goals, plans, strategies, and priorities be routinely monitored, evaluated, and updated? UPARR asked that a specific program for the annual monitoring, evaluating, and updating of the complete Action Program be outlined.

STEPS IN THE PROCESS

The planning process adopted by the team developing the Parks and Leisure Services Plan is shown in Figure 8.1. The process consisted of three phases: inventory and analysis, goals setting and plan development, and plan implementation.

Phase one: Inventory and analysis. The team examined eight areas of concern related to leisure services and communitywide planning and redevelopment efforts. Regarding the leisure services system, this examination included, among others, a review of the history of the parks and recreation system, current efforts to improve and expand open space and programs, characteristics of the user of the public parks, how the leisure system is maintained and managed, and leisure activities in which the private sector was a major provider. Local park services provided by other government agencies, primarily the county and state, were likewise inventoried. The examination also looked at other efforts to improve and revitalize the community, ranging from the city's comprehensive plans and the goals established for managing growth and change, to public works, renewal, and economic development projects. Five specific analyses came out of these reviews.

(1) *The adequacy of parks space and conditions.* The analysis revealed, among other problems, important shortages in park space

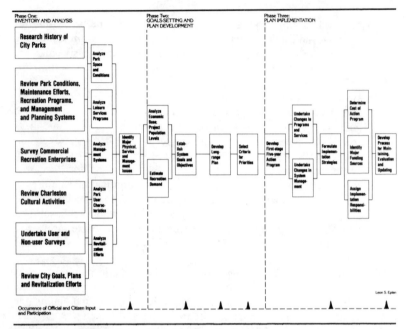

Figure 8.1   Charleston Leisure Services Planning Process

throughout the city's suburban areas, where growth had been taking place at a steady pace. To some extent quasi-public organizations had been filling unmet needs, but nonresidents had also begun to utilize city facilities, which contributed to the shortages and overcrowding. On the other hand, despite the increasing use of parks in the older city on the historic Peninsula by tourists, the inner-city space needs, with a few exceptions, appeared to be adequately met. However, Peninsula parks were found to be badly maintained, which reduced their use and usefulness. Finally, the analysis revealed that space being devoted to passive recreation throughout the city was insufficient, especially within the inner areas, where the population was aging.

(2) *The adequacy of leisure services programs.* The analysis indicated several problems. Most important was the mismatch between park and recreation programming and the diverse residential population, considerable duplication in facilities and in the offerings of providers, difficulties that certain populations faced in gaining access to programs with limited offerings, minimal levels of programming specifically targeted at the elderly, inadequate financial support for most publicly provided

programs, and the avoidance by cultural and park program providers to utilize each others' facilities.

(3) *The adequacy of the management system*. The analysis examined three areas related to management. The first concerned organizational structure and policies. Organizational units in some cases had similar or overlapping functions, lines of authority were neither simple nor clear, citizen input was competitive and not routinely utilized, and organizational goals were not well defined. The second area related to management and coordination. Among the findings was that staff assignments did not always reflect agreed-on priorities, coordination between Leisure Services and other public providers was uneven and ad hoc, and no ongoing process for comprehensive planning had been established. The third management area related to finances, where it was found, among other conclusions, that few efforts were being made to leverage limited program dollars and alternative sources of revenue were not being fully utilized.

(4) *The characteristics of the park user*. Two surveys were undertaken: in-park, face-to-face interviews with people using particular facilities; and telephone interviews of a representative sample of residents. These helped to identify personal characteristics of the user, popular recreation activities routinely engaged in, frequently used facilities, and reasons for choosing specific facilities over others—especially facilities not located near a resident's home. The telephone interviews revealed information on the personal characteristics of households, activities household members participated in, and specific demographic data. Calls were made to noncity as well as city residents.

(5) *Other revitalization efforts and how these would relate to the park system*. Charleston has been engaged in several activities intended to improve the livability of the community and increase its economic vitality. The analysis sought to relate these to the efforts to revitalize the park system in order to achieve common goals.

From these analyses came a sizable list of leisure services issues—physical, service, and management—that were selected to be addressed in the plan.

Phase two: Goals-setting and plan development. The purpose of the second phase was to prepare an overall, long-range plan for the leisure services system and establish priorities among the projects and programs described in the plan. To move through this phase, five major tasks were identified.

(1) *Population and Economic Base Study*. A review was made of the

demographics and economy of Charleston and its three-county region. Trends and important changes in both of these were then tied to their potential importance to the leisure services system. The rapidly developing tourist sector, for example, was described in terms of its impact on parks and recreation facilities.

(2) *Recreation demand.* Measuring the demand for recreation is one of the most difficult and complex tasks confronting park planners. Patterns of usage, desire patterns, and consumption characteristics vary widely among cities and populations within cities. Nonetheless, the process in Charleston carefully constructed estimates of demand.

Recreation demand was divided into active, facility-oriented activities and passive, unstructured activities. The first group consisted of eight types of activities, such as tennis, basketball, and softball. The second included six passive-type activities, including walking for pleasure, jogging, bicycling, and visiting zoos, museums, or historical sites.

Demand estimates for the 14 activities were made for 1980 (the base year), 1985, and 1990. For each, the active, structured facility demand for 1980 was compared with existing supply for the entire city, as well as for each of 11 neighborhood planning units to determine current shortages on a subarea basis. Additional demands generated in areas lying outside the city were also made since many noncity residents utilize city facilities. Demand absorbed by other suppliers (other governments and private sector) was factored out prior to the estimates.

Demand for passive, unstructured activities was estimated differently. Studies by South Carolina on the participation of the Charleston area population in various passive activities during the year were used to estimate demand (South Carolina, 1978). Walking, picnicking, and visiting museums and historic sites were found to be the most popular activities, followed by bicycling and tennis (tie), jogging and fishing. Based upon the percentage of population participating at least once a year in each of these activities, the total annual median activity occasions could then be estimated, for the entire city and by planning subarea. To determine demand, each activity had to be translated into a measurable standard (miles, picnic tables, acres), and then compared with supply.

(3) *Goals and objectives of the leisure plan.* Both the long-range plan and its companion, the five-year Action Program, were drawn on the basis of a carefully structured series of goals and objectives. The starting point for the goals-setting effort was a review of previously utilized and/or adopted city goals. Charleston's main planning guide had been

its Land Use and Housing Plan, adopted two years previously, which had made extensive use of goals and objectives. The overall goal of that Plan was accompanied by 14 specific objectives, several of which dealt with revitalization, with two specifically aimed at improving the leisure services system. It was from this Plan's implementation section that the recommendation to prepare a leisure services plan emerged.

Four main sources were used to develop the goals for the Leisure Services Plan: the in-park surveys and telephone interviews; discussions with the Leisure Services board; in-depth interviews conducted with 13 key individuals, including the mayor, other elected officials and staff, and neighborhood leaders; and the analysis of facilities, programs, and management system. From this effort emerged a total of eight goals (defined as a desired future state or condition) and 16 objectives (a statement that served to measure or more precisely define the dimensions of a goal).

(4) *Long-range plan.* The plan described the demands for both the active, structured, and the passive, unstructured activities that were not being satisfied in 1980. Based on population projections, demand was also calculated for 1985 and 1990. These were then broken down for each of the city's 11 planning areas. In terms of the active, structured group, those parks or other publicly owned properties that could best accommodate the additional facilities received initial attention. Parks having an oversupply of active facilities were examined next. In cases where oversupplied facilities could easily be transferred to parks in the undersupply category, changes were recommended. Finally, where need was indicated but no facilities existed, new acquisitions were recommended.

It was assumed that the city would try to satisfy only a small portion of the demand for activities. Most of these would be provided by others, including other public agencies, quasi-public groups, or private companies. A large portion of unstructured recreation, however, would be satisfied by the individual, such as walking for pleasure along a street or in a park. How much of the demand currently and in the future would be satisfied by whomever was based on the results of a Delphi survey of 25 recreation suppliers representing both the public and private sectors (State of Georgia, 1977).

(5) *Priorities.* In all, the demand studies, plus the addition of a few already proposed facilities, resulted in recommendations on a total of 43 projects in 40 existing and proposed parks and recreation facilities. This does not include other recommendations pertaining to improvements to

the operations of current recreation programs as well as to the management of the leisure services agencies.

It was clear that Charleston would not be able to undertake such an ambitious program quickly. Cutbacks in federal funds, a slow-growing local tax base, and rising operating costs suggested the need to spread out the time required for implementation. The planning team, therefore, provided a list of criteria for selecting the most needed and appropriate projects. Factors upon which the criteria were based were drawn from an assessment of the park information previously assembled, desires expressed by public officials and citizens, and the consistency of a particular project with the goals and objectives adopted for the plan. As a result, weight was given to a proposed recommendation based upon four considerations:

— A slight emphasis was given to projects favoring passive recreation over active recreation.
— A slight emphasis was given to targeting improvements toward certain population groups, such as the poor, elderly, and tourists, rather than toward spreading the improvements evenly throughout the city.
— No particular emphasis was given to enlarging the present system over improving existing facilities; both were judged of equal importance.
— Projects already under construction or that had funds earmarked for them received greater weight.

Applying these criteria to the 43 recommended projects produced three lists: 19 projects were placed on the Highest Priority list, 16 projects made the Second Priority list, and eight were on the Third Priority list. A generalized estimate was made of the cost of constructing each of the 43 recommended projects.

Phase three: Plan implementation. The 19 projects on the Highest Priority list, together with a number of other needed maintenance projects, program additions, and management changes, thus became the five-year action program. It was around these activities that this third plan implementation phase of the Parks and Leisure Services Plan was developed. In all, seven tasks were identified for the implementation of the first-stage, five-year program.

(1) *Program and services changes.* These related primarily to the unbalanced location of programs, some duplication of services, unclear program responsiveness, and uncertain sources of support for program administration and operations. Recommendations for addressing these problems included:

—Placing more programs, especially those requiring large outdoor spaces, in the growing suburban areas.

—Eliminating duplication of services through joint programming with other providers.

—Increasing the emphasis on neighborhood preferences in programming at specific parks and playgrounds.

—Identifying new sources of financial support for programming activities.

—Better utilizing available services of cultural groups and organizations.

(2) *Management changes.* Several vital changes were proposed in parks management:

—Suggestions related to changes in organizational structure and policy included more clearly defining roles and responsibilities, reorganizing certain bureaus, decentralizing a number of operations for better accountability, strengthening linkages with other public and private providers, and clarifying policies related to the role of the city in leisure services.

—Recommendations related to management and coordination suggested preparing a Master Maintenance Plan, reducing time-consuming maintenance tasks and establishing new contractual arrangements with other public bodies.

—Financing changes included initiating certain user fees, creating a self-sustaining Ecological Research Center, and better marketing of the system's special facilities.

(3) *Implementation strategies.* As indicated, considerable funds would be needed, beyond the city's financial capacity, in order to complete all of the proposed projects. A group of strategies was devised to help overcome resource and other limitations. The term *strategies* referred to courses of action adopted for directing of the available resources and actions, including the approaches that would be utilized to implement the plan.

The Action Program recommended that four strategies be used in directing the available monies, manpower, planning, and energies:

—The program focused on several techniques for leveraging city tax funds.

—Attention was given to ways to increase the park system by means other than outright purchase of land, an expensive course in a mature community. Possible alternatives to park expansion by fee simple purchases included greater utilization of the considerable amounts of estuaries and wetlands surrounding the city, greater use of nonpark public lands (such as educational institutions and transportation rights of way),

and wider use of the city's police powers (such as exactions and use of scenic easements).
— Strategies were devised for improving the maintenance of the park system. These dealt primarily with improving worker productivity and with additional sources of revenues for maintenance through fees, charges, and earmarked taxes.
— Suggestions were made regarding ways to utilize the private sector to help maintain and support the system, such as cooperative arrangements with organizations to operate programs and to utilize neighborhood groups to maintain miniparks.

(4) *Cost of the first phase*. At this point in the process, a more detailed estimate was prepared of the costs of constructing the 19 projects and other highest-priority programs.

(5) *Funding resources*. Estimates were made of the expected level of future recreation funds available for leisure services and special facilities. Past patterns of resources for both capital projects and operations were reviewed and projected until 1985, the year when all of the highest priority projects were expected finally to be underway. It was determined that all but four of the highest-priority projects could be funded from these sources, and other sources were recommended.

(6) *Implementation responsibilities*. The plan designated a specific agency that would have the responsibility for each of the 11 tasks described and for ongoing activities.

(7) *Process for plan evaluation and update*. Procedures were outlined for periodically assessing the plan and updating the various tasks described in the process. A schedule for this procedure was devised, one that was specifically tied to the city's annual general fund budget and that of the Revenue Sharing and Community Development Block Grant programs. Four major tasks, including the data collection, interviews, goals and objectives, and revenue projections, were recognized as being particularly important for periodic evaluation and update.

LESSONS FROM THE
CHARLESTON EXPERIENCE

Charleston serves as an example of where a national resolve to address a critical issue has worked well on the local scene. The nation's concern over its urban parks, expressed and documented in the Department of the Interior's National Urban Recreation Study, was translated into legislation, guidelines, and funds. Charleston used both the guidelines and funds to launch an ambitious program to rehabilitate its parks and open spaces. Over the past five years, that schedule has been faithfully followed. Slowly, the system is being revitalized and recreation programs improved and expanded. Most important, people are returning to parts of the city they had long abandoned and to parks they had largely ignored.

A number of useful, if not unique, lessons have been gained from Charleston's park planning efforts. First, immediate recreation needs require that they be placed in the broadest context. Allocation of recreation resources is, after all, a highly political decision. There are few better ways for an elected official to deliver a popular service than to create or refurbish a park. Thus it is important to reach some agreement on system goals *at the outset*, to formulate a plan based on the desire to obtain these goals, and then to place currently proposed as well as future projects within the context of the plan. This process helps to diffuse parochial interests as well as balance political decisions with other needs and longer-term considerations.

Second, a structured planning process also serves another important purpose. It provides the opportunity for the city to express a vision, not only for the park system, but for its broader concerns. Once expressed, park and leisure interests can then be placed within this context—for example, preserving the community's environment, maintaining the health and well-being of the people, revitalizing the physical fabric, or preparing for the community's future. As Gold (1980) has stated, there needs to be a determination to "build cities in parks, instead of parks in cities. . . . The idea of parks or recreation as an isolated set of spaces or experiences in cities is passé." The primary focus thereby becomes the need to serve people living in cities, or those visiting and utilizing cities, to build a total integrated environment—schools, streets, neighborhoods, shopping, and parks.

Participation of people in the park planning process is essential to its success, not only to find agreement on the kind of society desired, or goals to be obtained and on the plan itself, but on implementation actions as well. Involvement establishes proprietary relationships between the park system and the public and creates a lasting and valuable constituency in behalf of recreation and a commitment to carrying out the plan. Experience since the development of Charleston's Parks and Leisure Services Plan has emphasized the value of a constituency that would continuously support a carefully developed implementation program, one that provides the basis for programming the longer-term actions required if the system is to be revitalized, expanded, and reoriented.

Finally, no planning process will be successful if it does not have a built-in mechanism for periodic review, evaluation, and update. Especially in an urban setting, conditions repeatedly change: information becomes old and unreliable, revenue sources shift, agency responsibilities are altered, new technologies are introduced, outside forces intervene. Plans, if not updated continually, quickly become outdated. More important, people change, their attitudes and goals as well as demographic characteristics. Timetables, therefore, need to be established *at the beginning* of the implementation period that mandate how the process will retain its freshness and relevance. The success of the planning effort rests on its ability to perform and continue to perform over time.

REFERENCES

City of Charleston, South Carolina (1980-1981) Parks and Leisure Services Plan. Charleston: Department of Planning and Urban Development.

CONROY, P. (1980) Lords of Discipline. Boston: Houghton Mifflin.

CRANZ, G. (1978) "Changing Roles of Urban Parks." Landscape 22: 3.

GOLD, S. M. (1980) Recreation Planning and Design. New York: McGraw-Hill.

SHIVERS, J. S. and J. W. HALPER (1981) The Crisis in Urban Recreational Services. East Brunswick, NJ: Associated University Presses.

State of Georgia (1977) Comprehensive Outdoor Recreation Plan. Atlanta: Georgia Department of Natural Resources.

State of South Carolina (1978) Columbia: South Carolina Department of Parks, Recreation and Tourism.

U.S. Congress (1970) Public Law 91-190. Washington, DC: Government Printing Office.

U.S. Department of Housing and Urban Development (1978) The President's 1978 National Urban Policy Report. Washington, DC: author.

U.S. Department of the Interior (1978) National Urban Recreation Study, Executive Report. Washington, DC: author.

U.S. Department of the Interior (1979) Uniform Criteria for Preparation of Local Recovery Action Programs, Interim Rule. Washington, DC: author.

9

Transportation Infrastructure: Current and Projected Needs

CATHERINE ROSS

TRANSPORTATION INFRASTRUCTURE includes all the physical systems necessary to move people and goods, for example, roads, bridges, tunnels, interstate highways, pedestrianways, parking facilities, buses, ports, harbors, canals, waterways, railways, taxi fleets, airports, terminals, busways, and docks. While not exhaustive, this list indicates how extensive and varied is the transportation infrastructure system (American Society of Civil Engineers, 1984).

This chapter focuses primarily on highways and mass transit. First, it examines the concept of "needs" for both transportation categories. Although the federal government has played a major role in the development of standards and procedures for evaluating needs, a comprehensive, widely accepted framework for needs assessment still does not exist. Second, the chapter considers the federal government's role in transportation planning, its historical development, and current policy directions—especially the emphasis on privatization. Finally, the outlook and impetus for change in transportation planning are considered.

INFRASTRUCTURE EVALUATION

Although procedures and guidelines exist for evaluating the condition of infrastructure, these vary and have not been followed by many governments. Nevertheless, the federal government has played a major role in the development of standards and procedures. This is a direct result of federal governmental requirements for evaluation in conjunction with the allocation of program dollars (Hatry, 1982).

Despite federal efforts, there is great need for the development of procedures and standards that constitute a comprehensive ongoing framework within which assessment takes place. A comprehensive evaluation would include:

(A) Engineering-type indicators, such as bridge condition ratings.
(B) Performance indicators, such as the number of transit breakdowns.
(C) Service level/impact indicators, such as time lost due to breakdowns or cost associated with such occurrences.
(D) Maintenance unit-costs such as transit vehicles, road segments, and so on (Hatry, 1982).

One example of a comprehensive evaluation system is the Responsive Public Services Program of Savannah, Georgia. Every two years a survey is made of all planning areas. Assessments are made of the general livability and conditions of public facilities such as streets, water, sewer, and so on. This information is the basis for the development of the service improvement and the capital improvement program (Hatry, 1982).

Procedures for evaluating transportation systems are more refined than in other infrastructure areas. Roads and bridges have procedures sufficiently in place that it is possible to assess them. The National Bridge Inspection Program, established in 1968, has a rating scheme that is applicable nationally. Bridges are evaluated every two years as prescribed by federal law. The government publishes bridge inspection standards, yet gives each state great latitude in their implementation. Unfortunately, this has resulted in great variance in the method and extent of implementation.

A number of organizations, including the Federal Highway Administration (FHWA) and the American Association of State Highway and Transportation Officials (AASHTO), has developed street evaluation procedures. Nevertheless, local governments have generally not developed formal systems with which to conduct assessments of streets (Hatry, 1982). However, as with bridge evaluations, these methods do represent an attempt at objectivity. Moreover, these evaluations may soon be facilitated by the development of new, more appropriate and responsive computer technologies. Ideally, this technology would permit quick, objective, simple, and cost-effective assessment of the transportation infrastructure.

Even if appropriate measures or standards for monitoring and evaluating the infrastructure existed, governments would still need information on the relative cost of the improvements. Such data would help to answer the question of whether facilities should be replaced, rehabilitated, or maintenance levels altered.[1]

Thus the outputs of the evaluation must be helpful in identifying the costs associated with a given improvement or need. Officials must know operating, maintenance, replacement and investment costs. In a period of scarce resources, it is imperative that improved procedures be developed to assist decision makers in identifying the full range of costs. The allocation of significantly more dollars to infrastructure will not be cost-effective unless it is accompanied by improved planning and management of entire systems.

INFRASTRUCTURE NEEDS: HIGHWAYS

The determination of needs is particularly critical, given the lack of investment and the continuing decline of the transportation infrastructure (Lee, 1986). While there has been a general identification of the transportation infrastructure problem, it is often not discussed in a definitive manner.

Estimates of current highway expenditures are around $45 billion a year across all governmental levels. Replacement estimates of the current capital are approximately $3 trillion.[2] The evaluation of the condition of highways generally focuses on the interstate system. Though the system is not yet complete, it suffers from accelerating deterioration. The Federal-Aid System, of which the interstate system is one part, makes up 20% of the nation's roads, but carries 80% of total traffic. It includes 260,000 miles of major Primary System arterials, more than 40,000 miles of interstate routes; approximately 400,000 miles of rural collector roads in the Secondary System; 125,000 miles in the Urban System; and 260,000 bridges (Congressional Budget Office, 1983) (See Table 9.1).

In 1956, the Highway Trust Fund was created to assure a sound financial basis for the initiation and construction of the interstate highway system. The federal government decides what routes are to be included on the interstate system. The majority of federal spending on highways is financed by user taxes with the motor fuel tax most important. In excess of 95% of government highway expenditures are financed by users fees.

TABLE 9.1

Major Parts and Physical Status of the Nation's Highways,
by Financing Source

Highways by Financing Category	Route Miles	Percentage of Total Vehicle Miles
Federal-Aid Highway System		
Interstate	41,216	19.0
Primary[b]	259,240	29.5
Secondary	398,108	8.7
Urban	124,115	21.9
Bridges (number	(259,950)	—[c]
Total federal-aid	822,679	79.1[b]
Nonfederal-Aid System		
Roads	3,034,179	20.9
Bridges (number)	(313,700)	—[c]
Total roads	3,856,858	100.0

Percentage of Capital Spending Provided by Federal Government[a]	Percentage in Poor Condition	Percentage in Fair Condition
91	8.2	34.1
70	8.9	51.5
25	13.9	62.4
20	10.7	59.8
70	10.5	15.5[d]
50	11.5[e]	57.2[e]
—[f]	—[f]	—[f]
—[f]	33.4	27.4
—[f]	—[f]	—[f]

SOURCE: Congressional Budget Office (1983).
a. U.S. Department of Transportation (1982: iv-14). These estimates exclude maintenance.
b. Excludes interstate mileage.
c. Not applicable because vehicle miles are the same as for roads.
d. These bridges do not have adequate capacity for existing traffic or do not meet current design standards despite adequately sound structure.
e. Excludes bridges.
f. Data not available.

Generally, the interstate highway is built to last for a minimum of twenty years before major rehabilitation is required. Since construction of the system began in 1956, many of its sections are far older than the 20-year guidepost. Estimates are that more than 40% of the system needs to be rehabilitated, with 75% projected by 1990 (Congressional Budget

Office, 1983). The large jump in rehabilitation needs by 1990 is the result of deterioration accelerating as roads enter the last quarter of their design lives.

Other aspects of the Federal-Aid network are also in need of repair. This includes Primary, Secondary, and Urban systems. While these have generally been rated in better condition than the interstate system, without increased investment and rehabilitation they will continue to deteriorate. This is also true for roads not in the Federal-Aid System.

The Federal Highway Administration contends that 23% of the nation's bridges are structurally deficient. This accounts for approximately 10% of those in the Federal-Aid System and 33% of other bridges. Those that receive federal funds are larger and more expensive.

The Congressional Budget Office estimates it would cost $23.2 billion dollars to repair interstate routes, other Federal-Aid highways, and completion of the interstate system. Under current policy, the federal government would be responsible for $13.1 billion annually. In 1983, about 85% of the available monies administered by the Department of Transportation was spent on programs for the Federal-Aid System.

If the focus is on maintaining the existing system, Lee (1986) has estimated it would require $82 billion per year. This figure does not include land acquisition costs or interest payments.

FHWA estimates that costs under existing policy would approach $2.8 billion per year through 1989 to repair and maintain sections of the interstate. Of this amount, $2.5 billion would constitute the federal share (see Table 9.2). The costs of preventing further deterioration of the Primary, Secondary, and Urban systems, across levels of government, would be $67 billion for the same time period. Estimates for rehabilitating or replacing deficient bridges approximate $40.5 billion. Half of this would be allocated to improving bridges on the Federal-Aid System (Congressional Budget Office, 1983).

During the last 25 years local governments throughout the country have increased their expenditures on public transit. In 1982, all 50 states had established public transportation programs, focusing primarily on aid to local systems (McDowell, 1984). A major problem at the local level is the inadequacy of evaluation and assessment of transportation infrastructure needs. Most local governments do not conduct regular evaluations of streets and roads. Even where these do exist there is little or no relationship between these and the financial planning component of local government. The need for analytical techniques and methods to assist in making hard choices in investment is likely to increase. Many

TABLE 9.2
Costs Associated with Major National Highway Needs of the Federal-Aid System (1983-1990)

Area of Need	Effective Federal Share of Spending (in percentage)[a]	Average Annual Authorizations (in billions of dollars)		
		Total Estimated Needs	Federal Share of Estimated Needs	State and Local Share of Estimated Needs
Complete Interstate System by 1990	90	4.5	4.1	0.4
Interstate repair	90	2.8	2.5	0.3
Interstate reconstruction	25[b]	3.6	0.9	2.7
Primary	70	3.9	2.7	1.2
Secondary	20	3.2	0.6	2.6
Urban	20	2.7	0.5	2.2
Bridge repair	70	2.5	1.8[c]	0.7
Total[d]	56	23.2	13.1	10.1

SOURCE: Congressional Budget Office (1983).

a. Department of Transportation (1982: iv-14). These represent federal share of highway spending after accounting for state-only projects.

b. Congressional Budget Office assumption.

c. Federal Highway Administration (1982). Assumes an eight-year program and is restricted to the federal-aid system.

d. Excludes interstate transfer grants for highways, safety, recreational roads, and roads off the federal-aid system. Needs for roads and bridges off the federal-aid system are difficult to estimate but could reach $4 billion to $5 billion a year.

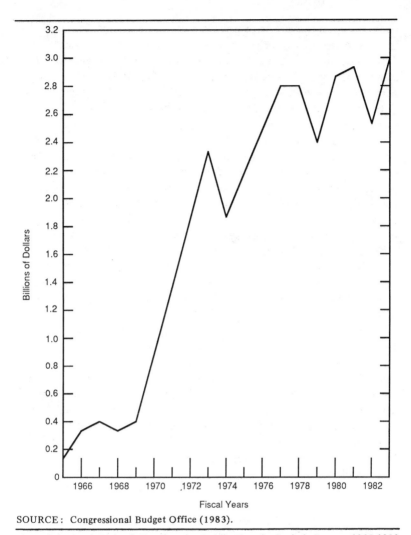

SOURCE: Congressional Budget Office (1983).

Figure 9.1 Total Federal Funding for Public Transit Capital Grants, 1965-1983

local decisions are typically made at the agency level, with the executive branch making final decisions. This model needs to be altered. There is an important need to increase centralization in order to enhance planning and decision making.

Federal involvement in mass transit began in 1983. This involvement was the result of the failure of a large number of privately held companies. The government assisted municipalities in taking control of these in order to assure the provision of public transportation. The decade of the 1970s saw unprecedented growth in aid for mass transportation and increased flexibility in the kinds of expenditures permitted by the federal government (see Figure 9.1). Recently, the government has favored rehabilitation of existing vehicles and curtailment of the construction of new rail systems.

To estimate future needs, it is necessary to examine the condition of existing facilities and project future service demands. Normal maintenance of rolling stock has been deferred in many of the cities with large public transportation systems. The Urban Mass Transportation Authority (UMTA) and the American Public Transit Association (APTA) estimate a need for a total expenditures of $5.5 billion a year to modernize and repair transit systems as well as to expand rail capacity. Of this amount; $3.3 billion would be for repair and modernization. UMTA estimates $2.2 billion would be needed annually to rehabilitate existing rolling stock, track, and other facilities (Congressional Budget Office, 1983). Based on a survey, UMTA estimates an annual need of $500 million to accomplish rail rolling stock modernization.

Another $1.1 billion is needed annually for bus systems. Of this, approximately $610 million annually would be allocated for repair and maintenance. In total, 75% of this amount would be concentrated in only 17% of the urban areas. The replacement of bus garages would require another $500 million annually. Expansions to existing rail systems and new construction in other cities would require $2.2 billion annually. This is so, even when there is general agreement that the large-scale systems such as in Atlanta, Washington, D.C., and San Francisco will probably not be undertaken in other cities in the foreseeable future.

PROBLEMS WITH FEDERAL POLICIES

Many existing policies evolved at a time when there was pressing need for initial construction or other goals that have changed substantially. Current federal policy evolved in response to a number of issues, including equity to assure participation of economically deprived groups, need for coordination and central control for specific facilities and services, and facility construction for poorer regions of the country.

The problem of encouraging local areas to invest in capital rather than in maintenance is a major shortcoming of current policy. UMTA permits automatic replacement of vehicles once they are twelve years of age. It is not clear that this is more cost-effective than rehabilitating these vehicles.

The federal government has become less willing in recent years to underwrite the cost of maintaining and improving the transit infrastructure. Thus local areas will have to finance a greater share of their transportation costs. While states have generally increased their aid to local governments, this still accounts for only a small portion of transportation expenditures.

Creative financing techniques will be increasingly important. One such approach is the "Capital Investment Enterprise Fund" where the state provides capital investment funds to any agency that experiences a net savings that would be returned to the fund for use on other projects or by other agencies (Hatry, 1982). Ultimately, the fund would be self-sustaining. A widely used approach is the use of dedicated local taxes to finance transit improvements and service. Moreover, some rethinking of the federal to state matching ratio is appropriate. This would, at the minimum, cause more careful consideration of projects undertaken. Additionally, a change in criteria to target those areas most in need may potentially reduce costs.

Federal expenditures on transportation infrastructure have increased in recent times. What is needed is not more money, but a more effective approach and balance between funds spent on capital and those for maintenance.

National policy must be altered to foster more effective investment and be more responsive to transportation infrastructure needs. The relationship between capital and maintenance must be more balanced. This requires more spending on maintenance, the development of flexible standards, and more attention on research and possible solutions to problems plaguing the transportation infrastructure.

A number of more innovative programs should also be funded, experimented with, and evaluated. These include a corporation that would provide subsidized loans nationally, a capital budgeting process to guide federal investment, and increased flexibility in federal standards to facilitate local adaptability (Advisory Commission on Intergovernmental Relations, 1984).

STATE AND LOCAL POLICIES

Local areas have steadily increased their transportation infrastructure expenditures. Voters have been approving bond issues at higher levels and motor fuel taxes have been increased. Some states are proposing state banks or funds that would subsidize loans. One New Jersey proposal would use existing federal grants that would be repaid as loans on a revolving basis. Other suggestions include establishing single-purpose agencies to build and maintain infrastructure and decentralizing the administrative and fiscal functions. Such a separation would probably result in expanded roles for state governments so they would do more of the planning and management of facilities.

A primary way for local and state governments to increase their financial capability is to increase user-charges. Between 1977 and 1982 local governments expanded the monies received from such charges by approximately 5%. User-charges are attractive for a number of reasons, but primarily because they link costs to use, thus resulting in greater economic efficiency. Both users and providers are more fiscally responsive when they must pay the full cost. This greatly reduces willingness to support unnecessary or costly projects. Facilities are generally better maintained and more accurately represent community preferences. User-charges are an attractive mechanism for underwriting infrastructure costs (Advisory Commission on Intergovernmental Relations, 1984).

Local and state funds are generally spent on roads not on the Federal-Aid System. A large amount goes toward the Secondary and Urban systems, and maintenance. Approximately 80% of local and state spending is financed by user taxes. Generally, local areas have been improving their financial situation by reducing expenditures and increasing revenues. This results in a greater capacity to finance the physical infrastructure (Advisory Commission on Intergovernmental Relations, 1984).

The market for tax-exempt debt has changed dramatically, and municipalities are employing a number of unique financing mechanisms. These include zero-coupon municipal bonds that are sold at a discount and do not pay interest, tax-exempt commercial paper that is a short-term flexible method, and notes or letters of credit guaranteeing repayment.[3] In some instances, sale-leaseback procedures are utilized to allow governments to take advantage of tax breaks available to corporations.

Special assessment districts may function in a variety of ways. They may be assembled for a one time assessment or they may operate on an ongoing basis. Special benefit districts have been established in a number of municipalities where charges against property owners in the district are used for development of the transit system or other transportation improvements.

Increasingly, the private sector is involved in the provision of transportation service and facilities. This is being accomplished through joint development, creative financing techniques, and expanded opportunities for private sector participation. Joint development permits the coordination of private land development and public transportation expenditures to facilitate economic development. In some instances this has been used to rehabilitate terminals, improve subways, bus terminals, truck facilities, pedestrian facilities, and so on.

The public sector has increased its willingness to pass along costs to developers through impact fees or exactions. These are tied to the impact of the proposed development on affected streets and roads. In some instances when the transportation facilities will be affected negatively, the developer may be required to construct the road or pay an assessed fee for improvements. Broward County, Florida uses the Traffic Impact System (TRIPS). It is a computerized traffic model that calculates the fee through simulation of expected impacts of proposed developments. These costs are then passed on to the developer (Ross, 1984).

TRANSPORTATION INFRASTRUCTURE: OUTLOOK AND IMPETUS FOR CHANGE

Improving the transportation infrastructure provides opportunities for enhancing the quality of life. For example, if the federal government targets some programs to depressed areas, the funds would create employment opportunities as well as increase the competitive position of these communities in attracting economic development.

There is a need for more research on infrastructure problems. The determination of cost-effective solutions and evaluations of experimental programs would be of immense value to future planning. A conference on infrastructure by the National Science Foundation and the American Society of Civil Engineers served as the backdrop for a call to establish an Infrastructure Research Center. Such a center would encompass infrastructure-related engineering and serve as a focal point for macro-level research undertakings (American Society of Civil Engineers, 1984). An equally important responsibility for the center would be the dissemination of research results.

Increasingly, federal involvement in provision of the infrastructure must focus on the opportunities for investment and potential return rather than a project-specific orientation. This approach assures the economic feasibility of candidate projects.

Private sector involvement in public transportation is addressed in sections 3(e) and 8(e) of the Urban Mass Transportation Act (1984). It stipulates that local transportation programs encourage to the greatest extent possible the participation of private enterprise. The Surface Transportation Assistance Act (1983) strengthened this commitment. It required local providers to consult private sector interests in plan development, provide opportunity to comment on proposed plans, and consider these views in final plan preparation. In October 1984, UMTA issued guidelines to promote greater reliance on the private sector and in November 1985, UMTA announced it would give priority consideration in discretionary grant awards to those applicants demonstrating commitment to private sector involvement (Ross, 1988). This thrust at the federal level is timely because of the increased need for private sector involvement in financing the transportation infrastructure. However, a cautionary note is in order. It would be most unfortunate that in our eagerness to embrace private solutions, that the public nature and purpose of our transportation system is forgotten. The needs of transit dependent populations—the poor, elderly, and handicapped, must be met and protected.

NOTES

1. Hatry has conducted extensive research on evaluation and problems of infrastructure evaluation are clearly outlined.

2. In his paper, "Highway Infrastructure Needs," Lee (1986) discusses replacement value of existing capital stock and compares his finding to results reported by others.

3. Numerous examples of innovative financing mechanisms are discussed in the Advisory Commission's Report (1984).

REFERENCES

Advisory Commission On Intergovernmental Relations (1984) Financing Public Physical Infrastructure. Washington, DC: author.

American Society of Civil Engineers (1984) Research Needs Related to the Nation's Infrastructure. New York: author.

CATANESE, A. J. and J. C. SNYDER (1979) Introduction to Urban Planning. New York: McGraw-Hill.

Congressional Budget Office (1983) Public Works Infrastructure: Policy Considerations for the 1980s. Washington, DC: Government Printing Office.

General Accounting Office (1985) 20 Years of Federal Mass Transit Assistance: How Has Mass Transit Changed? Washington, DC: Superintendent of Documents.

HATRY, H. P. (1982) Maintaining the Existing Infrastructure: Overview of Current Issues and Practices in Local Government Planning. Washington, DC: U.S. Department of Housing and Urban Development.

LEE, D. B. (1986) Highway Infrastructure Needs. Cambridge, MA: Transportation System Center.

McDOWELL, B. D. (1984) "Governmental actors and factors in mass transit." Intergovernmental Perspective 10: 7-13.

ROSS, C. L. et al. (1984) Synthesis of Planning Practice for Small and Medium-Sized Communities. Washington, DC: Transportation Research Board.

ROSS, C. L. et al. (1987) "Urban transportation planning," in Catanese and Snyder (eds.) Introduction to Urban Planning. New York: McGraw-Hill.

U.S. Department of Transportation (1984) The Status of the Nation's Local Public Transportation: Conditions and Performance. Washington, DC: Urban Mass Transportation Administration.

Part IV

**Political, Environmental, and
Equity Issues in Infrastructure Planning**

10

The Politics of Infrastructure:
Robert Moses and the Verrazano Bridge

JON J. LINES
ELLEN L. PARKER

THIS CHAPTER is a case study of policy planning and practice in the construction of a major infrastructure project—New York City's Verrazano Narrows Bridge. Planned and built in the 1950s by two of the more important agencies in the New York metropolitan region, the Triborough Bridge and Tunnel Authority (TBTA) and the Port of New York Authority (PNYA), the bridge was designed to connect the relatively undeveloped borough of Staten Island with the mainland at Brooklyn.

In planning the bridge, one issue that arose was whether the two authorities should build the bridge to accommodate commuter rail facilities. This was a relatively minor aspect of the $300 million project. However, it had a broader importance. First, the decision would affect the ability of the city of New York to provide rail transportation between Staten Island and Brooklyn, a major concern in a city that relies so heavily on commuter rail transportation. Second, and more germane to this chapter, the debate between the advocates of improved rail transit and the Authorities planning the bridge illustrates how differing institutional perceptions of the problem can have far-reaching policy implications in metropolitan transportation policy.

THE TRAFFIC PROBLEM AND
THE "ROAD VERSUS RAIL" DEBATE

Commuter transportation was a major policy issue in the New York metropolitan area after World War II. The existing stock of regional highways and bridges, most of which were built in the 1920s and 1930s, was unable to handle the increasing volume of traffic in the postwar years. Long lines of vehicles on Hudson and East River crossings, severely congested Manhattan streets, and crowded commuter rail and subway systems were daily annoyances for metropolitan area commuters in the 1950s.

Two categories of solutions to the "traffic problem" ultimately emerged. The first was to expand and upgrade the mass transit network. If efficient and comfortable rail transit could be provided between the growing suburban communities and the central city, commuters would have an alternative to the automobile, and the congestion on the overburdened arterial facilities would be reduced. The second was to build new and expanded vehicular arterials, particularly new bridges and high-speed expressways capable of handling a large traffic volume. Advocates of this view maintained motorists drove by free choice, and would not use transit even if better facilities were available.

Of course, these were not mutually exclusive alternatives. In an important contemporary study of the New York region's political institutions, Robert Wood (1961: 131-132) argued that "conceivably, a disinterested observer might determine the optimum combination of rail and highway facilities required to move the greatest number of people with maximum ease and comfort at the lowest cost."

There was, however, no "disinterested observer," and the issue was not ascertaining the "optimum combination of rail and highway facilities." Regional transportation policy was a political process, as Wood (1961: 131) noted:

> The wide disparities between the rail and auto agencies with respect to financial resources, organizational arrangements, legal responsibility, and attitudes are at the heart of the [New York] Region's transportation politics. These disparities dictate sharply contrasting definitions of transportation "needs" and sharply contrasting philosophies of "the public interest." Each agency becomes convinced that its own program best promotes the general welfare, and the stage is set for controversy.

Ultimately, policy outcomes are a product of organizational capacity, and the "solution" to the problem is defined by the strengths and biases of the organization preparing the plan. "What matters is not a determination of which set of assumptions is 'right' according to the criterion of some outside party," asserts Wood (1961: 133-134). "What matters is which agencies possess the financial and political capacity to translate their own goals into operating programs."

THE JOINT STUDIES: THE
PUBLIC AUTHORITY'S RESPONSE
TO THE TRAFFIC PROBLEM

The postwar increase in vehicular traffic and the consequent congestion problem was keenly felt by the TBTA and PNYA. Studies done by the Port Authority found that trans-Hudson bridges and tunnels were handling nearly double the prewar volume of traffic, and that traffic was steadily increasing:

During the twenty-year period prior to 1948, trans-Hudson traffic increased less than a million and a half vehicles a year. . . . The full scale resumption of private automobile manufacture in 1947 and 1948 brought with it an accelerated rate of traffic growth. The annual increase of trans-Hudson traffic jumped from a million and a half to from 3,500,000 to 5,700,000 vehicle crossings a year. By 1954, nearly 73,300,000 vehicles, almost double the pre-war volume, were crossing the Hudson River annually [TBTA and PNYA, 1954: 13].

Triborough facilities were similarly overburdened. Traffic over the Triborough Bridge, Bronx Whitestone Bridge, Queens Midtown Tunnel, and the Henry Hudson Bridge in 1954 was more than double the volume of 1946.

The solution adopted by the two Authorities was simple—build more arterials. Both Authorities had been actively engaged in road building since the war ended. The Port Authority began construction of a third tube to the Lincoln Tunnel in the late 1940s, and had plans to build a second deck of the George Washington Bridge and a new 125th Street bridge between New Jersey and Manhattan. The Triborough was committed to the Throgs Neck Bridge, designed to alleviate the congestion on the Bronx-Whitestone Bridge, and was examining the feasibility of a Narrows Crossing. In addition, the Triborough's chairman, Robert Moses, characteristically had ambitious plans for new regional arterials throughout New York City, Long Island, and Westchester County.

In 1954, the TBTA and the PNYA reached an agreement to undertake a study to determine the feasibility of building a complex of new arterial highways and bridges. The final report, *Joint Study of Arterial Facilities, New York-New Jersey Region* (1954) proposed three bridge projects: the Throgs Neck Bridge, a second deck of the George Washington Bridge, and a Narrows Bridge. The two Authorities agreed to finance the $400 million bridge projects from their own revenues by issuing bonds backed by the tolls to be collected on the new bridges. The construction of the new arterial "connections" to existing and new highways was to be managed by the Authorities, and financed by federal-state highway programs.

The Joint Study was enthusiastically endorsed at the time of its announcement. The *New York Times* (1954) gave it front page coverage, and in an associated editorial praised this new initiative:

> Announcement that the Port of New York Authority and the Triborough Bridge and Tunnel Authority will make immediately a "comprehensive study of all major phases of the arterial traffic problem in the New York-New Jersey metropolitan area" is the most encouraging development of recent times relating to the traffic problem.
>
> A most welcome feature of this enterprise is the fact that the two great authorities, responsible for such great benefits to the metropolitan area, are joining in this cooperative venture of exploration. It is a survey-partnership rich in possibilities. . . . The mere fact that this study is being made, and at considerable expense, is pretty fair earnest that this is one traffic study that will provide action in one direction or another.

Despite these high expectations, the Joint Study was a transportation program of limited scope. The Triborough and Port Authorities explicitly concentrated their study on vehicular arterial construction, emphasizing that transit had to be considered as a separate issue. Asserting that improving transit would have relatively little impact on the number of automobile passengers, the Authorities concluded that the solution to traffic congestion had to be based in the construction of improved roads and bridges for private automobile usage (TBTA and PNYA, 1954: 9).

It is not surprising the Authorities chose to define the problem in this limited way. The emphasis on vehicular facilities was due to the organizational structure of the TBTA and the PNYA, and the way in which this affected their historic and current agenda. Both agencies were constituted as public authorities. The PNYA had been created by interstate compact between New York and New Jersey to "coordinate" transportation (particularly rail) in the New York-New Jersey Port District; the Triborough Bridge Authority (the predecessor to the TBTA) had been established by New York state law to finance and build a specific project, the Triborough Bridge. As public authorities, both the Triborough and the Port Authority relied on revenue bond financing to raise capital. Under the enabling legislation creating the Authorities, their revenue bonds were not backed by the "full faith and credit" of the public tax base (state or municipal). The only income backing the revenue bonds was the revenue generated by user-fees on the projects the bonds financed. To ensure investors would purchase the Authorities' revenue bonds, there had to be reasonable certainty that the project would generate revenues adequate to cover not only bond interest and principal, but also ongoing operational administrative and maintenance costs.

Historically, the projects that best met these criteria were toll facilities such as highways and bridges. In the case of the Triborough and the Port Authorities, the debt service on the bonds was paid by vehicular tolls on their bridges. Both these agencies initially built their revenue base on the acquisition and construction of vehicular facilities and control over the toll revenues these facilities generated. The Triborough was created in 1933 for precisely this reason (Lines et al., 1986). The Port Authority was created in 1921 with a much broader agenda, but it was not until it implemented a trans-Hudson toll bridge program in the 1930s that the PNYA achieved financial self-sufficiency (Bird, 1949; Danielson and Doig, 1982). Rapid transit, on the other hand, was traditionally a deficit-ridden operation. Rail facilities were expensive to build and operate, and political pressures kept fares below the cost of providing the service.

Since the Triborough and Port Authorities relied on bonds sold to private investors for capital, vehicular arterials that charged tolls were the basis of their financial self-sufficiency. The Authorities avoided integrating rapid transit in their arterial plans because it was incapable of generating revenues to support itself. The Joint Study reflected this emphasis on revenue-generating facilities. Adequate rapid transit services for the region may have been a laudable goal in its own right, but if it did not pay for itself, it was an issue the Authorities were not willing, or able, to address.

THE POSITION OF THE
RAPID TRANSIT ADVOCATES

The Port and Triborough Authorities never seriously considered the possibility of using the Joint Studies projects to expand rapid transit services. They were, however, sensitive to the "road versus rail" debates then emerging in the local political arena. The Port Authority had just survived an attack on their involvement in Joint Studies by a New Jersey state senator, Malcolm Forbes. The "Forbes Resolution" introduced into the New Jersey senate in the spring of 1954 would have forced the Port Authority to suspend construction on any new projects until the release of preliminary studies by transit commissions in New York and New Jersey. Forbes was attempting to force the Port Authority to assume a major responsibility for commuter transit in New Jersey by holding the Joint Studies projects hostage.

The two distinct perspectives on the transit issue were apparent from testimony before the New Jersey Senate Committee on Federal and Interstate Relations. Goodhue Livingston, a well-known member of the New York City Planning Commission, voiced an eloquent attack on the Port Authority, and the regional authority structure in general. Livingston testified that under the current structure, the Authorities would never address transit issues. He accused the Triborough and Port Authorities of avoiding any responsibility for rapid rail transit, arguing the Authorities had a vested interest in building vehicular arterials because they relied on the tolls from these arterials to support their organizations. The very nature of the authority structure was at the core of the problem:

> In many ways the set-up of these Authorities is an obsolete one and calls for much revision before it becomes too late. These Authorities have an aroma of an East India Company, arrogant and forgetful of the fact that they were constituted by the people to serve the public who live within this immense region and not simply to pursue an easy course in order to point with pride to their swelled resources [Livingston, 1954].

Testifying the same day as Livingston, Austin Tobin, the Executive Director of the PNYA, presented the Port Authority's argument. He cited numerous studies undertaken by the Port Authority and other agencies that indicated the need for hundreds of millions of dollars in capital improvements on regional transit lines. Tobin concluded that rail transit was not self-sufficient and hence could not be supported by the sale of revenue bonds that were the mainstay of Authority financing. Forcing the Authority into rapid transit would endanger its very existence:

> The principle of self-support is the whole strength of the Port Authority's ability to carry forward the programs of terminal and transportation development entrusted to it by the two States, and to do so on a revenue bond basis; that the Port Authority's credit structure would be seriously impaired if there was any implication that the Port Authority was even considering the financing of rail transit; that any amendment to the Port Compact under which the Port Authority would have recourse to public subsidy from tax levying sources in support of its projects would destroy the entire concept and character of the Authority [Tobin, 1954].

The Forbes Resolution was the precursor of a larger debate over the issue of authority involvement in providing rapid transit. The individual state transit commissions were merged in June 1954 to form a single bistate transit commission, the Metropolitan Rapid Transit Commission (MRTC). The perspective of the MRTC was clearly stated in its first Interim Report. It stressed that "the problem of mass transportation of people and merchandise is inevitably intermingled with that of automobile and truck transportation, and any over-all approach must seriously consider the interrelationships between the two" (MRTC, 1955).

From the beginning, the MRTC questioned the Authorities' exclusive focus on arterials as the solution to the traffic problem. The report indicated that "an adequate, modernized and scientific transportation system [integrating road and rail facilities], planned to invigorate the present and the future, is as essential to the whole Metropolitan organism as is the circulation of the blood to the whole human body" (MRTC, 1955).

This "road versus rail" debate was regionwide (Doig, 1966). The debate over transit on the Verrazano Narrows Bridge epitomized the issues, conflicts, and disparate viewpoints of the main actors, the MRTC, the TBTA, and the PNYA.

RAPID TRANSIT AND THE
VERRAZANO NARROWS BRIDGE

The Joint Study of the TBTA and the PNYA had proposed a number of new bridges and arterials, but the Verrazano Narrows Bridge was the cornerstone of the plan. It was the largest and single most expensive project of the three bridge projects, and it potentially had a number of significant impacts. By providing an efficient vehicular crossing between Staten Island and Brooklyn, it could stimulate development on Staten Island, the City's most underdeveloped borough. The bridge was also an important link in the arterial plan for the region. By connecting the Staten Island Expressway to the New York mainland, the Verrazano Narrows Bridge would complete a network of arterials between New Jersey and Long Island. This new route, which would enable through-traffic to bypass Manhattan, would be faster and more direct than the existing route that necessitated crossing the Holland Tunnel and lower Manhattan's congested streets. Also, to the Port Authority's benefit, the traffic over this new route between New Jersey and Long Island would cross over the Port Authority bridges to New Jersey on the west side of Staten Island. The toll revenues generated would help to alleviate the deficits those bridges suffered.

The Joint Study report summarized the rationale behind its planning and the potential impacts of the projects on regional development. A major concern of the Study was the creation of a more efficient arterial plan for automobile traffic around the region:

> It is recommended that a twelve-lane double deck bridge be constructed to provide a direct, fast route, bypassing Manhattan, for the large block of traffic between Union county and New Jersey to the south and the Brooklyn waterfront and industrial and residential areas of Brooklyn, Queens, Nassau and Suffolk counties [TBTA and PNYA, 1954: 21-25].

The report also predicted the project would stimulate development on Staten Island:

> For the first time the Borough of Richmond [Staten Island] would have a quick, convenient vehicular interchange with its four sister Boroughs in Greater New York. It is expected that this, the last large undeveloped area adjacent to Manhattan, would enjoy a significant economic improvement. Population would be at least tripled by 1975; the development of the Borough would be integrated with the expanding economy of New Jersey and Long Island [TBTA and PNYA, 1954: 21-25].

All of these anticipated impacts, however, were premised on the automobile. The final Joint Study report deliberately did not address the issue of mass transit to Staten Island. This was not an oversight: The Authorities explicitly defined transit as an issue not in their purview.

Given the magnitude of the anticipated impacts of the bridge on transportation and development patterns, mass transit was clearly an important issue. There was considerable popular support for rapid rail as a solution to traffic congestion, and the MRTC study underscored the need to recognize transit issues in regional planning. The political lobbying in New Jersey to force the PNYA to assume a responsibility for rapid transit was further evidence of the growing importance of the transit question. It is not surprising that the Joint Study and its proposal for the Verrazano Narrows Bridge became a target for transit advocates.

The Authorities had expected criticism from the transit advocates, and their stance on this issue was the subject of a great deal of discussion and disagreement between Austin Tobin, executive director of the Port Authority and Robert Moses, chairman of the Triborough Bridge and Tunnel Authority. In a letter to Moses, Tobin argued that the final Joint Studies report should mention that the Narrows Bridge could structurally accommodate rapid transit if the City ever decided to extend the subway system to Staten Island. Although he did not favor building the Narrows Bridge to accommodate transit, Tobin wished to defuse the transit advocates, fearing their attacks may jeopardize the entire project. He contended that a nod to future transit needs would "spike the guns of those individuals and organizations who might try to use the rapid transit argument as a device for opposing the bridge itself" (Tobin, 1954b).

Tobin firmly believed an extension of the transit lines over the bridge was "financially impossible," but he was sensitive to criticisms that the Authorities had ignored the issue of transit. In his opinion, it was important to address the criticisms directly, and not avoid the issues. "Such a short reference to the bridge strength would cut the ground from under those who might argue that our planning of the bridge has been blind to the possible future needs for giving rapid transit service to Staten Island" (Tobin, 1954b).

Moses was unwilling to make this token concession, believing that it was misleading and that it would raise false expectations. He argued that the Fourth Avenue Subway line in Brooklyn, the transit line to which the Narrows line would connect, was inadequate to handle new transit services. It was highly improbable the city would finance new subway extensions to the Brooklyn line or the Narrows Bridge. These circumstances led the TBTA leadership to conclude that rapid transit on the Narrows Bridge was simply not a possibility. Echoing Moses's views on the matter, TBTA General Manager George Spargo (1954) wrote to Tobin:

I don't see why we should try to kid people on Staten Island about the possibility of ultimately building rapid transit on the Narrows Bridge. While it is physically possible to do this I don't expect that it will ever happen . . .

I think we should take on the opposition and get it over with in our joint report.

In the final Joint Study report, the Triborough's view prevailed. The Joint Study dismissed claims that the city might extend the subway from Brooklyn to Staten Island over the Narrows Bridge. "According to the New York City Transit Authority, the existing Fourth Avenue Subway Line in Brooklyn is now operating at capacity, both as to its ability to handle new equipment and additional passengers on the available cars" (TBTA and PNYA, 1954: 30). An entirely new subway line would be needed to accommodate the increased demand on the system, including additional tunnel facilities over the East River. The Authorities concluded "the enormous cost of such a subway expansion would present an insurmountable burden to transit financing" (TBTA and PNYA, 1954: 30).

The Authorities found additional reasons for their dismissal of the transit issue. If subway trains were to travel the bridge, a less steep grade would be necessary. The grade of the bridge was determined by the need to maintain certain minimum vertical clearances over the Narrows as required in the bridge permit granted by the Army, and the need to minimize disruption of the bridge approaches on the surrounding area. The proposed grade was too steep for standard trains to negotiate, and lowering the height of the bridge would interfere with navigation in the Narrows. To accommodate subway cars, therefore, the approaches would have to be extended through residential neighborhoods of Brooklyn, necessitating increased land condemnation and dislocation. Moses was aware that opposition was sure to arise in Brooklyn from residents who would be dislocated as a result of the construction of the Bridge's approaches, and wanted to forestall it as much as possible. "It is clear that such a rail approach through residential areas, particularly in the Bay Ridge section of Brooklyn, would have a most adverse effect on residential properties in this area" (TBTA and PNYA, 1954: 30). It did not make sense to endure these adverse effects and risk additional opposition to the bridge project in order to provide for a transit line that would never be built.

Transit advocates were not dissuaded by the Authorities' logic, however. Even before the MRTC became substantively involved in the issue in 1956, the Staten Island Chamber of Commerce began lobbying the TBTA for rail transit on the bridge. At a minimum, the Chamber was hoping to convince the Authorities to provide the necessary width to accommodate two lanes of rail tracks in the hope that rail services could be provided at some future date.

MOSES AND THE STATEN ISLAND CHAMBER OF COMMERCE

Narrows Bridge transit was discussed in a series of correspondence between Moses and Arthur O. Hedquist, executive secretary of the Staten Island Chamber of Commerce. The chamber was one of the staunchest advocates for the bridge from the beginning. Yet the chamber also felt that rapid transit was necessary if traffic congestion on the crossing were to be avoided. In 1955, the chamber authored a report on transit issues that discussed the matter of Staten Island.

Noting that over 50% of New York City's vacant land was located on Staten Island, the chamber report predicted a population increase from 200,000 to 700,000 residents by 1975. Many of these residents, employed in areas of New York other than Staten Island, would commute to work. Present commuter traffic on the ferries was estimated at 40,000; with the projected population increase, the chamber estimated there would be 140,000 commuters per day within twenty years. Under these circumstances, the report concluded: "To construct the Narrows Bridge without regard for mass transportation by rail will be a tragedy and indicates an ineffectual planning for the future needs of the City of New York" (Staten Island Chamber of Commerce, 1955).

The Staten Island Chamber of Commerce dismissed the Authorities' arguments that, however desirable, rapid transit tracks were not feasible on the bridge. The chamber cited the statistics from the New York City Transit Authority's first Annual Report to dispute the claim that the city's existing subway connections were incapable of handling additional passengers. This report indicated that the Fourth Avenue subway line could handle up to 111 additional cars in peak hours (Staten Island Chamber of Commerce, 1955). Even if the Authorities' claim that the subway system could not handle the additional transit load from a Narrows link were correct, the chamber contended that rapid transit would still be a sensible investment for the future: "Even if . . . a new subway in Brooklyn were required, the advantages to the City of the development of real estate on Staten Island due to the provision of rapid transit would make such construction highly desirable" (Staten Island Chamber of Commerce, 1955). The chamber also argued that it was technologically possible for trains to negotiate the grade of the bridge. New subway cars developed by General Electric, which were less than half the weight of New York's transit cars, could easily manage the proposed grade on the bridge.

Hedquist (1955) concluded that "the necessary expenditures to so construct the Narrows Bridge now [to accommodate rapid transit tracks] will be infinitesimal compared to the cost that would be involved 5-10 years, or even 20 years, hence." Moses, however, was more concerned with the difficulties of getting the bridge built than he was for any future rapid transit construction problems. "It is going to be sufficiently difficult to get the bridge without rapid transit," replied Moses (1955). "With that addition [rapid transit], it would be impossible."

The debate between the Staten Island Chamber of Commerce and the two Authorities (TBTA and PNYA) over the provision of transit on the Verrazano Narrows Bridge captured the attention of Governor Harriman of New York by the end of 1955. In September, Harriman requested a response from the Triborough and Port Authorities to the chamber's proposals. Austin Tobin, executive director of PNYA, replied on behalf of the Authorities by listing the apparently contradictory statements made by the New York City Transit Authority regarding the capacity of the Fourth Avenue subway in Brooklyn, and Transit Authority plans to extend the line. Tobin implied that the chamber's position, based on Transit Authority information, was flawed because the Transit Authority had no coherent plan for extending transit to the Island. "These statements by officials of the Transit Authority," claimed Tobin (1955), "appear to be so confusing that it is impossible to accurately determine their position on this matter."

DISPARATE PERCEPTIONS
OF RAPID TRANSIT NEED

The debate was the result of "disparate perceptions." The PNYA and the TBTA believed that rapid transit was not vital to Staten Island's development. In some ways, however, the Authorities' stance missed the point. Rapid transit would have an important impact on the kinds of development that would occur, and on broader issues of transportation planning. Specifically, transit was needed to avoid traffic congestion that would logically increase in intensity as the Island developed. To the transit advocates, the issue was not whether the city's subway system would ever be built to accommodate additional Narrows Bridge service. Their argument was that if would be more cost-efficient to build the bridge with the capacity to accommodate transit now than to build new facilities for transit in the future.

The Authorities had a much different perspective on the problem. They were in the business of providing automobile facilities. Transit issues were not their responsibility, and concerned about the security of their bonds, they felt they could not afford to become involved in deficit-ridden transit projects. They were concerned about the immediate added costs of providing the facilities for transit, which they would have to shoulder with no commitment of when, if ever, tracks would actually be built, and who would pay for them. It seemed useless and financially unsound to invest in the capacity for transit when there were no concrete plans for an extension of transit rails over the bridge.

The case of transit on the Verrazano Narrows Bridge illustrates the Authorities' limited perception of their role in the transportation system of the metropolitan region. The Authorities were not being asked to subsidize rapid transit directly, but merely to ensure the bridge could structurally accommodate transit in case in the future financing to extend the lines became available. The financial commitment required, while considerable, was only about 5%-10% over the cost of the entire project. While they could have "afforded" the additional expense, the Triborough and the Port Authorities felt no obligation to invest Authority moneys in transit facilities. The increase in the cost of the bridge—and the increase in the amount to be bonded—to provide accommodations for future rail tracks that, in the Authorities' assessment, would never be built anyway, seemed ludicrous. It was certainly not an investment they could expect their bondholders to back.

Tobin, in his response to Governor Harriman's inquiry into the matter of transit on the Verrazano Bridge, enclosed a "draft reply" for the governor's signature to be sent to Hedquist at the Staten Island Chamber of Commerce. In this "draft reply," Tobin detailed what was to become the Authorities' position throughout the remainder of this debate. Given the financial improbability of a new subway and East

River tubes being built, "it would appear that the added cost and other difficulties that would be involved in providing space for rapid transit tracks on the Narrows Bridge would not be a sound investment" (Tobin, 1955).

The "additional cost" argument was reiterated by the TBTA less than a week after Tobin's letter to Harriman. When asked to report on "the real story about the grade on the bridge [and] would the subway trains be able to make it" (Spargo, 1955) Arthur Hodgkiss, assistant manager of the TBTA, replied with a two page memo that admitted that the grade of the bridge would not prevent the use of commuter rail transit.

Hodgkiss went one step further and provided a detailed cost estimate for building the structure to accommodate the proposed transit tracks. According to the TBTA's engineering consultant's estimates, an additional $6 million would be needed to widen the bridge itself and another $4 million would be necessary to alter the approaches to the bridge in order to accommodate the trains. This $10 million would be paid directly out of Authority moneys. In addition, $3.5 million would have to be spent for property acquisition on the "expressway right-of-way" (the Seventh Avenue expressway connections to the bridge) and $2 million more on actual expressway construction. These additional costs, totaling $5.5 million, would not be covered under the provisions of the state and federal programs that the Authority relied on to pay for associated expressways. The Authority would not incur this cost, but Hodgkiss noted "without doubt the City or some other agency would be required to pay the additional costs involved" (Hodgkiss, 1956). In total, therefore, the additional cost of making the bridge suitable for transit rails was $15.5 million, paid partially by the Authority, and partially by the city or some other agency. This was approximately 5% of the total cost of $300 million for the entire project.

By early 1956, the MRTC began to get involved in the Narrows Bridge transit issue under its intrastate study agenda. This unwelcome bit of news came to the TBTA via a letter from Roger Gilman of the Port of New York Authority to Arthur Hodgkiss in January of 1956 (Gilman, 1956a). TBTA General Manager George Spargo was then informed that the MRTC was using its $150 thousand allocation to "study rapid transit on the Narrows Bridge, the idea being to extend the Fourth Avenue Subway across the Narrows into Staten Island" (Hodgkiss, 1956).

MOSES CONFRONTS THE MRTC

Moses was determined to meet the MRTC head on. In a letter to Charles Tuttle, MRTC co-chairman, and an old adversary from Moses's Long Island Parks Commission days in the 1920s, he pointed out the apparent inability of the Fourth Avenue subway to handle the volume of traffic that would be generated by a Staten Island line, and the Transit Authority's inability to construct new subway connections in Brooklyn. In light of the inadequacy of the current transit system, he questioned the value of incurring additional expenses providing for future facilities. Moses argued the estimated $10 million that accommodating train tracks on the bridge would cost the Authority directly was not a worthwhile use of funds. He noted that the Port Authority had designed the George Washington Bridge to accommodate future transit and in the twenty-five years of the bridge's operation "not the slightest interest has been evidenced by any railroad of installing rapid transit on the bridge." Similar facilities on the Narrows Bridge seemed to him an equal waste: "No responsible organization has approached us on the construction of rail on the Narrows Bridge and no offer is expected" (Moses, 1956a). The crux of Moses's (1956a) position, however, was the financial ability of the Authority to finance such an expansion of the bridge:

> The Authority does not have recourse to taxes and must rely upon income to finance its revenue bonds. The members, as responsible public officials, cannot agree to what in their opinion would be a waste of $10,000,000 in anticipation of a most improbable rapid transit system for Staten Island. If the bridge is to be strengthened for this purpose, some other agency will have to supply the additional funds. The Authority will not.

Unswayed by Moses's attack, the MRTC announced its plans to proceed with the Narrows Bridge study in its *Interim Report*, issued in March 1956. On March 13, it announced its employment of the consulting firm of Day and Zimmerman to conduct the New York transit study, including the Narrows Bridge issue (MRTC, 1956). Tuttle wrote Moses shortly thereafter noting that the Commission's preliminary investigations indicated that planned improvements of the Brooklyn subway system would result in adequate capacity to handle Staten Island rail service by 1962. While the Commission's "views and recommendations will naturally await the [Day and Zimmerman's transit] study's conclusion," Tuttle (1956) closed the letter with a rather clear statement of intent:

> The future development of the vast potentials of Staten Island and the adjoining territory in New Jersey can scarcely be kept dependent upon vehicular transportation solely and the limited and time-consuming ferries, but requires in all prudence and foresight that mass transportation by rapid transit also be considered, particularly as to whether comparatively small expenditures now would save vastly greater expenditure later or prevent denial of rapid transit travel to and from Staten Island at all.

Moses's response cut to the heart of the Authority's position. It was not so much that the Authority opposed rapid transit per se, or even that it was unwilling to take a role in its development. Rather, the Authority was unable to do so, due to the fiscal and institutional limits it faced as a public Authority:

> It is not a question of reluctance on the part of members of the [TBTA] to spend an additional sum of $10,000,000 on the Narrows Bridge in order to provide facilities for future rapid transit. It is that even if we could sell bonds without public credit for such a dubious purpose to prudent investors, we would not have a moral right to spend this money in anticipation of a rapid transit system that has no chance of materializing when we have no agreement with any responsible bonder to repay the investment and no possibility of retrieving it except through toll revenues on motor vehicles. Where is the sum, between half a billion and a billion dollars to build a new rapid transit line in Brooklyn with yards, equipment and trains, leading into Manhattan [Moses, 1956b]?

Beyond the financial question of the "moral right" of the Triborough to finance an additional $10 million for transit on the bridge, Moses had a fundamental distrust of the direction the Commission study was taking. He was concerned that the transit issue may jeopardize the entire Verrazano project. In a letter to New York City's Mayor Wagner regarding a committee put together to study the city's transit needs in cooperation with the MRTC, Moses unabashedly displayed his hostility toward the MRTC's agenda. He admitted the value of reviewing New York City's plan for transit facilities, but he questioned the motives of the MRTC study. Transit "is a subsidized operation," Moses (1956c) noted, and recommendations for extending any rail lines "can only result in an increase in subsidy." The MRTC was not concerned with the solution of the commuter problem, but rather, with shifting the burden of the deficits incurred by transit from the railroads themselves to the public sector, and, in particular, to New York City. Without being specific, Moses (1956c) warned Mayor Wagner not to allow important projects (such as the Verrazano Bridge) to be postponed while the results of the MRTC study were awaited:

> The wholly unrealistic and biased approach of the Transit Commission to the transit problem can only lead to unnecessary embarrassment to your administration and to those who are directly responsible for the arterial highway program. There will be all kinds of pressures to delay any action under the new federal and state highway program until all of these wholly unrelated problems have been discussed at length in town meetings in the villages of New Jersey, Westchester, Nassau and Suffolk without regard for a particular interest in New York City's pressing problems. You can be sure that suburban areas will not agree to pay their share of the inevitable costs and that they will expect New York City to take on most of the burden.

By April 1956, Governor Harriman again entered the transit debate. While not actually endorsing the MRTC's position, he expressed concern over the direction the Authorities were taking in the planning of the bridge. Harriman wrote to Donald Lowe, Chairman of the PNYA, concerning an April PNYA Board meeting that authorized engineering work in connection with the Narrows Bridge. "I assume," wrote the Governor,

> that this preliminary work will not be such as to commit the Port Authority or the Triborough Bridge Authority on the question of whether or not the bridge should be designed so as to accommodate rapid transit facilities in the future. As I understand it, this question is within the area of studies being actively carried out by the Metropolitan Rapid Transit Committee. I hope that no final decisions will be made until the results of that study are available [Harriman, 1956].

Harriman's interest in the issue generated a considerable amount of effort on the part of both Authorities to justify their position. In response to Harriman's letter, the PNYA composed a five page report entitled "Rail Transit on the Narrows Bridge," which it forwarded to the Triborough for review. In it, the Authority detailed its views on the Narrows Bridge transit issue. The major reasons for the Port Authority's objections to rapid transit were already known, namely, the unlikelihood of a Brooklyn extension of the subway system, and the additional cost of widening the bridge to accommodate transit. However, they did introduce a new issue, the necessity of altering the design of the approaches to the bridge to accommodate tracks. The Authorities had already negotiated an agreement with the Army for the acquisition of land at Forts Hamilton and Wadsworth. This agreement had been designed to minimize the taking of residential land that was already becoming a major issue in the Bay Ridge section of Brooklyn. Forcing the Authorities to provide space for transit would "demand complete re-design of these ramps and a renegotiation of the entire agreement with the Army. In all likelihood, it would destroy any such prospect for such an agreement since the land takings in Forts Hamilton and Wadsworth would have to be increased to an extent that would in our judgment be unacceptable to the Army" (PNYA, 1956).

For the first time, the Authorities made a direct threat that they would not build the Narrows Bridge if forced to pay for the additional cost involved in providing space for future rail transit tracks. Claiming the bridge to be financially marginal as it was originally designed, the Authorities argued the cost of adding facilities for transit, estimated at over $10 million, would make it "practically impossible to market the bonds for financing the bridge" (PNYA, 1956). If the Authorities were forced to make provision for the "remote possibility that fixed rail lines might some day be installed on the bridge," they wanted the assurance that they would not be forced to finance it themselves. "The only alternative would appear to be for the Metropolitan Rapid Transit Commission or some other agency or agencies to commit itself *now* to finance all the additional cost for strengthening the structure and providing the added ramp structures" (PNYA, 1956). Without such a commitment, the Authorities were unwilling to undertake the project. In summarizing the five pages of argument against rapid transit, the Port Authority concluded, "the investment of the substantial funds needed to re-plan and re-design the Narrows Bridge in order to provide for some future possibility that is speculative and improbable to say the least, would not be in the public interest and would require that they re-examine the feasibility of the entire Narrows Bridge project" (PNYA, 1956).

MOSES RESPONDS TO THE
PORT AUTHORITY REPORT

After reviewing the Port Authority's report, Moses sent the governor a seven-point analysis that outlined the Port Authority's points. The analysis also stated the Triborough's concern that the additional cost of providing transit could not be financed from tolls without raising these tolls to an unacceptable level (defined as being "comparable to the Hudson River crossings to New Jersey"). Furthermore, Moses added a new dimension to the debate by "upping the ante" on the bridge, claiming that the additional cost for providing transit was not $10 to $12 million, as had been contended, but $50 million (Moses, 1956d). This estimate was based on an analysis done by Othmar Ammann, of Ammann and Whitney, consulting engineers to the Triborough Bridge and Tunnel Authority. Ammann's analysis argued that the $10 to $12 million cost was based on reserving two of the twelve planned vehicular lanes for transit. However, under current traffic projections, this substitution would result in the Narrows Bridge reaching its capacity within 15 to 20 years after completion. "Provision for rapid transit tracks," Ammann concluded, "would therefore have to be made at the expense of needed vehicular capacity or else at considerable additional cost to the project at this time" (Ammann, 1956a). Ammann estimated the cost of *adding* two lanes for transit to be approximately $50 million, or almost one-fourth of the projected cost of the bridge as originally planned (Ammann, 1956b).

This information gave Moses additional ammunition against the transit plan. Concluding his letter to Governor Harriman, Moses (1956d) made no direct threat to reconsider the bridge project, but his language made the Triborough's position clear in no uncertain terms:

> The Authorities cannot on any basis gamble on the additional $50,000,000 cost of a marginal project with the vague possibility of securing a modest return in the indeterminate future. The Authorities were established to build needed public facilities to be paid for out of user fees and without obligating the City and State. The Commissioners are in a unique position having not only a public trust but also a responsibility for business like administration to the bond holders of the Authorities. They cannot conscientiously recommend substantial expenditures for which they can expect no direct or indirect return.

This 300% increase in the estimated cost of providing space for transit tracks on the Narrows Bridge generated considerable confusion in the governor's office. More details were requested, and Ammann's drawings and analysis were sent to Albany. Moses, however, was not satisfied with simply explaining the new cost estimates. In an internal TBTA memo, he expanded the scope of his attack, noting that he wanted to "go way beyond a few cost figures on adding rapid transit to the Narrows Bridge." He wanted to include a discussion of the transit needs on Staten Island and in Brooklyn in order to show the magnitude of problems and to undermine the position of the Transit Authority and the MRTC. "Obviously the Transit Authority people are talking sheer nonsense when they refer to the possibility of carrying traffic over the existing Brooklyn Line without a new subway, yards, tunnel to Manhattan, etc." (Moses, 1956e). Moses emphasized the fact that neither the bond holders nor the Port Authority would accept the additional costs for transit.

These points were contained in a letter to the governor's office (Moses, 1956f). The governor's office responded by expressing confusion over the new cost estimates. Harriman's secretary, Jonathan Bingham, noted that the Triborough's estimates of $56 million did not match the figure of $3.5 million quoted by the Port Authority (Bingham, 1956). The governor's office forwarded the TBTA's estimates to the Transit Authority for comment.

Moses's response to these criticisms was direct. He berated both the Transit Authority and their "perfectly preposterous position that they can pour additional rapid transit into existing lines in Brooklyn"; and Tuttle, who Moses (1956g) felt was responsible for "all this agitation." Furthermore, Moses noted, Tuttle and the Transit Authority were obstructing the entire Narrows Bridge project by interfering with the Authorities' decision-making process, and by advocating unrealistic projects without the least bit of knowledge of how they were to be funded. Complaining that "forward progress is being interrupted by asking others to substitute their judgment for ours [PNYA and TBTA]," Moses (1956e) accused the Transit Authority of being fiscally unsound:

> The Transit Authority finances no permanent improvements out of revenues and . . . it is self-supporting at most only as to operation. In other words, all public improvements by the Transit Authority have to be paid for by the City of New York out of Capital Budget which is already terrifically overburdened.

Moses concluded with the allegation that Transit Authority plans for extending transit to Staten Island were illusionary. Drawing on his experience on the City Planning Commission working on the Capital Budget, he claimed "the Transit Authority has a dozen projects involving City capital funds which will come years ahead of any such scheme as rapid transit to Staten Island" (Moses, 1956g). The projects could be financed only if the city's debt limit were increased by constitutional amendment, a prospect Moses did not support since it would affect the tax level.

The issue came to a head the following autumn with the publication of the Day and Zimmerman report, prepared by the MRTC's consultant on the Narrows Bridge project. Day and Zimmerman estimated annual deficits from a Staten Island Transit system at between $2.227 and $5.257 million. Construction costs of a cross-Island train line were estimated at between $38.5 and $43.5 million, plus the additional $10 million for the bridge crossing originally presented by the Authorities. The consultants also noted that the additional space needed to accommodate transit facilities on Staten Island's Clove Lake Expressway would probably not be eligible for funding under the federal-state highway program that was paying for the expressways. The city would have to incur this additional burden itself (Gilman, 1956b).

The issue was resolved when the MRTC published its interim report in January 1957. In a rather long and detailed analysis, the Commission noted that if the transit line were built, the city would be confronted with annual deficits ranging from $5 to $6.5 million, depending on whether the $10 or the $50 million estimate for the Narrows Bridge expense was used, to operate and pay for the new system. Significantly, the MRTC accepted the fact that the Authorities refused to finance the provision of transit on the bridge, and calculated these deficits based on the assumption that the city would have to incur this expense. The MRTC did not question the basic assumption that public transit was a noteworthy public good, but it posed the question of whether the costs of this service were offset by the benefits. The MRTC (1957) ultimately answered this question by stating "nearly equal public convenience and public benefits could be obtained from . . . direct bus service from various parts of Staten Island across the Narrows Bridge to the present subway station . . . or to any other desirable subway transfer point in Brooklyn. The initial capital investment and the annual cost to the City to provide such alternative service would be comparatively small."

CONCLUSION

The TBTA won this battle, but ultimately lost the war. While the Authority was able to avoid providing transit on the Verrazano Narrows Bridge, it was ultimately forced to face the issue of rapid transit as one aspect of the transportation problem. In 1968, a little more than a decade after the Verrazano Narrows debate played itself out, Governor Nelson Rockefeller engineered the creation of a new public transportation authority, the Metropolitan Transit Authority (MTA). The MTA consisted of a merger of a number of existing public transportation agencies: the New York City Transit Authority, the Manhattan and Bronx Surface Operating Authority, the Long Island Railroad, Penn Central Railroad, New Haven Railroad, and the Staten Island Rapid Transit Service. The TBTA was absorbed into the MTA, ostensibly to provide a "balanced regional approach," but the motive was more accurately to provide a revenue source to defray transit costs (Caro, 1975: 1132-1144).

With this merger, Governor Rockefeller accomplished what the transit advocates in the 1950s were unable to do: force the public authorities to accept responsibility for the issue of mass transit. To a large degree, however, the transit advocates' failure was due to their misunderstanding of the organizational environment within which the debate over transit occurred. Rockefeller's success was possible only after a complete redefinition of the Authority's organizational structure.

There was not a direct relationship between the actions of the transit coalition in the 1950s and Rockefeller's creation of the MTA in the 1960s. The debate over the Verrazano Narrows Bridge, however, can be seen as the first step in the process. The MRTC and its allies did not consider the possibility of asking the TBTA and the PNYA to finance transit itself; they only requested the Authorities build their bridges so that a transit agency could provide rail service in the future. This was the first step, however, to a realization that public authorities, with their lucrative source of toll revenues generated by their arterial projects, could help subsidize the expenses of public transit.

The creation of the MTA, of course, never "solved" the commuter rail problem or the traffic problem of metropolitan New York. It has, however, created a new type of regional transportation agency that has its own form of control over resources. A different organizational environment was created. As the organizational self-definition of the public authorities in the 1950s precluded the TBTA or the PNYA from accepting any responsibility for transit, the new institutional structure of the hybrid arterial-transit authorities determines the current agenda of the MTA. Any solution to the problems of traffic congestion and transit in the metropolitan area must take this into account.

The "politics of policy" is crucial to the construction of infrastructure. Often far more important than "objective analysis," the political interaction among organizations has a decisive impact on infrastructure planning. In fact, as shown in this case study, objective analysis is one of many weapons used in the political policy struggle.

REFERENCES

AMMANN, O. H. (1956a) Personal communication to Robert Moses (April 19).

AMMANN, O. H. (1956b) Personal communication to Arthur Hodgkiss, Assistant General Manager, Triborough Bridge and Tunnel Authority (July 5).

BINGHAM, J. B. (1956) Personal communication to Robert Moses (July 13).

BIRD, F. L. (1949) A Study of the Port of New York Authority. New York: Dun & Bradstreet.

CARO, R. A. (1975) The Power Broker: Robert Moses and the Fall of New York. New York: Vintage.

DANIELSON, M. N. and J. W. DOIG (1982) New York: The Politics of Urban and Regional Development. Berkeley: Univ. of California Press.

DOIG, J. W. (1966) Metropolitan Transportation Politics and the New York Region. New York: Columbia Univ. Press.

GILMAN, R. H. (1956a) Personal communication to Arthur Hodgkiss, Assistant General Manager, Triborough Bridge and Tunnel Authority (January 18).

GILMAN, R. H. (1956b) Memo to Austin Tobin (October 4).

HARRIMAN, W. A. (1956) Personal communication to Donald Lowe, Chairman, Port of New York Authority (April 27).

HEDQUIST, A. S. (1955) Personal communication to Robert Moses, Chairman of Triborough Bridge and Tunnel Authority (August 22).

HODGKISS, A. S. (1955) Memo to George Spargo, General Manager, Triborough Bridge and Tunnel Authority (October 14).

HODGKISS, A. S. (1956) Memo to George Spargo (January 20).

LINES, J. L., E. L. PARKER, and D. C. PERRY (1986) "Building the public works machine: Robert Moses and the public authority," in M. Schoolman and A. Magid (eds.) Reindustrializing New York State: Strategies, Implications, Challenges. Albany: State Univ. of New York Press.

LIVINGSTON, G., Jr. (1954) Statement at Public Hearing on Senate Concurrent Resolution No. 9, before the [New Jersey] Senate Committee on Federal and Interstate Relations (April 7).

Metropolitan Rapid Transit Commission (1955) Interim Report on the Activities of the Commission. New York: author.

Metropolitan Rapid Transit Commission (1956) Interim Report on the Activities of the Commission During 1955. New York: author.

Metropolitan Rapid Transit Commission (1957) Interim Report on the Activities of the Commission During 1956. New York: author.

MOSES, R. (1955) Personal communication to Arthur Hedquist, Executive Secretary, Staten Island Chamber of Commerce (September 1).

MOSES, R. (1956a) Personal communication to Charles H. Tuttle, Co-Chairman, Metropolitan Rapid Transit Commission (January 24).

MOSES, R. (1956b) Personal communication to Charles H. Tuttle (February 28).

MOSES, R. (1956c) Personal communication to Hon. Robert F. Wagner, Mayor, New York City (March 29).

MOSES, R. (1956d) Personal communication to Averill Harriman, Governor, State of New York (June 8).

MOSES, R. (1956e) Memo to Arthur Hodgkiss (July 3).

MOSES, R. (1956f) Personal communication to Jonathan B. Bingham, Secretary to Governor Harriman (July 10).

MOSES, R. (1956g) Personal communication to Jonathan Bingham (July 17).

New York Times (1954) "The whole traffic picture." (January 15).

Port of New York Authority (1956) "Rail Transit on the Narrows Bridge." (unpublished)

SPARGO, G. (1954) Personal communication to Austin Tobin, Executive Director, Port of New York Authority (December 22).

SPARGO, G. (1955) Memo to Arthur S. Hodgkiss, Assistant General Manager, Triborough Bridge and Tunnel Authority (October 4).

Staten Island Chamber of Commerce (1955) Report as to Necessity for Rapid Transit Facilities as Part of the Proposed Narrows Bridge (August).

TOBIN, A. J. (1954a) Statement at Public Hearing on Senate Concurrent Resolution No. 9, before the [New Jersey] Senate Committee on Federal and Interstate Relations (April 7).

TOBIN, A. J. (1954b) Personal communication to George Spargo, General Manager, Triborough Bridge and Tunnel Authority (December 8).

TOBIN, A. J. (1955) Personal communication to Daniel P. Moynihan, Assistant to the Secretary of the Governor (September 30).

Triborough Bridge and Tunnel Authority and Port of New York Authority (1954) Joint Study of Arterial Facilities, New York-New Jersey Region. New York: authors.

TUTTLE, C. H. (1956) Personal communication to Robert Moses (March 15).

WOOD, R. S. (1961) 1400 Governments: The Political Economy of the New York Metropolitan Region. New York: Doubleday.

11

Predicting Impacts of
Infrastructure on Land Use

LEONARD ORTOLANO

THE NATIONAL ENVIRONMENTAL POLICY ACT of 1969 (NEPA) has had an important influence on the planning and design of physical infrastructure in the United States. The Act requires that all agencies of the federal government prepare an environmental assessment of proposed major actions that might significantly affect the "quality of the human environment." A substantial fraction of such federal agency actions involve physical infrastructure.[1] In some instances, the actions consist of federal projects such as dams built by the U.S. Army Corps of Engineers. In other cases, the federal decisions affecting infrastructure involve the issuance of permits or licenses. An example is the Nuclear Regulatory Commission's decision to grant a utility a license to construct a nuclear power plant. The influence of NEPA has not been restricted to federal agencies. Using NEPA as a model, many state and local governments have established environmental impact reporting requirements for decisions involving the development of new infrastructure.

Some environmental impacts of infrastructure projects are direct. An example is the increased noise adjacent to a new stretch of highway. Other impacts are indirect, such as changes in land use caused by new infrastructure development.

The chapter focuses on the indirect impacts of infrastructure on land

AUTHOR'S NOTE: *This chapter benefited from review comments offered by James E. Moore II and Olga Varveri of the Department of Civil Engineering at Stanford, and Jay M. Stein of the Department of Environmental Design and Planning, SUNY—Buffalo.*

use. It first explores the nature of these impacts and then examines two principal land use prediction strategies: expert judgment and mathematical models. Advantages and disadvantages of these strategies are explored from the perspective of planners charged with assessing the environmental impacts of typical infrastructure projects. Issues central to the process of predicting how infrastructure affects land use are considered in the chapter's final section.

INFRASTRUCTURE-LAND USE INTERACTIONS

Infrastructure projects frequently influence the intensity and pattern of land use.[2] For example, consider the case of a new segment of interstate highway that is built a short distance from what was once the main road through a town. After the new segment of interstate is completed, commercial development on the former main road falls off, and new motels and eateries are constructed near the interchanges of the new highway.[3] The new development initiates its own set of impacts on traffic congestion, noise, and so forth. Another example is a city whose population growth is constrained by its existing water supply. Following the development of a new source of water, the town experiences an intense wave of residential development to satisfy the "pent up" demand for new housing.

Although the influence of infrastructure on land use can involve significant environmental effects, such effects are often treated superficially in environmental impact assessments. One reason for this relates to the institutional settings in which land use and infrastructure planning occurs. Land use planning and decision making is typically carried out by city and county governments. In contrast, major infrastructure projects, such as interstate highways and large dams, are developed by state and federal agencies. Meyer and Miller (1984: 181) elaborate on this point in the context of urban transportation and land use planning:

> Different agencies and people are responsible for and trained to do transportation planning and analysis on one hand and land use (or "urban") planning and analysis on the other. To be sure an urban planning department may well be concerned with both transportation and land use issues, but typically, even in such cases, a relatively *autonomous* "transportation group" will exist within the planning department to deal with transportation issues [emphasis added].[4]

Another reason why infrastructure-land use interactions are often analyzed inadequately is that the underlying cause-effect relations are difficult to infer, complex, and poorly understood. This is illustrated by the previous highway and water supply examples. A new segment of interstate highway doesn't always lead to a shift in commercial development.[5] Moreover, even when a shift occurs, the *net* environmental effect (i.e., the difference in environmental impacts of new commercial development with and without the new interstate) may not be significant from anything but a very localized perspective. In other words, the new commercial development might have taken place anyway, in which case the new road would only shift the location of development by a short distance. Similarly, in the water supply example, can it really be said that the new water supply "caused" new housing development? After all, who would locate in a place only because water is available?

FORECASTING STRATEGIES

Although many methods for predicting the impacts of infrastructure on land use have been developed, forecasting specialists do not agree on which methods are the most useful. Existing prediction procedures generally follow two quite different strategies: expert judgment and mathematical modeling. Expert judgment methods usually rely on a process for involving a variety of "experts" including land use and infrastructure planners, and persons familiar with the local development context—city council members, private developers, local agency planners, industrial and commercial businesspeople, and community groups. The judgments of such experts are used to evaluate quantitative and qualitative factors unique to the area being considered. Sometimes the perspectives of the various experts are coordinated and aggregated using one of the so-called judgmental forecasting procedures, such as the "Delphi method."[6]

The second approach to forecasting the land use impacts of infrastructure projects relies on mathematical models.[7] Data on land use attributes are collected and used to estimate coefficients in one or more equations. Examples of attributes include the unit cost of land and the availability of public services and facilities, including infrastructure. The "output" from using these equations includes the land use changes expected as a result of providing new infrastructure.

For the most part, mathematical models used in predicting land use impacts are very complex and require extensive data. They call for much more data and expertise than is typically available in studies that assess the environmental impacts of infrastructure projects. Moreover, the geographic scale of analysis is generally quite large; predictions are usually not made, for example, at the level of a city block. Assessments of the land use impacts of particular infrastructure projects would, ideally, be at a much more "micro" level than the highly aggregated outputs of mathematical models.

The sections that follow provide case studies illustrating the two major land use forecasting strategies. The first section considers an application of expert judgment to assess the land use impacts of alternative transportation systems. The second examines a mathematical model developed for persons with little modeling expertise. It is used to predict the land use impacts of a proposed wastewater treatment project.

FORECASTS BASED ON EXPERT JUDGMENT

The case study demonstrating the application of expert judgment to forecast land use impacts is based on the Delphi method. This method has been used in numerous contexts, most of which have little to do with land use planning.[8] In recent years, however, Davis (1975), Ervin (1977), and others have experimented with the Delphi method as a technique for urban and regional planning. Before introducing the case, the central features of the method are outlined.

OVERVIEW OF THE DELPHI METHOD

The Delphi method is a technique used by analysts to obtain and refine the opinions of a group of informed individuals, referred to collectively as a Delphi panel.[9] Members of a panel are selected because of their knowledge of the issues under study. A typical panel has about 8 to 12 members.

The basic instrument used in the Delphi technique is a questionnaire that elicits quantitative responses to specific questions and encourages comments that help clarify those responses. The questionnaire is submitted to the panelists on several occasions in an iterative fashion. Starting with the second iteration, statistical and verbal summaries of panel members' responses in the previous iteration are submitted to the panelists with a blank copy of the questionnaire. Panelists are asked to review their previous responses and, if appropriate, to revise them in light of information in the summaries. This process continues until a satisfactory agreement among panelists has been reached or responses do not change between successive iterations. The objective of the iterative process is to obtain reasonable agreement on all questions and to provide a means of communication among panelists that maintains the anonymity of individual panel members. This anonymity reduces the likelihood that participants' opinions will be affected by panel members who, in an ordinary meeting format, would be influential because of their personal style or professional stature. Use of question-naires administered iteratively also reduces social pressures to obtain a group consensus.

IMPLEMENTING THE FORECASTING PROCEDURE

A case study to examine the usefulness of the Delphi method in predicting land use impacts was reported by Cavalli-Sforza and Ortolano (1984). The case concerns transportation system investments in Santa Clara County, California. The county includes the city of San Jose and is dominated by the semiconductor and computer industry ("Silicon Valley"). It is experiencing rapid growth and suffering from severe peak-hour traffic congestion.

Three alternative transportation systems in Santa Clara County distinguished by transportation mode and particular investments have been examined:

- Alternative I—Emphasis on *highway* system improvements.
- Alternative II—Emphasis on *bus* system improvements and incentives for car and van pooling.
- Alternative III—Emphasis on *rail* system improvements (commuter train and "light rail"), with special high-density residential and commercial zoning policies for station areas.

Based on a preliminary survey, about 30 potential members of a Delphi panel were identified. Of these, 12 "local experts" were selected. Their backgrounds were as follows: urban economist, housing specialist, transportation agency analyst/engineer (2), private transportation consultant (2), regional planning agency analyst, county transportation commissioner, neighborhood association representative, local politi-cal activist, Chamber of Commerce member, and school district superintendent.

The composition of the final Delphi panel was less than ideal because it overrepresented professional transportation analysts and planners, while not including public utility, private business, land development or real estate "experts." Unfortunately, prospective panelists in these occupations who were interested in the study felt that too much time would be required for their participation. To some extent, however, their viewpoints were represented by other panelists.

A questionnaire was used to elicit the judgmental forecasts of panel members regarding several transportation-land use variables potentially affected by the three previously mentioned transportation alternatives. Forecasts were obtained for population, housing, employment, commute patterns, and choice of transit mode. The area of analysis was the city of San Jose; it was divided into four zones. For each transportation program, all variables were predicted for each of two time periods: 1990 and 2000. For any particular alternative and year, the value of each variable was predicted for each of the four zones.

DELPHI FORECAST RESULTS

The final forecasts of land use and other variables were based on three iterations (or rounds) of the Delphi questionnaire. For most of the variables included in the study, the behavior of the medians and other statistical descriptors of the distributions of responses during rounds 2 and 3 met conventional criteria for terminating a Delphi exercise.[10]

Figure 11.1 illustrates results obtained using the Delphi method. These results, which are for commercial employment in four sections of San Jose, indicate that panelists felt the rail emphasis alternative (III) would stimulate commercial development relative to the other transportation programs. The forecasts show much of the increase in commercial employment occurring in central San Jose—the zone containing the city's downtown area. Accessibility to that zone would be improved greatly by the rail investments.

ASSESSMENT OF FORECASTING PROCEDURE

The case study forecasting exercise revealed some problems in using the Delphi technique to predict land use impacts of infrastructure. The principal difficulties were in getting the questionnaires completed, returned, and summarized in a timely fashion. This is reflected by the 18 months it took to complete the three rounds of the Delphi method. Such a time duration is unacceptably long for a method that is to be useful in practice. There were, however, three factors that account for the excessive time. First, and foremost, the questionnaire itself was long and

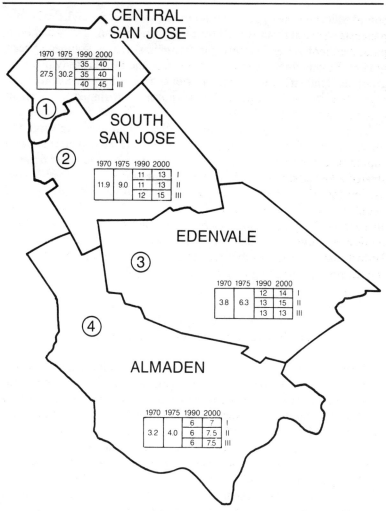

CENTRAL
SAN JOSE

1970	1975	1990	2000	
27.5	30.2	35	40	I
		35	40	II
		40	45	III

①

SOUTH
SAN JOSE

②

1970	1975	1990	2000	
11.9	9.0	11	13	I
		11	13	II
		12	15	III

EDENVALE

③

1970	1975	1990	2000	
3.8	6.3	12	14	I
		13	15	II
		13	13	III

④

ALMADEN

1970	1975	1990	2000	
3.2	4.0	6	7	I
		6	7.5	II
		6	7.5	III

SOURCE: Cavilli-Sforza and Ortolano (1984). Reprinted with permission of the
American Society of Civil Engineers.

**Figure 11.1   Forecasts of Commercial Employment (all table entries are medians
of responses in thousands)**

complex; it could easily take four hours to complete. Second, the Delphi panelists were not remunerated for their participation. If they had been paid, their motivation to return questionnaires on time would have been greater. Finally, the researchers conducting the Delphi study included graduate students whose course work and other responsibilities, together with unavoidable student turnover, contributed to delays in completing the study.

To successfully use the Delphi method in forecasting land use impacts, questionnaires should be kept short and Delphi panel members should be compensated for their time. The case study exercise demonstrated a key advantage of judgmental approaches to forecasting land use impacts: the inclusion of the intuitions, opinions, and judgments of people familiar with the local area and key variables affecting land use. In general, judgmental approaches can often be implemented using modest amounts of data, staff expertise, and computing facilities. Unfortunately, little information is available on the accuracy of land use impact predictions using judgmental methods.

AN ILLUSTRATIVE
MATHEMATICAL MODELING APPROACH

During the 1970s many researchers attempted to develop mathematical modeling procedures that would predict the indirect environmental impacts of infrastructure projects.[11] Some of these modeling approaches contained a "module" for predicting land use impacts. Once land use changes were predicted, other procedures (e.g., traffic assignment methods and air pollutant dispersion models) could be used to trace effects of the expected changes in land use. Very often, the mathematical modeling approaches relied on multiple-regression analysis.[12]

The discussion here focuses on a forecasting approach that was developed under the sponsorship of the U.S. Environmental Protection Agency and was intended to be useful in a wide variety of contexts. The approach examined is the "Growth Effects of Major Land Use Projects" (GEMLUP) procedure for predicting indirect impacts of new wastewater collection systems.[13] The method was developed to provide a way of estimating whether proposed wastewater collection facilities would influence land use, traffic congestion, and air quality. Although GEMLUP contains several parts, the focus here is on its land use module.[14] The following review of GEMLUP illustrates some general ideas about the use of multiple-regression equations as tools for predicting land use changes.

OVERVIEW OF THE GEMLUP PROCEDURE

The GEMLUP forecasting procedure uses a set of nine independent, statistically derived equations to estimate land use characteristics (e.g., dwelling units per 10,000 acres) ten years beyond year t, the base year used in the analysis. It is presumed that year t is the year in which the proposed project's new or expanded collection system first carried wastewater flows. The procedure forecasts several different categories of land use including residential, manufacturing, and commercial. Each prediction is for the area of analysis as a whole; there is no spatial disaggregation of the model's forecasts.

The procedures used in developing the equations can be sketched out by considering the GEMLUP equation for predicting "RES," the total residential development in the area of analysis. The developers of GEMLUP postulated "independent variables" such as the number of acres of vacant, developable land, the price of land and median family income (see Table 11.1).

Selection of the independent variables was based, in part, on an underlying theory of the factors that GEMLUP's developers felt would influence residential development (the "dependent variable").[15] The selection was also influenced by data availability and a determination of which independent variables would give the best results, where "best" was defined using standard statistical measures, such as the coefficient of multiple determination. The model developers postulated a linear relationship for how the independent variables affect the dependent variable.[16]

As shown in Table 11.1, the hypothesized relationship among the variables has seven constants $(C_1, C_2, \ldots, C_7)$, one multiplying each independent variable and an additive constant. The relationship is useless in forecasting until these constants are determined. In the case of GEMLUP, this determination was made by gathering estimates for the dependent variable and each of the six independent variables for forty different physical settings. In other words, a particular area of analysis was selected and then estimates were made of residential development (RES), median price of an acre of residential land divided by median family income (LAND), and so forth. Estimates were based on land use maps, data from the U.S. Census, county and city planning office records, and so on. The data gathering process was repeated for forty different areas of analysis. Using standard statistical methods, the data

TABLE 11.1
The GEMLUP Equation for Predicting Total Residential
Development in the Area of Analysis

Dependent Variable
    RES = total residential development in the area of analysis in year t + 10 (dwelling units per 10,000 acres).

Independent Variables
    VACANT = vacant, developable land in the area of analysis (in year t) divided by the area of analysis minus vacant undevelopable land (in year t).

    LAND = median price of an acre of vacant, residential land in year t divided by median family income in year t.

    RECAP1 = collection reserve, the ratio of postproject wastewater collection capacity minus peak wastewater flow to peak wastewater flow (x100).

    MANJOB = number of manufacturing workers residing in the area of analysis in year t divided by total census tract area in square miles.

    STAY = nonmobility, the percentage of families in year t who were in the same house in year (t + 5).

    DRIVE = driver density, 100s of workers who drive to work in year t in the county divided by the area of the county.

Functional Form of the Relationship Among Variables
$$RES = C_1\,VACANT + C_2\,LAND + C_3\,RECAP1 + C_4\,MANJOB + C_5\,STAY + C_6\,DRIVE + C_7$$

Forecasting Equation
$$RES = -8692\;VACANT + 5347\;LAND + 16.42\;RECAP1 + 11.24\,MANJOB - 18{,}804\,STAY + 497.2\,DRIVE + 13{,}466$$

from all forty areas provided numerical estimates of the coefficients, C_1, C_2, ..., C_7. The resulting equation is at the bottom of Table 11.1.

IMPLEMENTATION OF GEMLUP

The GEMLUP procedure was designed to provide a useful way of predicting the land use impacts of a particular type of infrastructure investment: expansion of wastewater collection capacity. To test the procedure's practicability, researchers at Stanford University employed GEMLUP to predict land use impacts of a wastewater management program in the Livermore-Amador Valley in northern California.[17] During the early 1970s, the Valley's population growth was severely constrained by the absence of adequate wastewater management facilities, and thus a case study application of GEMLUP in this context appeared appropriate.[18]

Applying GEMLUP in this context produced erroneous results. The residential equation predicted 127,000 dwelling units in the study area for 1985, an unrealistic increase from the estimated 17,000 dwelling units in 1975. As another example, GEMLUP produced a negative estimate for the area of commercial land use, a physical impossibility.

ASSESSMENT OF THE
FORECASTING PROCEDURE

The above mentioned shortcomings of GEMLUP illustrate difficulties commonly experienced in using multiple-regression equations to predict land use changes. An equation such as the one in Table 11.1 cannot be transported for use in a context substantially different (in either temporal or spatial dimensions) from the cases used to estimate the equation's coefficients.

Difficulties in the Livermore-Amador Valley forecasting exercise arose, in part, because the case study area was different in several important respects from most of the 40 areas used in estimating the constants in the GEMLUP equations. For example, the astronomical price ($100,000 per acre) of residential land in the Livermore-Amador Valley—in proximity to the high growth San Francisco Bay area—produced a value of 6.2 for the LAND variable in the equation for computing total residential dwelling units (RES). This value far exceeds both the average (0.537) and the maximum (2.55) of the LAND variable in the 40 cases used to develop the predictive equations. The influence of the extraordinarily high value for LAND in the Livermore-Amador case was sufficient to swamp the effects of other variables in the predictive equation.

Another difficulty in using the RES equation for the Livermore-Amador Valley case concerns GEMLUP's lack of transferability over time. Inflation was the cause of this problem. Two variables in particular, land cost and income, were significantly affected by the high inflation rates characteristic of the 1970s. The inclusion of inflation-sensitive variables caused the GEMLUP land use prediction equations to be obsolete shortly after they were derived.[19]

The poor performance of the GEMLUP equations raises important questions about statistical models for predicting land use. The developers of GEMLUP claimed that it was applicable to a wide variety of wastewater management projects, and that was one reason it was selected for case study purposes.[20] However, it is clear from the Livermore-Amador Valley results that equations based on 40 cases can produce very poor results. Moreover, even assuming that the number and kinds of cases used in developing the GEMLUP equations provided coverage of all cases likely to be important to GEMLUP's users, the inclusion of inflation-sensitive variables caused the equations to be obsolete.

One final limitation of statistical modeling procedures such as GEMLUP concerns their logical structure or lack thereof. The key element in developing the GEMLUP equations appears to have been the production of a good model, where "good" is narrowly defined using standard statistical measures. In the case of the equation for RES, the result (notwithstanding its statistical properties) is a model that must be viewed as a "black box." It has no apparent logic. Indeed, studying the structure of the equation yields several counterintuitive results. For example, the negative coefficient for "VACANT" indicates that residential development potential decreases as the availability of vacant, developable land increases. The developers of GEMLUP correctly caution potential users *not* to interpret individual coefficients in the predictive equations. These coefficients have no meaning in the usual cause-effect sense. Indeed, the predictive equations do little to inform GEMLUP's users about causal relationships between wastewater facility construction and regional growth.

Although GEMLUP and other mathematical models for predicting land use impacts of infrastructure appear to be more rigorous than purely judgmental approaches such as the Delphi method, the rigor is sometimes more apparent then real. In fact, as the discussion above suggests, blind adherence to the computational procedures of GEMLUP can yield quantitative estimates that are absurd and much further afield than anything one would expect from the Delphi method.

There is reason to be cautious of land use forecasts based on mathematical models, but there is no reason to withdraw from using such models. Indeed, as is illustrated in a survey by Tang (1975), there are numerous examples of regression models that have been applied successfully in forecasting land use variables such as property values.

The difference between the approaches typically followed in the regression studies cited by Tang and the approach employed in GEMLUP is that the models included in Tang's work were generally developed for a single, well-circumscribed study area. For GEMLUP to be applied in that fashion it would be necessary to reestimate the coefficients in the equations (such as the one for RES) for a particular area. This would not create difficulties in a research study. However, in the context of environmental impact assessments for proposed infrastructure projects, the time and budget needed to gather data and estimate coefficients in a regression equation are often unavailable. Moreover the expertise required to construct mathematical models competently is specialized and may not be available to many infrastructure planning units. Although the needed expertise could be obtained from consultants, the costs would generally be excessive for impact assessments on typical projects. Indeed, the desire to avoid incurring high costs and obtaining modeling expertise on a routine basis provided some of the motivation for developing GEMLUP. Clearly, as illustrated by the Livermore-Amador Valley exercise, it is not simple to develop a single model robust enough to give meaningful results in the many contexts in which infrastructure projects are developed.

IMPORTANT UNANSWERED QUESTIONS

The above described experiences with the Delphi method and GEMLUP give a sense of the field as a whole. Unfortunately, there currently is no consensus on how best to predict the land use impacts of infrastructure projects. There are, of course, several promising approaches. The troublesome problem, however, is that approaches that can yield accurate results typically require more time and funds than are commonly available to infrastructure agencies in preparing environmental impact assessments.

In addition to the difficulty in finding a widely acceptable analytic approach to forecasting, there are other problems in analyzing the land use impacts of infrastructure. These concern the distinction between induced and displaced growth. In this context, induced growth is an increase in development that occurs because of the infrastructure facility. In contrast, displaced growth is development that would have occurred in the region anyway, but occurs in a different location as a result of the infrastructure project.

Models such as GEMLUP are poorly suited for analyzing distinctions between induced and displaced growth. This occurs because the area of analysis is typically only a portion of a region, and what goes on outside the area of analysis remains unexamined. Moreover, GEMLUP does not provide spatially disaggregated forecasts—a necessity if questions of induced and displaced growth are to be investigated.

Other models, such as the Lowry model and its derivatives, permit an analysis of spatial changes within a region.[21] In these cases, regional population and employment are treated as constants established outside of the modeling context. These models are therefore not well suited to examine induced growth. However, because they allocate regional employment and population among zones, they could potentially be used to study the effect of new infrastructure in displacing growth.

A notion tied directly to the concept of displaced growth concerns the difference between a regional and a local (i.e., area of analysis) perspective. Again, GEMLUP provides an interesting case in point because it considers only a portion of a region. Impacts that appear negative (positive) from a local viewpoint may not look as bad (good) from a regional perspective. Consider, for example, residential development caused by new wastewater management facilities in the Livermore-Amador Valley. It would be hard to argue that such residential development is "new" to the San Francisco Bay area. Assuming it is not, the population increase in the Livermore-Amador Valley is associated with a corresponding (but not necessarily equal) decrease in growth in another portion of the region.

The distinction between a regional and a local perspective can be taken one step further by considering how displacements in land use affect air quality. It may be the case that an increase in wastewater treatment facilities in the Livermore-Amador Valley leads to substantial population growth in the Valley and, correspondingly, more auto trips and more automobile-generated air pollutant emissions in the Valley. If these trips by new Livermore-Amador Valley residents are offset partially by trips not taken in portions of the region that would have otherwise absorbed the growth, then an analysis of regional air quality impacts should account for this. From a regionwide perspective, it could be that the air quality impacts are not as bad as they appear when the Livermore-Amador Valley is considered in isolation.

CONCLUSIONS

The prediction of land use impacts is clearly complex. Moreover the incompleteness of existing theories about land use and economic development and how they are influenced by infrastructure changes must be recognized. Mathematical models, when developed for a particular study area and infrastructure facility, can be useful. However, models whose coefficients have not been estimated for a particular context can yield very misleading results.

Despite the analytic complexities and the limitations of existing forecasting methods, the impacts of infrastructure on land use can be significant and the effects are potentially too important to ignore. Moreover, laws such as NEPA and its equivalents at the state level require that land use impacts be accounted for in infrastructure planning.

In assessing land use impacts, infrastructure planning units should consider using both mathematical models and expert judgment. For areas that have been studied extensively by land use modelers, there may be mathematical models available that can be adapted to yield insights into effects of a proposed project. In the case of major projects with potentially significant impacts, it may be appropriate to spend the resources needed to construct a new mathematical model for the circumstances in question. Alternatively, it may be productive to employ an expert judgment forecasting procedure such as the Delphi method. In all cases, local experts can be asked to generate scenarios of conditions with and without a proposed infrastructure project so that decision makers can be alerted to potential land use impacts.

NOTES

1. For an introduction to NEPA and its influence on infrastructure planning, see Ortolano (1983: Chs. 6 and 11).

2. Case histories documenting the land use impacts of infrastructure are abundant. Well-known studies include Warner's (1978) analysis of how street railways, waterworks, and sewer lines influenced the development of Boston's suburbs, and Kharl's (1982: Ch. 5) account of how the Owens Valley water supply affected real estate development in Southern California. Numerous contemporary examples of the impact of new transportation facilities on land development are given by Stanback and Knight (1976: Ch. 2) and Ayer and Hocking (1986). For additional examples of the link between water resources and land use, see Carson et al. (1973: 75-78) and Ortolano (1973: Ch. 8).

3. An extension of this example involves the reciprocal impacts of the new land use patterns on the transportation system. As elaborated by Putman (1983), the new land use pattern can influence the demand for transportation facilities. Putman's examples concern the commonly observed circumstance in which new highways, designed to relieve congestion, are themselves congested shortly after they are built. The effect of a new highway, in these cases, is to make adjacent lands more attractive for development. The induced development puts increased pressure on the transportation network causing a demand for increased highway capacity. Although such reciprocal impacts between land use and infrastructure are potentially important, they are beyond the scope of this chapter. Putman's discussion provides an introduction to the research undertaken to understand these complex interactions.

4. Meyer and Miller (1984: 181) go on to argue that this "institutional dichotomy encourages planners and analysts to think of 'transportation problems' and 'land use problems' as independent entities." The lack of integration of infrastructure planning and land use planning is certainly not restricted to the transportation area. For examples

documenting that water resources planners sometimes fail to account for land use impacts and related environmental consequences of federal water projects, see Randolph (1976: 5.13-5.16).

5. Siccardi's (1986) analysis of federal efforts to use highway construction to stimulate economic development in rural population centers is instructive. His analysis of highway projects in 35 "growth centers" led him to conclude that "the construction of highways alone cannot be an economic development process; at least the effects of highways become blurred as one of many elements of such a process." Siccardi also questions whether highway construction alone would have any effects on growth centers in sparsely populated portions of the western United States.

6. For an introduction to the Delphi method and other expert opinions (or judgmental) methods for making forecasts, see Porter et al. (1980: 122-131).

7. The mathematical modeling approaches most commonly reported in the literature can be categorized as follows:

(i)   Conventional Multiple-Regression Equations—Statistical analysis procedures have been used to derive single (or independent, multiple) equation models for predicting variables such as land use density, employment, population, and property value. An example, summarized by Meyer and Miller (1984), is a regression equation used to predict how retail sales in downtown Denver would be affected by alternate transportation control plans. A survey of the many regression studies undertaken to estimate the impact of transportation facilities on property values is presented by Tang (1975).

(ii) Interdependent Regression Equations—Attempts have been made to employ linked sets of regression equations to model the complex interactions among variables affecting land use. To make predictions of land use impacts, these equations must be solved simultaneously. A well-known example is the EMPIRIC Activity Allocation Model that has been applied in Boston, Atlanta, and several other North American cities.

(iii) The Lowry Model and Its Derivatives—In 1964, Lowry developed a model for predicting how a given population would distribute itself among different zones within a region. The factors influencing this "allocation" of people included employment, transportation, and the "attractiveness" of different zones. Since the mid-1960s, numerous extensions of the Lowry model have been developed. A noteworthy example is Putman's (1983) integration of Lowry-type models with transportation systems analysis models for predicting the number and distribution of trips.

(iv) Dynamic Simulations—In this type of analysis, changes in land use are represented as outcomes of a dynamic process representing interactions between land use-related activities and infrastructure policies. Methods in this category include the systems dynamics approach, cross-impact simulations, and stochastic processes models. An example is the systems dynamics model for analyzing land use impacts of transportation facilities developed by Mehta and Dajani (1981). The utility of systems dynamics models in forecasting land use has not been assessed thoroughly.

(v)   Multiple-Market Equilibrium Models—Urban economists, regional scientists, and others have built models to describe the location of households and firms in urban areas. Many of these models are not especially sensitive to physical infrastructure. The work by Anas (1982) is a notable exception. He integrated the models of urban economists and transportation specialists to produce a multimarket equilibrium model that can be used to analyze transportation investments. His model forecasts residential location, housing rent patterns, and metropolitan commuting choices.

For surveys of mathematical models developed to forecast the effects of infrastructure on land use, see Dajani and Ortolano (1979) and Meyer and Miller (1984). The latter is concerned exclusively with transportation plans and projects.

8. See, for example, Brockhaus and Michelson (1977) and Linstone and Turoff (1975).

9. This discussion includes several paragraphs previously published in the *Journal of Transportation Engineering*: Cavalli-Sforza and Ortolano (1984: 324-339). The author acknowledges the permission of the American Society of Civil Engineers for the use of this copyrighted work. He also thanks Violetta Cavalli-Sforza for agreeing to have the coauthored material appear herein.

10. These criteria, which are based on convergence and stability of panelists' responses, are summarized in Cavalli-Sforza et al. (1982).

11. For a review of some of these methods, see Urban System Research Engineering (1979).

12. Readers interested in the details of multiple-regression analysis are referred to standard textbooks in statistics (e.g., Draper and Smith, 1966) and econometrics (e.g., Maddala, 1977).

13. Prior to conducting the case study described below, the author considered the GEMLUP approach to be potentially the most practicable of the several methods for predicting secondary impacts of wastewater management projects reviewed by Urban Systems Research Engineering (1979).

14. Strictly speaking, the model considered herein is GEMLUP-II and is documented by Guldberg et al. (1977) and Guldberg and D'Agostino (1978). GEMLUP-I preceded it and was intended to predict indirect (or "secondary") effects of major residential and industrial development projects; see Benesh et al. (1976).

15. The variable selection process involved a preliminary "path analysis" to test a "causal model" of the factors believed to be affected by wastewater management facilities. This yielded a model consisting of simultaneous equations that was viewed as unworkable as a forecasting tool. Following this, a system of independent equations was derived using traditional multiple-regression analysis procedures. The terms in these equations, illustrated by Table 11.1, "cannot be examined to deduce the strength and direction of causal relationships" (Guldberg et al., 1977: 268). For a more complete discussion see the original GEMLUP-II documentation: Guldberg et al. (1978) and Guldberg and D'Agostino (1978).

16. A linear relationship is one in which, aside from a constant term, all terms involve only a single variable raised to the first power. The GEMLUP documentation does not indicate precisely how it was decided that a linear relationship was appropriate.

17. The researchers included two Stanford faculty members, the author and Professor Greig Harvey, and two graduate students, Violetta Cavalli-Sforza and Frank Sweeney. All were members of the Department of Civil Engineering at Stanford University during the early 1980s when the study was conducted. The discussion of GEMLUP relies on unpublished reports of the joint study effort. The contributions of my coinvestigators are acknowledged.

18. Although the case study results are unpublished, details on the Livermore-Amador Valley wastewater management problem are available in Arthur D. Little, Inc. and Thomas Reid and Associates (1974) and U.S. Environmental Protection Agency (1975).

19. One way of dealing with problems caused by inflation is to express all dollar estimates in "real" as opposed to "nominal" terms. The latter consists of dollars at their reported values in any particular time period. In contrast, "real" monetary estimates are given in terms of dollars in a specified base year. The documentation of GEMLUP is ambiguous on this point, but it seems to indicate that nominal dollars were used.

20. See, generally, Guldberg and D'Agostino (1978: 1-1-1-8). In addition, see supra note 13.

21. For an introduction to the Lowry model and its derivatives, see Dajani and Ortolano (1979).

REFERENCES

ANAS, A. (1982) Residential Location Markets and Urban Transportation: Economic Theory, Econometrics and Policy Analysis with Discrete Choice Models. New York: Academic Press.

Arthur D. Little, Inc. and Thomas Reid and Associates (1974) Environmental Impact Report Supplemental Analysis: Population Growth and Air Quality in the Livermore-Amador Valley. Document No. C-77102. Prepared for the Valley Community Services District Stage III Waste Water Treatment Plant Enlargement.

AYER, L. L. and R. J. HOCKING (1986) "Land Development Impacts of Transit Construction." J. of Transportation Engineering 112, 1: 77-87.

BENESH, F., P. GULDBERG, and R. D'AGOSTINO (1976) Growth Effects of Major Land Use Projects, Vol. 3. Summary. Report No. EPA-450/3-76-012C. Research Triangle Park, NC: U.S. Environmental Protection Agency.

BROCKHAUS, W. L. and J. F. MICKELSON (1977) "An analysis of prior Delphi applications and some observations on its future applicability." Technical Forecasting and Social Change 10 (summer).

CARSON, J. M., G. W. RIVKIN, and M. D. RIVKIN (1973) Community Growth and Water Resources Policy. New York: Praeger.

CAVALLI-SFORZA, V. and L. ORTOLANO (1984) "Delphi forecasts of land use: transportation interactions." J. of Transportation Engineering 110, 3: 324-339.

CAVALLI-SFORZA, V., L. ORTOLANO et al. (1982) Transit Facilities and Land Use: An Application of the Delphi Method. Report No. IPM-15. Stanford, California: Stanford Univ., Department of Civil Engineering.

DAJANI, J. S. and L. ORTOLANO [eds.] (1979) Methods of Forecasting the Reciprocal Impacts of Infrastructure Development and Land-Use. Report No. IPM-11. Stanford, CA: Stanford Univ., Department of Civil Engineering.

DAVIS, J. M. (1975) "Land use forecasting: a Delphi approach." Ph.D. dissertation, University of Georgia, Athens.

DRAPER, N. R. and H. SMITH (1966) Applied Regression Analysis. New York: John Wiley.

ERVIN, O. L. (1977) "A Delphi study of regional industrial land-use." Rev. of Regional Studies 7, 1: 42-58.

GULDBERG, P. H., F. H. BENESH, and T. McCURDY (1977) "Secondary impacts of major land use projects." J. of the Amer. Institute of Planners 43, 7: 260-270.

GULDBERG, P. H. and R. B. D'AGOSTINO (1978) Growth Effects of Major Land Use Projects (Wastewater Facilities). Volume II: Summary, Predictive Equations, and Worksheets. Report No. EPA-450/3-78-014b. Research Triangle Park, NC: U.S. Environmental Protection Agency.

GULDBERG, P. H., R. B. D'AGOSTINO, and R. D. CUNNINGHAM (1978) Growth Effects of Major Land Use Projects (Wastewater Facilities), Volume I: Model Specification and Causal Analysis. Report No. EPA-450/3-78-014a. Research Triangle Park, NC: U.S. Environmental Protection Agency.

KHARL, W. L. (1982) Water and Power: The Conflict over Los Angeles' Water Supply in the Owens Valley. Berkeley: Univ. of California Press.

LINSTONE, H. A. and M. TUROFF [eds.] (1975) The Delphi Method: Techniques and Applications. Reading, MA: Addison-Wesley.

MADDALA, G. S. (1977) Econometrics. New York: McGraw-Hill.

MEHTA, S. and J. S. DAJANI (1981) SILUS: The Stanford Infrastructure and Land Use System. Report No. IPM-12. Stanford, CA: Stanford Univ., Department of Civil Engineering.

MEYER, M. D. and E. J. MILLER (1984) Urban Transportation Planning: A Decision-Oriented Approach. New York: McGraw-Hill.

ORTOLANO, L. [ed.] (1973) Analyzing the Environmental Impacts of Water Projects. IWR Report 73-3. Alexandria, VI: U.S. Army Engineers Institute for Water Resources.

ORTOLANO, L. (1984) Environmental Planning and Decision Making. New York: John Wiley.

PORTER, A. L. et al. (1980) A Guidebook for Technology Assessment and Impact Analysis. New York: North Holland.

PUTMAN, S. H. (1983) Integrated Urban Models: Policy Analysis of Transportation and Land Use. London: Pion Limited.

RANDOLPH, J. (1976) "Influence of NEPA on corps of engineers water planning in California." Ph.D. dissertation, Stanford University, Stanford, CA.

SICCARDI, A. J. (1986) "Economic effects of transit and highway construction and rehabilitation." J. of Transportation Engineering 112, 1: 63-76.

STANBACK, T. M., Jr. and R. V. KNIGHT (1976) Suburbanization and the City. Montclair, NJ: Allanheld Osmon.

TANG, F. (1975) Detection and Estimation of Transportation Impact with Models of Suburban Residential Property Sales Prices. Monograph No. 5.

U.S. Environmental Protection Agency (1975) Draft Environmental Impact Statement: Proposed Wastewater Management Program, Livermore-Amador Valley, Alameda County, California. Document No. C-06-1031-010. San Francisco, CA: Region IX, U.S. Environmental Protection Agency.

Urban System Research Engineering (1979) Air Quality Reviews for Wastewater Management Facilities: A Guidebook on Procedures and Methods. Draft of report prepared for the U.S. Environmental Protection Agency, Office of Transportation and Land Policy, Washington DC, under contract No. 68- 01-4790.

WARNER, S. B., Jr. (1978) Streetcar Suburbs: The Process of Growth in Boston (1870-1900). Second Edition. Cambridge, MA: Harvard Univ. Press.

12

Equity and Distributional Issues in Infrastructure Planning: A Theoretical Perspective

TIMOTHY BEATLEY

THE PLANNING AND MANAGEMENT of public infrastructure holds important questions for social equity. Public decisions concerning such infrastructure often affect people's lives in fundamental ways, both in terms of how such investments are *financed* and how they are *located* in the physical and social environment. This chapter examines some alternative ways to identify and measure the equity or inequity of these infrastructure decisions. In the process it raises a number of broad/fundamental questions about how society should be organized, how income should be distributed, and how public decisions should be made in a representative-democratic context.

The presentation that follows suggests that equity in infrastructure planning can be addressed by asking, debating and explicitly answering several fundamental questions. These include the following: (1) What ethical concepts or principles are relevant in determining an equitable distribution of the benefits and burdens of public infrastructure? (2) How should the relevant public or moral community be defined? and (3) How and by whom should decisions about public infrastructure be made? Although the discussion below is organized around these three questions, they do not involve conceptually distinct categories of concepts, but are closely related.

WHAT ETHICAL CONCEPTS
OR PRINCIPLES ARE
RELEVANT TO EQUITABLE
INFRASTRUCTURE PLANNING?

MARKET FAILURE
AND UTILITARIAN ETHICS

The utilitarian approach to public infrastructure planning is one that attempts to maximize overall aggregate social welfare. As J. S. Mill (1961: 194) explains, "The creed which accepts as the foundation, utility, or the Greatest-Happiness Principle, holds that actions are right in proportion as they tend to promote happiness, wrong as they tend to produce the reverse of happiness." The debate over how to define the concept of utility or benefit has raged for centuries, from those who have defined it in more sensory terms (e.g., pleasure, absence of pain) and others defining it in broader human developmental terms (e.g., personal growth and fulfillment, social and political participation). Despite such disagreements, the central notion of maximizing such benefits or utility on a societal or community level is central to most utilitarians.

Many planners and public officials, whether cognizant of it or not, depend heavily on the utilitarian paradigm. It focuses not on who benefits or bears the costs of infrastructure programs or decisions, but rather their net result, that is, the quantity of benefits and costs across all individuals in the jurisdiction (however this is delineated, see below). The contemporary public planning embodiment of the utilitarian paradigm, benefit-cost analysis, views as desirable public investments, and infrastructure projects that are, first, likely to yield benefits in excess of costs, and, second, likely to maximize the ratio of benefits to costs (i.e., net aggregate utility). For instance, we may choose one particular type of public capital investment—say the construction of a downtown convention center over another type of investment—perhaps an industrial park, because it is predicted that the former will generate greater levels of employment, higher tax revenues, and a higher commercial multiple effect, ceteris paribus. The maximal net benefit alternative is to be chosen regardless of the *kinds* of employment that are generated, *who* is likely to benefit from tax base increases, *which* local establishments are likely to benefit from increased commercial trade, and so on.

The conceptual and practical problems of benefit-cost assessment are numerous (e.g., Tribe, 1974; Thompson, 1980; Mishan, 1975). There are, for example, significant questions of how we define and calculate benefits and costs, the discount rates used in estimating future benefits and costs, and social welfare functions.

Concern over market failure also generally falls within the utilitarian paradigm. When markets function properly they serve to maximize social welfare by permitting individuals to choose packages of goods and services that maximize personal welfare.[1] Through Pareto-efficient transactions, individuals are able to maximize their welfare. The type and extent of public infrastructure investments are in turn often founded on the failure, for various reasons (from the external nature of benefits and costs to high transactions costs to problems of information), of the market system. Public goods theory can justify the building of public highways and lighthouses (to cite classic examples) to maximize social welfare (see Moore, 1978). An important practical result from an equity standpoint is that the strict Pareto-standard, typically used to defend the ethics of market transactions, is replaced by the Potential or Compensatory Pareto-Standard (Kaldor-Hicks Standard; see Kaldor, 1939; Hicks, 1939). Here economists and planners hypothesize about what individuals would be *willing to pay*, and the requirement of an actual economic transaction becomes moot. That is, the socially efficient outcome is the one in which those who benefit from the outcome *could* compensate those who are harmed, yielding a net social outcome. Thus the planner or public official chooses one infrastructure alternative over another because it yields a higher net return, regardless of who is harmed, or the community's inability to compensate them for these effects.

THE RAWLSIAN DIFFERENCE PRINCIPLE

John Rawls (1971), in his seminal work *A Theory of Justice*, presents a compelling ethical framework that can be used to evaluate the equity of infrastructure planning. Directly attacking the utilitarian model, Rawls constructs a hypothetical "original position" in which individuals in a state of equality, and divorced of specific information about their personal attributes and life circumstances (under a "veil of ignorance"), decide upon the fundamental principles of justice by which to guide social institutions and legislation (see Beatley, 1984). Rawls argues for the need for such principles by characterizing society as an inherently cooperative venture, and one in which a person's life benefits and burdens are fundamentally arbitrary from a moral point of view. Rawls (1971: 302) derives from this framework his Two Principles of Justice:

> *First Principle*: Each person is to have an equal right to the most extensive total system of equal basic liberties compatible with a similar system of liberty for all.
>
> *Second Principle*: Social and economic inequalities are to be arranged so that they are both (a) to the greatest benefit of the least advantaged, consistent with the just savings principle, and (b) attached to offices and positions open to all under conditions of fair equality of opportunity.

The second principle—specifically the so-called *Difference Principle*—holds the greatest implication for determining the equity of public infrastructure decisions. It directs planners and public officials involved in infrastructure decisions to adopt those financing and locational policies that serve to maximize benefits for members of the least-advantaged economic and social group. Public institutions and policies focus on improving the conditions of the "average" member of this group. Once this has been attained, the Rawlsian planner seeks to implement the *lexical difference principle*, which directs him or her to maximize benefits to members of the next least-advantaged group. Thus in sharp contrast to the utilitarian ethic, planners and policymakers under the Rawlsian framework are not willing to accept public infrastructure decisions that may produce the greatest or greater net social benefit unless they also result in maximal benefit to the least advantaged.

A number of practical problems, however, exist in implementing the Difference Principle. An initial difficulty is in delineating relevant social groups, that is, how will the least-advantaged group be defined? Moreover, assuming that such groups have been delineated, how do we know when we have actually achieved the Difference Principle, or rather when we have gone too far (i.e., when the long-run effects of cumulative infrastructure and other decisions actually serve to lower the life prospects of the least advantaged)? As with several of the categories of standards discussed here, there may be substantial disagreement concerning which public decisions and actions will best implement the Difference Principle. Specifically, Rawls argues that this is accomplished through the provision of "primary goods," or things that all rational individuals can be said to want regardless of what their life plan may turn out to be. Obviously, much disagreement about which items can be said to be primary goods and which are not may exist (and the extent to which they are "interchangeable").

Despite these practical difficulties, the Rawlsian imperative can be operationalized. Its greatest limitation is that the infrastructure planner or policymaker may be faced with political and administrative parameters that reduce the opportunities to take actions that truly advance the interests of the least-advantaged groups. Infrastructure decisions, however, often have tremendous impacts on the least advantaged. For example, the construction of Interstate 40 through North Nashville resulted in the wholesale destruction of minority and low-income businesses (e.g., see Seley, 1983). While most infrastructure decisions are not likely to offer such clear and definitive contrasts between what is equitable and what is inequitable, many will provide opportunities at the margin for advancing the Rawlsian ideal. For instance, incremental efforts to tie public infrastructure to the provision of low- and moderate-income housing, or to minimize the disruption that such projects may create for low- and moderate-income neighborhoods, may generate large cumulative positive effects.

EQUALITY AND EQUAL OPPORTUNITY

The concept of equality has been an unquestioned philosophical component of the American social and political ethos, and remains a theme of relatively high currency. Arguments that infrastructure planning ought to promote equality can take many forms depending upon the precise definition given to the concept (e.g., see Rae, 1981; Dworkin, 1981). An *equal share* conception may suggest that the costs and benefits of certain public facilities ought to be distributed equally among individuals and groups in the community. For instance, such a standard might justify allocating funds for road and street improvements in even lumps to different geographical sectors or neighborhoods in the localities. On the financing side, it may suggest that individuals in the community ought to be required to make *equal sacrifices* in providing needed public infrastructure. As a further example, it may suggest that certain LULU's ("locally unwanted land uses") or NIMBY's ("Not in my back yard") that involve public investments, such as group homes or certain land uses/activities that generate large amounts of noise and traffic, ought to be located such that their negative impacts are equally distributed. A standard of *equal chance* may be appropriate in cases where the manifestation of future benefits or costs from infrastructure investments is uncertain. Such a principle may prevent public investments involving dangerous activities or occurrences (e.g., toxic waste facilities, dangerous transportation facilities, structures that increase the chance of flooding and other natural disasters) from being placed near certain individuals or groups already subjected to high levels of risk.

A more radical notion involves *equality of outcomes*. This suggests that public infrastructure planning, in acknowledgement of the intrinsic moral equality of man, ought to bring about social and economic conditions that place individuals on equal footing in terms of income and resources although tastes and lifestyles will differ. Locating public infrastructure in a particular neighborhood may be justified by reducing the levels of inequality among this particular social group and others in the locality. Such a standard may support amounts of these investments substantially higher than would be required under an equal shares standard.

A *compensatory* standard of equality is one that contends that a history of discrimination or unfair social practices justifies certain infrastructural investments to compensate or make up for these past inequities. The ethical foundation of such a standard is the contention that certain groups or classes would be in a more advanced economic and social position and that such investments are necessary to place these groups where they would have been had these unjust practices not existed.[2]

The notion of equality perhaps most consistent with the history and market philosophy of the United States is that of *equality of opportunity*; the belief that all individuals ought to be afforded the chance to enhance their life prospects and to develop and apply their skills and abilities to the fullest extent. In the past this has often been defined narrowly to address restrictions placed upon access to jobs, education, legal services, and so on (e.g., legal due process, discrimination on the basis of race or sex). In recent years, a more expanded notion of equality of opportunity has gained favor—one that acknowledges that serious concern with the equity or fairness of social starting points requires that all individuals have access to a basic and essential set of primary goods. Rawls (1971), for instance, qualifies the workings of the Difference Principle by what he calls the *principle of fair equality of opportunity*. Rawls (1971: 275) speculates upon what serious attention to such a standard would require:

> I assume also that there is fair (as opposed to formal) equality of opportunity. This means that in addition to maintaining the usual kinds

of overhead capital, the government tries to ensure equal chances of education and culture for persons similarly endowed and motivated either by subsidizing private schools or by establishing a public school system. It also enforces and underwrites equality of opportunity in economic activities and in free choice of occupation. This is achieved by policing the conduct of firms and private associations and by preventing the establishment of monopolistic restrictions and barriers to the more desirable positions. Finally, the government guarantees a social minimum either by family allowances and special payments for sickness and employment, or more systematically by such devices as a graded income supplement (a so-called negative income tax).

While Rawls is not very specific about how this principle of fair equality of opportunity would function, it has important implications for public infrastructure planning. Public investments, from sewer and water facilities to public roads to educational facilities, affect, in quite fundamental ways, the extent to which this type of "substantive" equality of opportunity is achieved (e.g., see Badcock, 1984). Of course, even assuming agreement on the need to attain some level of substantive equality of opportunity, exactly what constitutes such a level will be a hotly contested issue—one upon which reasonable people will disagree.

RIGHTS, DUTIES, AND SOCIAL NEEDS

Politicians and policy analysts often agree on the need for certain actions and policies on grounds of equity, yet may disagree about the precise ethical justification or definition of equity. Those arguing for minimum levels of certain public investments and infrastructure to ensure a substantive equality of opportunity may be joined by those who support a similar package of investments but for different reasons. They may believe that all individuals are by virtue of their being human entitled to a certain social minimum (see Feinberg, 1980). Western society traditionally thinks in terms of "negative" rights or freedoms ("I have a right to privacy, and to be left alone!" "I have a right to private property and to protect it against trespassers!" and so on) and less in terms of the *positive rights* (i.e., the right to food, clothing, shelter).[3]

A major problem with this justifying approach is the difficult question of what constitutes the "minimum entitlement." Moreover, practical ambiguity may exist over the precise scope of these rights (individuals may have the positive right to a minimum level of transportation/mobility, but does this entitle every individual to own an automobile?). The question of permissible tradeoffs between social minima is also encountered in the practical debate. That is, can some degree of the minimum social right to housing be traded off in exchange for a more extensive amount of some other social right, perhaps education? Movement in this direction, however, approaches the utilitarian position.

One way to get around this quagmire is to introduce the concept of *need*. It can be argued that certain kinds of public infrastructure and investments, in certain quantities, are *needed* by individuals and groups. For need to be meaningful requires the delineation of a goal or objective or desired social outcome. Certain public investments, such as public sewer and water service, may be needed to ensure public health, that is, people's survival. Other investments may be needed to ensure the creation/sustaining of intimate and family-oriented neighborhoods. In turn, these are needed to ensure the safety and emotional security of individuals.

Numerous public facilities and service decisions are of course made according to more narrowly defined conceptions of need, defined less in terms of ultimate human needs, and more in terms of functional intermediate needs. A neighborhood may *need* greater allocations of certain public services, such as public streets and roads, because its residents have historically exhibited a lower usage of mass transit, and a greater usage of automobiles. A greater need for parks may exist in lower-income neighborhoods because here private leisure spaces and recreational opportunities are fewer (see Lucy, 1981: 454-455).

The equity criterion of *ability to pay* frequently used in financing public infrastructure holds an interesting relationship to the concept of need. While not a precise theoretical fit, ability to pay appears, from an ethical perspective, almost an inverse of social need. It seems fair to ask individuals with larger incomes and greater amounts of property to assume larger shares of the costs of such public investments because these individuals *need* these resources less to satisfy their basic human needs, that is, housing and food. To require less economically well-off individuals to assume greater contributions, or even equal contributions, would amount to an infringement on their ability to satisfy basic needs. An ability-to-pay criterion is consistent with the intuitive ethical logic that those who have the most can afford the most, and this may of course serve to advance more fundamental social concepts of justice, such as the Rawlsian Difference Principle or the satisfaction of basic positive rights or human needs.

CULPABILITY AND DESERT

Many equity questions that arise in the financing and planning of public infrastructure involve considerations of *desert*, broadly defined. The concept is used here to encompass desert of both the benefits and burdens associated with such public investments. There has been, for instance, a long and controversial debate over who should bear the costs of community growth. The *benefit principle* is one traditional response, suggesting that those individuals and groups who directly benefit from a service or facility ought to bear the costs of its provision, *and* ought to bear these costs in *proportion* to their benefits received (Beatley and Kaiser, 1983). The increasing popularity of user fees and impact fees is a reflection of the intuitive ethical appeal of such a standard (e.g., see Hagman and Misczynski, 1978). Many beneficiaries of such public investments may not be "users" in the traditional sense (i.e., individuals benefiting directly from sewer and water hookups for example) but may benefit more indirectly. Individuals who own land adjoining a new highway or other large public investment may experience tremendous increases in land values. As a further example, downtown businesses may reap large profits from the provision of new public infrastructure, such as a parking deck or a public square. A corollary standard is that of the principle of *culpability*, which argues that individuals and groups must assume responsibility for the costs or disbenefits their activities impose on others, for instance in the form of water pollution or traffic congestion.

The concept of desert may also provide an interesting ethical defense of distributing the costs of infrastructure based on wealth and property. That is, it can be argued that individuals with greater income and/or property wealth, should be taxed at least in proportion to these resources, since they have more that is being protected (through police, fire, roads, and so on).

EXPECTATIONS AND PROMISE MAKING

Disputes concerning the appropriate extent, location, and financing of public infrastructure often result from conflicting or unrealized expectations. Residents of a certain neighborhood, for example, may be indignant because expectations they had for certain public investments, for example, road and street improvements, did not prove to be forthcoming.[4] Similarly, residents of a rural county may have formed expectations that certain growth-inducing public investments (e.g., the construction of a new segment of interstate) would not be made and are shocked and disappointed when such improvements occur. It can be argued that equitable public investment/infrastructure policies and decisions acknowledge and respect the formation of reasonable or legitimate expectations.

An initial perspective on such considerations of equity is to evaluate the legitimacy of expectations in terms of their source (see Beatley, 1985a). On one extreme would be personal and group expectations based upon *explicit promises* (e.g., exhibited in many forms from the inclusion of a project in the local capital improvements program to a verbal commitment from a public official). On the other extreme would be public expectations created by general economic and social conditions (e.g., "it only makes sense that a new school would be built here"). Demands based on the former should hold substantially greater moral weight than those founded on the latter.

Many infrastructure issues also involve *implicit* or *tacit promises* (see Rubin, 1972-1973). Tacit promises are made through repetitive public actions and a continuous chain of past public policy in this area, for instance, by a locality's refusal to permit the extension of certain public facilities into particular locations (e.g., sewer and water extensions outside of a designated urban service boundary). Over a long period of time its continual reaffirmation of this intention can be construed as a tacit promise that such policies will continue into the future. Numerous factors (e.g., continuity, consistency, opportunities for passive valida-tion) will influence the legitimacy of the expectations founded on such tacit promises.[5] Generally speaking, the ethical foundation is that individuals and groups have adjusted their actions, behavior, and plans under presumably good faith assumptions about future conditions.

HOW SHOULD THE RELEVANT
PUBLIC BE DEFINED?

The desirability of particular infrastructure decisions, and the application of the concepts and principles as described above, depends on defining the relevant public. One approach is to define the relevant public according to social and economic groups. As we have seen, if the Rawlsian Difference Principle is embraced, the focus of public in-vestments and infrastructure is on improving the conditions of the members of the worst-off groups in the community. The discussion below, however, argues that planners and policymakers ought to consider an *expanded* conception of the public.

INTERTEMPORAL EQUITY

Decisions concerning the financing, location, and the like of public infrastructure typically entail costs and benefits that occur over a relatively long period of time.[6] An important issue, however, concerns which temporal groups ethical obligations are owed to. Should concern be only with current residents, or with future generations? How far into the future do our ethical obligations extend? How are the interests, needs, preferences, and so on, of this future public to be determined?

Concern about intergenerational equity is increasingly found in contemporary political and philosophical debate, particularly with respect to the natural environment (e.g., see Partridge, 1981; Attfield, 1983). Rawls incorporates this into his ethical framework by placing a constraint on the Difference Principle—the "just savings principle." This requires present generations to adopt a reasonable rate of investment and savings to ensure that just institutions are protected in the future. This accumulation must encompass "not only factories and machines, and so on, but also knowledge and culture, as well as the techniques and skills, that make possible just institutions and the fair value of liberty" (Rawls, 1971: 288). Thus public infrastructure policies and decisions must protect for future generations a range of resources and social investments. Defining the precise extent of obligation (or the savings or accumulation rate in Rawls's terminology), however, is difficult.

Principles of desert may appear of particular relevance in guiding decision about public infrastructure. French (1983), for instance, presents the case of a city considering the construction of a domed sports stadium where bond payment will be borne in large degree by future residents. Is there an ethical obligation "not to inflict the expense for the projects of the present upon the pocketbooks of the future?" (French, 1983: 84). The notion of desert is violated if the benefits obtained from such a project do not extend at least as far into the future as do the financial encumbrances. Similarly, such considerations are also relevant to public projects that benefit present residents, but place certain risks or disamenities on future residents, for example, hazardous waste disposal facilities.

INTERJURISDICTIONAL EQUITY

An important consideration in public infrastructure planning is the extent to which public officials and residents in one locality or jurisdiction owe certain obligations to residents in other jurisdictions. The impacts of infrastructure decisions are often not readily confined by neat jurisdictional boundaries. For instance, one locality's failure to make necessary waste treatment plant improvements/expansion may serve to jeopardize the health and safety of downstream communities. Extending urban growth-related infrastructure in a particularly sensitive environmental habitat can jeopardize an adjoining locality's source of drinking water. Positively, a locality's efforts to revitalize its downtown can generate employment and economic benefits beyond its jurisdictional boundaries.

What are the precise ethical obligations and duties owed beyond local boundaries? At a minimum, one local town's decisions concerning infrastructure should take reasonable care to minimize the negative effects of its projects on contiguous localities. Moreover, a locality's obligation should extend to assuming its fair share of the costs of such public goods as affordable housing, improvements to the regional transportation network, and improvements essential to accommodate economic growth (i.e., no locality has a right to thrust its problems onto other localities). Elsewhere, I have argued that the Rawlsian Difference Principle can and should be applied on an interjurisdictional basis (see Beatley, 1984).

A major barrier to this type of ethical behavior is the *assurance problem*.[7] Is it fair for one community to assume an extra degree of ethical concern or care for the extralocal impacts of its infrastructure planning and decision making when similarly situated jurisdictions do not acknowledge similar obligations? If each jurisdiction could be assured that others would act in similar ways, they would perceive this additional reasonable care to be fair. For instance, one locality may be willing to make necessary pollution-control investments if it can be assured that other polluting jurisdictions will make similar sacrifices.[8] These contributions or sacrifices need not be equal, but must be equitable, that is, more affluent localities may be asked to bear proportionately larger shares of the costs of pollution reduction; localities receiving the largest benefits from polluting activities may be asked to assume large shares, and so on.

NONANTHROPOCENTRIC
EQUITY/INTERSPECIES EQUITY

A nonanthropocentric perspective concerns the tremendous impacts of infrastructure and public investments, mostly negative, on other forms of life. For instance, what is our ethical obligation to control and manage development projects carefully so as not to endanger nearly extinct animal species? The Tellico dam/Tennessee Snail Darter case is perhaps the most notorious of such dilemmas. Moreover, is there an obligation to consider the negative (or positive) effects infrastructure policy will have on all animal life, and even inanimate objects such as mountains and rivers?

A nonanthropocentric notion of equity would argue that animals and other forms of life contain intrinsic value and have the right to have their interests protected, regardless of what their instrumental value may be to people. Support for this idea has been growing in recent years (e.g., see Passmore, 1980; Regan and Singer, 1976; Regan, 1983; Attfield, 1983; Taylor, 1981), and holds considerable implication for the ethical legitimacy of many infrastructure projects. Respect for nonhuman life suggests that projects exercise reasonable care to avoid unnecessarily harming the rights and interests of other life forms.

HOW AND BY WHOM SHOULD
PUBLIC INFRASTRUCTURE
DECISIONS BE MADE?

An important set of ethical questions concerns who should be involved in infrastructure decision processes and who should have the authority and responsibility of making such important decisions? Whose interests should be represented in these decision-making processes, and whose interests are systematically ignored or misrepresented, and so on?

Infrastructure decisions and the overall decision-making framework can be evaluated according to the extent of *political equality* involved. There are several primary ways of examining this, and each is described below.

EQUALITY OF PARTICIPATION/
FORMAL POLITICAL ACCESS

A common conception of an equitable political or administrative process involves providing all affected parties with the opportunity to participate directly in decision processes. For instance, highway planning should involve a process whereby public officials examine broad community impacts and determine how affected individuals view alternative proposals. Better infrastructure decisions will be made when the needs, preferences, and desires of the community are fully examined. Community feedback, for example, may indicate that a new highway will cause widespread damage to neighborhood cohesion, friendship networks, and so on. Participation may also suggest the desirability of alternative highway routes that would minimize these impacts. More general participation processes can indicate that other public infrastructure investments, such as road maintenance or recreational improvements, are more desirable from a broader perspective than building the highway.

A major limitation, however, is the practical difficulty of gaining widespread participation. Moreover, many individuals often resent the need to participate, arguing that in a representative-democratic context, it is the appropriate function of elected officials to protect their interests (see Seley, 1983: 61-66).

Equality of influence. Political power and influence are not equally distributed among different actors and interests in the community. Thus an equitable infrastructure decision-making process may require that steps be taken to ensure the ability of different groups to influence political/administrative outcomes. No particular economic interest or political faction should be permitted to co-opt the outcomes of infrastructure planning. The research and literature in the community power field suggest several different political spheres in which substantial inequalities in political influence can develop, threatening the equity of resulting decisions. Political theorists often discuss these inequalities as developing in the three "faces" or dimensions of power (Gaventa, 1980; Lukes, 1974; Forester, 1982). A first face of power can be seen in the overt decisions about public infrastructure that occur in formal decision-making structures (e.g., city councils, planning commissions). Discussion here has historically centered on debate between elite theorists (e.g., Hunter, 1953) and pluralists (e.g., Dahl, 1961; Polsby, 1969). At this level the objective is *equality of decision making*. Attention is given to the ability of particular individuals, parties, and interests to prevail on relatively structured public investment questions (e.g., whether or not to make a specific proposed infrastructure investment, such as a sewer line or road).

Bachrach and Baratz (1970) are credited with expanding this

framework to include a second face of power that they called "non-decision making," in which the focus of attention shifts to the level of agenda setting and the ability of individuals and groups to inject their concerns into formal decision-making structures. The equity goal in this realm is thus one of *equality of interest expression*. Lukes (1974) has identified a third face of power in which the question becomes one of whether individuals and groups have been manipulated such that political demands do not even arise, nevertheless appear on public agendas or voted upon at formal decision-making levels (e.g., see Gaventa, 1981). The equity goal in this case is thus one of *equality of interest formation*.

Extreme inequalities in any of these realms of political influence raise questions of procedural or political fairness. The presence of such inequalities can both jeopardize the moral legitimacy of the resulting infrastructure decision(s) and call for public actions to correct for or reduce these inequalities. Numerous interventions can be taken, however, to correct for such inequalities, albeit often with low effectiveness. The distribution of information concerning the agenda-setting process, and efforts to educate individuals and groups in the community about how to get certain infrastructure issues off the ground, can help equalize power in the second face. Releasing information concerning the negative consequences of a proposed public infrastructure project, and perhaps carefully explaining it to affected parties, can adjust power relations in the first dimension (e.g., once informed opposition exists, the political costs of supporting such a proposal may be substantial). The planning process may enhance substantially the organization and ability of individuals and groups in the community to represent and defend, and even to formulate more precisely, their positions on key infrastructure issues.

Equality of representation. Decisions concerning public infrastructure occur within a representative democratic context, presenting an additional sphere in which inequalities can jeopardize the fairness of political results. The focus shifts from political processes and institutions to the personal responsibility of elected (and nonelected) representatives. At the most general level, an equitable political/decision-making process requires representatives (whether a city council person or a state legislator) to consider fully and incorporate into their voting and other decisions the interests of all groups in the community (or whatever the jurisdiction happens to be and/or however the relevant public is defined). Equality of representation is necessarily something more than reliance upon either participation and expression of constituent views or leaving infrastructure outcomes to the machinations of political power. Since not everyone in the community will participate, a representative cannot rely on participation. Similarly, representatives usually have to make decisions in situations of unequal influence. Equality of representation ideally would mean that elected officials represent all interests in the community, regardless of their actual participation in political processes or their possession of political power. This is an impossible ideal to achieve.

It is also unclear whether it is even desirable for representatives to exclusively follow the *current preferences* of constituents.[9] Take, as an example, the case of a coastal town considering whether to develop its pristine harbor/waterfront areas as a major commercial port and energy facility and whether to make the necessary capital investments to bring this development about. Because such a development is perceived as badly needed to counter high employment and a lagging local economy, there is considerable citizen support for the project. Members of the local governing body, however, are concerned about the long-term ecological and amenity damage this development can generate. It is possible that, at some point in the future, residents will regret that the development ever occurred. The actual infrastructure decision, reflecting a more expanded notion of constituent interest, could be considerably different than what might be indicated from citizen input and participation (see Beatley, 1985b).

CONCLUSIONS

This chapter has examined several serious and important equity issues concerning the planning of public infrastructure. These issues have been organized according to several key ethical questions. First, the chapter identified a number of ethical principles and concepts that are useful in evaluating infrastructure plans and policies. No one ethical principle will appeal to every person, and unique mixtures and combinations of different ethical standards and concepts will most likely result. Moreover, different infrastructure decisions and situations will call for unique and creative applications of these concepts. Second, several different ways of delimiting the relevant public have been identified. While no precise delimitation has been presented, as inclusive a definition as is practical has been advocated. Finally, potential procedural and political inequities have been examined under the question of how to make public infrastructure decisions. A number of possible realms of inequality were identified and it was argued that when these reach extreme levels the equity of the resulting infrastructure decisions is jeopardized.

The most important conclusion of this chapter is that planners, policymakers, and the public must begin to formulate and conceive of public infrastructure decisions and policy in ethical terms. There is a strong need for careful and politically inclusive debate about public infrastructure along equity dimensions.

NOTES

1. Efforts to maximize aggregate benefits need not, however, be based on market assumptions. For instance, the benefits of providing a particular public good may occur largely to individuals who would be unable to purchase the good under a perfectly functioning market system, that is, these benefits would not be counted under a utilitarian analysis that sought only to approximate what the unfettered market result would be.

2. It could be argued that programs and policies that advance a compensatory equality standard ought to incorporate a "punitive" component as well as a "restorative" component.

3. The notion of positive rights is similar to, if not one way to implement, the notion of "positive liberties." However, I conceive of positive rights as things that are basic human entitlements, irrespective of their influence on or purpose of helping people achieve other goals in life. Much of the positive liberties argument appears to center on the need for such substantive rights to ensure equality of opportunity, fulfillment of human potential, and so on. See Crocker, 1980, for a convincing argument for positive liberties.

4. This has been referred to as "transitional equity." See, for instance, Patton and Sawicki (1986: 153-156).

5. See Beatley (1985a) for a brief review of these factors and considerations.

6. A common approach to evaluating such future impacts is to convert them to present values through the selection of an appropriate discount rate. Such a methodology devalues the importance of benefits and costs occurring to future generations, and may thus be inconsistent with broader notions of equity.

7. Also described as the "free-rider" problem; for example, see Runge (1984).

8. Many localities may see little practical effect from their actions when the behavior of other localities is unchanged. In other words, a locality may even be willing to undertake a unilateral ethical response, but this is not rational if no discernible change in the environment results from their actions (reductions in pollution, traffic congestion, and so on). Institutional approaches to overcoming the assurance problem also obviously enhance the effectiveness of such ethical actions.

9. This is usually referred to as a distinction between "trustee" and "delegate" models of representation; see Pitkin (1967) for a discussion of various models of representation.

REFERENCES

ATTFIELD, R. (1983) The Ethics of Environmental Concern. New York: Columbia Univ. Press.

BACHRACH, P. and M. BARATZ (1970) Power and Poverty. New York: Oxford Univ. Press.

BADCOCK, B. (1984) Unfairly Structured Cities. Oxford: Basil Blackwell.

BEATLEY, T. (1984) "Applying moral principles to growth management." J. of the Amer. Planning Assn. 50, 4: 459-469.

BEATLEY, T. (1985a) "Expectations and promise-making in land use policy." Presented to the Association of Collegiate Schools of Planning, November 1-3, Atlanta, GE.

BEATLEY, T. (1985b) "Paternalism and land use planning: ethical bases and practical applications," pp. 53-70 in Attig et al. (eds.) Restraint of Liberty. Bowling Green, OH: Bowling Green State Univ.

BEATLEY, T. and E. J. KAISER (1983) Financing Community Infrastructure: An Exploratory Review and Assessment of Alternative Approaches. Raleigh: North Carolina Board of Science and Technology.

CROCKER, L. (1980) Positive Liberty: An Essay in Normative Political Philosophy. The Hague: Martinus Nijhoff.

DAHL, R. (1961) Who Governs? New Haven, CT: Yale Univ. Press.

DWORKIN, R. (1981a) "What is equality?" Parts 1 and 2, Philosophy and Public Affairs 10, 3: 185-246.

DWORKIN, R. (1981b) "What is equality?" Parts 1 and 2, Philosophy and Public Affairs 10, 4: 283-345.

FEINBERG, J. (1980) Rights, Justice and the Bounds of Liberty. Princeton, NJ: Princeton Univ. Press.

FORESTER, J. (1982) "Planning in the face of power." J. of the Amer. Planning Assn. 48 (winter): 67-87.

FRENCH, P. A. (1983) Ethics in Government. Englewood Cliffs, NJ: Prentice-Hall.

GAVENTA, J. (1980) Power and Powerlessness. Urbana: Univ. of Illinois Press.

HAGMAN, D. and D. MISCZYERSKI (1978) Windfalls for Wipeouts: Land Value Capture and Compensation. Chicago, IL: APA Planners Press.

HICKS J. R. (1939) "The foundations of welfare economics." Economic J. XLIX: 696-712.

HUNTER, F. (1953) Community Power Structure: A Study of Decisionmakers. Chapel Hill, NC: UNC Press.

KALDOR, N. (1939) "Welfare propositions in economics and interpersonal comparisons of utility." Economic J. XLIX: 549-552.

LUCY, W. (1981) "Equity and planning for local services." J. of the Amer. Planning Assn. 47, 4: 447-457.

LUKES, S. (1974) Power: A Radical View. New York: Macmillan.

MILL, J. S. (1961) On Liberty. London: Parker & Sons.

MISHAN, E. J. (1975) Economics for Social Decisions: Elements of Cost-Benefit Analysis. New York: Praeger.

MOORE, T. (1978) "Why allow planners to do what they do? A justification from economic theory." J. of the Amer. Institute of Planners 44, 4: 387-398.

PARTRIDGE, E. [ed.] (1981) Responsibilities to Future Generations. Buffalo, NY: Prometheus.

PASSMORE, J. (1980) Man's Responsibility for Nature. London: Duckworth.

PATTON, C. V. and D. S. SAWICKI (1986) Basic Methods of Policy Analysis and Planning. Englewood Cliffs, NJ: Prentice-Hall.

PITKIN, H. (1967) The Concept of Representation. Berkeley: Univ. of California Press.

POLSBY, N. (1969) Community Power and Political Theory. New Haven, CT: Yale Univ. Press.

RAE, D. (1981) Equalities. Cambridge, MA: Harvard Univ. Press.

RAWLS, J. (1971) A Theory of Justice. Cambridge, MA: Harvard Univ. Press.

REGAN, T. (1983) The Case for Animal Rights. Berkeley: Univ. of California Press.

REGAN, T. and P. SINGER [eds.] (1976) Animal Rights and Human Obligations. Englewood Cliffs, NJ: Prentice-Hall.

RUBEN, D. (1972-1973) "Tacit-promising." Ethics 83: 71-79.

RUNGE, C. F. (1984) "Institutions and the free rider: the assurance problem in collective action." J. of Politics (February): 154-181.

SELEY, J. E. (1983) The Politics of Public-Facility Planning. Lexington, MA: D.C. Heath.

TAYLOR, P. W. (1981) "The ethics of respect for nature." Environmental Ethics 3 (fall): 197-218.

THOMPSON, M. (1980) Benefit-Cost Analysis for Program Evaluation. Newbury Park, CA: Sage.

TRIBE, L. H. (1972) "Policy science: analysis of ideology." Philosophy and Public Affairs 2, 1: 66-110.

13

Equity Planning for Infrastructure: Applications

WILLIAM LUCY

EQUITY IS ONE of the important concepts that should be included in public infrastructure planning criteria. This chapter's focus is on ways to operationalize the concept of equity in infrastructure planning. The equity concept can be applied best to scattered and numerous capital items, such as streets, water lines, fire stations, parks, and branch libraries, so that geographic comparisons are feasible. Applying the equity concept to special facilities such as airports and sewage disposal plants is more difficult to operationalize.

This chapter covers equity concepts that I have found common in the thinking of analysts and practitioners, a brief treatment of measurement issues, steps to take in conducting equity planning, examples of localities that have included equity concepts in their capital improvement planning, and discussion of practitioners' diverse opinions about equity.

EQUITY CONCEPTS

Equity involves notions of fairness. It addresses the distribution of benefits and costs. Some of the equity meanings and their implications for planning have been discussed in Chapter 12. Here I will mention five interpretations of the concept that often have been applied. These are the beliefs that equity, under various circumstances, should be based on equality, need, demand, preference, or willingness-to-pay, or some combination of these concepts.

Equality. One commonly held idea is that equals should be treated equally. Leaving aside the problem of how one defines who is equal to whom for what purposes, there are two other practical problems that must be addressed. One concerns what equal treatment means when the public facilities in question are scattered, such as parks, schools, libraries, health centers, fire stations, rather than systematically connected to structures and their users, such as utilities, streets, and sidewalks. Second, the question is how to measure equal treatment when facilities and services have different and important aspects.

With scattered facilities, the traditional approach to measuring equity is to seek a threshold of adequacy. Neighborhood parks, for example, commonly are sought within one-half mile of all residents, a standard proposed by the National Recreation and Park Association (Gold, 1973). Fire station locations are influenced by fire insurance underwriters' criteria, which emphasize having stations near valuable property (Insurance Services Office, 1974). With these park and fire criteria, one can see quickly that some residents may stand to gain more than others. Using a criterion of locating a neighborhood park within x miles of every resident means that low-density, wealthier neighborhoods will have more parks. This result can be compensated for by having more acreage in each park in high-density neighborhoods—unlikely except where land was donated or acquired many decades ago, that is, Central Park and Prospect Park in New York City, Piedmont Park in Atlanta. Following the criterion of locating fire stations near to valuable public and private property, then fire stations also may be close to low-income and black neighborhoods, if costly commercial and manufacturing facilities are close to these areas. Moreover, the potential fire loss criterion may overlap another important criterion—the actual occurrence of fires, because fire incidence is much higher in poor than well-off neighborhoods.

These potential criteria for locating fire stations also suggest alternative measures of important characteristics of services. A number of measurement frameworks have been used (Hatry, 1977; Levy et al., 1974; Lineberry, 1977; Lucy et al., 1977; Lucy and Mladenka, 1978). They generally are variations on systems model concepts that include inputs (what goes into the service system) and outputs (what comes out of the service system). The variation I prefer uses the term *resources* in place of inputs and *results* in place of outputs. I also use the term *activities* to refer to processes that intervene between resources and results, and I use the term *impacts* to refer to how the physical and social environment may be changed by the presence of service results (see

---

Each infrastructure service has objectives

involving

Servicing population and influencing social conditions

by using

Resources
(expenditures, facilities, equipment)

and engaging in

Activities
(time frequency and duration)
having

Results
(direct consequences--intended and unintended, and
especially use of services--amount and ratio--and
reasons for non-use) and
leading to

Impacts
(changes in social conditions)

Figure 13.1 Infrastructure Service Analysis Framework

Figure 13.1). Examples of indicators of these concepts for several services are listed in Table 13.1.

Fire hydrants are an example of a type of facility that can be measured in several ways. Resource aspects of the service can be measured by whether some structures exceed a standard number of feet from a hydrant. The presence of the hydrant is intended to produce a result when the activity of attaching a hose to it is carried out. The result is measured in terms of volume and pressure of water flow per minute. An unintended result is the number of days in which the hydrant is inoperable, perhaps because of damage to the fixtures. Impacts, which are changes in the environment, could be measured by effects on fire insurance rates, property values, and by length of time properties remain on the market but unsold.

Considering actions to change the conditions measured by these indicators, the location of hydrants is easiest to change. Water flow, on

TABLE 13.1

Examples of Infrastructure Service Indicators

Resources

Expenditures ($ per 1,000 population or 100 households, $ per square mile, or $ per phenomenon such as $ per fire loss)

Facilities (neighborhood park acres per 1,000 residents, ratio of hard surfaced to other surfaced streets, ratio of improved lots with sewer lines within x feet to improved lots lacking such service)

Activities

Frequency (mass transit headways by neighborhood)

Duration (hours swimming pools, recreation centers, and libraries are open per week; response time for fire apparatus to arrive on the scene from receipt of call for service)

Results

Intended consequences (street roughness rating, water pressure at the tap, water flow per minute from hydrants, percentage hours per week of uninterrupted flow in sewers)

Unintended consequences (hours water lines, sewer lines, and fire hydrants are out of service; liability insurance losses attributable to street surface conditions; complaints about recreation centers, swimming pools, and branch libraries being closed)

Use of facilities by amount (number of mass transit, swimming pool, park, and library users per day) and by ratio of users to population (number of visits to branch libraries per day per population in the service area)

Nonuse of facilities by reasons (percentage of persons in service area not using a park because of anxiety about their personal safety, percentage of persons not using mass transit because of the distance of stops from residences and workplaces)

Impacts

Changes in social conditions (property values, abandonment, rates of private investment, arson rates, illnesses and deaths related to unsanitary conditions)

NOTE: Data for specific indicators, and impacts, of resources, activities, and results are obtained by gathering field data about facilities. These examples are illustrative, not exhaustive.

the other hand, is a function of capacity of the water system and of the height of the area served. Inoperable hydrants may be caused by vandalism as well as by age. Many conditions besides the quantity and quality of fire hydrants will influence insurance rates and property values. Each type of indicator, therefore, raises issues about how one should measure equality and what kind of equality one should achieve. Should one work toward equality of resources, results, or impacts, recognizing that each, in succession, tends to be more difficult to achieve? Which indicators of each aspect of a service system should be used to measure success? These are questions, however, that should not be answered until deliberations occur about other equity criteria.

Need. Basing equity on need necessarily implies that service distribution should be unequal. Those who need more service should get more, or they should pay less than others for the same service.

Measurement of need can be operationalized with two methods. One approach involves developing indicators based on demographic characteristics, such as income. Thus low income would indicate greater difficulty in purchasing services. This is especially true of services such as parks, libraries, and mass transit, which increasingly are being financed by user fees. Low-income people, of course, are less able to pay for small-scale infrastructure improvements (sidewalks, streets, water and sewer lines) through special assessments.

Other demographic variables also can be important indicators of need. For example, the age structure of a neighborhood, such as the number of children age 12 and under, is a useful indicator of need for neighborhood parks, play equipment in existing parks, elementary schools or school buses, and children's library books.

A second approach is to develop need measures based on quality of infrastructure conditions. Examples include age of infrastructure, peak load usage, and hours without water or sewer service due to equipment failures. Such indicators provide a reasonable basis for distributing services. For example, a higher level of service or more expenditures may be required in some areas for a limited time period to bring them up to community standards.

While there can be excellent reasons for an unequal distribution of services or expenditures, it is difficult to determine how much inequality is justified. While income levels may be a reasonable criterion for decisions about where to locate recreation centers, they are less appropriate for determining the frequency of street resurfacings. Low-income persons may need cheaper water, but they are not likely to need more water than others. No criterion is suitable for all purposes. In fact, most decisions should be based on multiple criteria, some of which may be in conflict with one another.

Demand. The demand criterion involves a political variation on economic market principles. That is, those who explicitly seek more of a service should receive more of it. Those who do not want more of a service should not have it imposed.

Demand can be identified in two ways. The first is based on use—units of water consumed, bus and subway ridership, visitors to a zoo. The second is through requests and complaints, that is, specific requests for more frequent or effective refuse collection, complaints about potholes in streets, or, much more broadly, basing votes in referenda and general elections on opinions about service quality.

The distributional implications of each type of demand indicator will vary, sometimes in ways that are difficult to discern. Low rates for domestic water use can benefit low-income people but also encourage wasteful practices, such as lawn watering, especially by the well-off. This could eventually strain system capacity and lead to a need for major infrastructure investments that may have been avoided by more diligent conservation pricing (Hanke, 1972). Basing branch library locations and book purchases on actual or predicted use will bias distribution toward residents of better-off neighborhoods, because libraries are used more by middle- than low-income people. Conversely, basing bus routes on proximity to low-income neighborhoods would be more consistent with use. Rider surveys show low-income persons to be the highest users (Census, 1980: 188).

Research about political activity shows higher-income groups to have higher rates of voter turnout and especially to be more active in the general political process (Verba and Nie, 1972: 334-343). Unfortunately, little information is known about differences among income groups in their propensity to lodge complaints if they are dissatisfied with service quality (Lucy, 1985; Sharp, 1982; Verba and Nie, 1972: 125-137).

Preference. The preference concept can limit deficiencies of the demand concept of equity. Demands are expressed, while preferences may be held silently. Demand is not always an accurate reflection of preference. People are not equal in their physical and verbal abilities to express themselves and in self-confidence. Furthermore, they have unequal financial resources and knowledge about how to access and influence the political and bureaucratic systems.

Use of services also may not reflect desire for them. The elderly may want to use, but avoid, some parks because they are intimidated by other users—young adult males. Poor accessibility of some services because of excessive distances to buses, parks, or libraries, may result in less use than is desired. Moreover, some users may be frustrated by the inappropriateness of the facilities, such as tennis courts being where potential users want basketball courts, or vice versa, with reduced use a consequence.

Accurately identifying preferences is a difficult task. Since both use and complaints are inadequate preference indicators, additional data should be collected through various citizen participation techniques, that is, surveys, interviews, or group discussions, when such information may contribute significantly to investment decisions.

Willingness-to-pay. The foundation of the concept of willingness-to-pay has two parts. One is that beneficiaries of services should pay for them, and nonbeneficiaries should not pay. The second is that preferences and demands are cheap, perhaps insincere, probably insufficiently thought through, unless personal discipline is required, which accompanies ranking preferences in the face of scarce resources.

Deficiencies of these arguments are equally apparent. The requirement of payment for use is administratively difficult for many services (including streets, police, and neighborhood parks). Willingness-to-pay does not help one choose locations for fire stations or schools. Since willingness-to-pay is related to ability-to-pay, it has the effect of applying market tests to public services for which the body politic often has decided, with considerable agreement among the localities of the 50 states, that ability-to-pay should be irrelevant. Elementary and secondary education and public safety (police and fire protection) are the most important examples. The social and political consequences would be unacceptable.

EQUITY CONCEPTS
AND FACILITY PLANNING

Equity concepts should be applied to facility planning in three processes. One is analytical. It concerns the current distribution of facilities and how that has changed in recent years. The second is deliberative. It concerns which equity concepts should be applied in which ways to facility planning subjects. The third is comparative across service functions. It concerns criteria, including equity concepts, that should be applied to all infrastructure projects.

DISTRIBUTION OF INFRASTRUCTURE

The first process involves describing infrastructure distribution. An inventory is essential—what exists where in terms of age, condition, and useful life. Such an inventory often will have been used in capital improvement programming. Descriptions become richer if they include results of service provision—users of parks, fire loss and suppression time, and vehicles per day using streets. Such data about use of facilities often can be related directly to decisions. For example, if many streets are similar in age, condition, and useful life (and more streets need treatment than can be repaved or resurfaced) then data about results, that is, such as amount of usage, often should determine priorities. However, other criteria, such as neighborhood development goals, may suggest otherwise. Data should be gathered for the physical facilities in place and also for infrastructure investments of the most recent three to five years. Analysts then can identify the pattern of facility distribution among many different types of facilities. They also can determine whether recent investment decisions have altered the previous pattern in ways the policymakers intended.

APPLYING INFRASTRUCTURE CONCEPTS

The second process involves deciding how equity concepts should be applied to infrastructure planning. This process should describe the ways in which concepts have been operationalized recently in the locality, and, if possible, in previous years. However, this is not an easy task. Distributional criteria rarely are written and may be purposely obfuscated. Formal analyses of decision-making processes about the distribution of infrastructure also are unusual. In this situation, discussions with infrastructure decision makers can have three advantages—it may yield information, identify uncertainty about which criteria have been and should be used, and more awareness and thoughtfulness about gainers and losers from infrastructure decisions in the community.

Deliberations about applying equity criteria should begin with conceptualizing equality. In interviews I have conducted, the idea that most often comes first to mind by elected officials and administrators is that services should be distributed equally. By this they seem to mean that everyone should get the same service. The question to ask then is: "To what extent and in which ways should the equality concept be applied to specific services?" for those services that involve scattered facilities (streets, parks, schools, libraries, fire stations, and others), equality can be achieved only if it is interpreted to mean a threshold of adequacy (having the facility within x distance). Discussion then can focus on how great the distance should be, what the characteristics of the facility should be, and whether one should measure the service using resource, activity, result, or even impact data. Concerns inevitably will include what constitutes need and demand for the service. This will lead to questions about how unequal service distribution should be and what inequality should be based on.

The concept of preference can be used to check whether demands should be regarded as substantial and sufficient. Preferences are most important to elicit in those cases for which nonusers and inarticulate users may have important concerns to have taken into account (such as concerns about parks and mass transit). The concept of willingness-to-pay can be used to determine whether direct beneficiaries should pay some or all of the cost through fees for service. In general, the more unusual and specialized the service (yoga classes offered by recreation departments), discretionary the activity (using the municipal golf course), and identifiable the users are (as with yoga and golf), the more appropriate it is to charge users the full cost of the service.

Another type of infrastructure service includes those linked directly to individual structures (residences, businesses, and public buildings). For services like water, sewerage, and refuse collection, equality is a more meaningful concept. Users of each structure can be equal in having the service connected directly to their property, although charges may be unequal because of varying costs of providing service.

Considerable equality also can be achieved in service characteristics—such as water taste and pressure. These qualities are determined mainly by filtration plants and pumping stations that serve substantial portions of service areas. Conversely, some reservoirs are more susceptible than others to taste problems associated with summer algae growth. Similarly, some areas are higher than others and can be served only by more powerful pumps. Moreover, cracked or corroded distribution rivers can result in lower pressure and more days without service. Each of these conditions involves issues about whether unequal outputs justify greater expenditures to reduce inequality.

The concept of willingness-to-pay is especially pertinent to services that are linked to individual structures. Beneficiaries are identifiable, and they can be billed for services received. How much beneficiaries should pay, however, is not simple to determine. Typical rate structures charge small users more than large users per unit of service. The rationale for declining block structures is not only that distribution costs to large users are lower than for smaller users, but also act as inducements for manufacturers to locate within a local jurisdiction. If large users require larger and more costly central facilities (reservoirs, trunk lines, filtration plants, and pumping stations) than would otherwise be needed, then small users may pay disproportionately for the costs of the system. These are issues that should be addressed through examination of the rate structure.

Related to this is the means by which the distribution system is financed. Are special assessments levied for new distribution connections? Who pays for replacement of outmoded, ineffective distribution facilities? Are the methods of finance consistently applied to each section of the jurisdiction? Special assessments are a means of forcing beneficiaries to pay for benefits received. This may seem an appropriate way to make better-off residents pay the full cost of service, especially in outlying areas that are expensive to serve. But the same criteria applied in low-income areas could have the effect of denying residents even the most rudimentary water service. If different methods of finance are to be used, then policymakers have the difficult task of specifying the criteria for such differences and the cut-off points for invoking them.

COMPARING DIVERSE FACILITIES

The third application of equity concepts to infrastructure planning concerns comparing diverse facilities. This involves applying general criteria to many different services and choosing among investment alternatives in light of jurisdictional goals. Two examples follow: St. Paul, Minnesota's distributional criteria in the context of other community goals; and Savannah, Georgia's policy of addressing inequalities in the distribution of some facilities.

St. Paul has a sophisticated capital improvement planning and budgeting system. The system includes a complex neighborhood participation process, as well as roles for administrators, planners, and council members. Decision making is facilitated with a 5-page rating sheet, which assigns points based on how well projects meet criteria. A 33-page Capital Allocation Policy describes the goals and principles and provides criteria for project decisions (St. Paul Department of Planning and Economic Development, 1984).

The St. Paul Capital Allocation Policy contains several equity concepts for determining the distribution of capital projects. These include an appropriate neighborhood or geographic distribution of projects. However, goals and principles are stated that imply that retaining better-off residents, stabilizing the tax base, and leveraging private investment also are important priorities.

In the St. Paul policy statement, one of the four major goals is to "strengthen the City's neighborhoods in order to make them better places to live." In addition, "the annual proportion of funds allocated to any area of the City is monitored over time to avoid excessive geographic concentration of improvements, and to assure that the needs of all areas of the City are being addressed." The neighborhood betterment strategy, in addition, is based on two principles: "To channel the majority of capital expenditures for neighborhood betterment to those areas where there is the greatest opportunity for stimulating private investment; and to make available a steady commitment of resources to other areas of the City so as to prevent deterioration and maintain their stability." Areas eligible for CDBG funds would have less claim on city capital expenditures than areas with better prospects for leveraging private investment.

Savannah initiated its "Responsive Public Services Program" in 1973. In his transmittal letter to the City Council describing the program, City Manager Arthur Mendonsa stated: "the city government through its service programs should seek to maintain each neighborhood at an acceptable level of livability.... From the study, it is clear that the level of services being provided in some of the neighborhoods is not effective." The Savannah analysis found that neighborhoods most deficient in fire hydrants, street paving, and sewers were poor and predominantly black. A recent analysis based on 1980 data showed the program has been successful in reducing infrastructure inequalities related to race and income. The analysis, however, did not explain the sources of funding or how the amount and percentage of funds spent in deficient neighborhoods compared with expenditures elsewhere (Toulmin, 1985).

OPINIONS ABOUT
DISTRIBUTIONAL EQUITY

According to preliminary research findings, decision makers differ considerably about how facilities should be distributed. One study (Lucy, 1985) of nine large cities and one urban county showed a diversity of opinions among park and library administrators in different jurisdictions. In addition, service administrators, chief executives, planners, budgeters, and local legislators in single jurisdictions also differed substantially in their opinions. Further research is needed about the basis for the opinions of decision makers on equity issues and how accountability is achieved.

Answers to the questions in the study illustrate the above point. The questions concerned the criteria that were used, or should be used, in making decisions about locating neighborhood parks and branch libraries. The questions were framed to embody the equity concepts of equality, need, and demand. For example, park administrators ranked requests (a demand measure) first and the maximum distance standard (an equality measure favoring lower-density, higher-income neighborhoods) second. The acreage and density standard (an equality rule skewed more to low- and moderate-income persons) ranked third. No criterion was ranked first by more than one-third of the respondents.

Library administrators were asked whether branch library locations should be based on a maximum distance standard, relating square footage to population density, circulation rates, citizen requests, or income of residents. For libraries, the maximum distance rule was ranked first by the most respondents, but each of the five criteria was ranked first by at least one respondent. In contrast with the park administrators, the library administrators put the citizen request criterion last. Library administrators gave more weight to low-income neighborhoods in location decisions than did park administrators.

Two questions were put to both park administrators and local government generalists—chief executives, legislators, budgeters, and planners. The answers are suggestive about a problem of accountability. In total, 51 park administrators and generalists were asked whether neighborhood park locations and acreage should be roughly proportionate to population density, and 36 said substantial reliance should be placed on that criterion. However, the park administrators agreed with their own local legislators in only three of eight jurisdictions. When asked whether citizen requests should influence neighborhood park location decisions, park administrators agreed with legislators in but two of seven jurisdictions. Surprisingly, only 7 of 19 legislators agreed with using the request criterion, in contrast with the lead role given to requests by the park administrators.

With libraries, the generalists and library administrators were asked whether residents should be within a standard number of miles of a branch library. All but one library administrator placed substantial reliance on this criterion, while a majority of the generalists opposed using it. Again, a split between administrators and local legislators appeared.

The diversity of opinions indicates that infrastructure location issues often are not purely technical questions to be determined by professionals. The value-laden influences on opinions are too obvious to accept claims that professional expertise should dominate decisions. Second, basic issues of accountability are raised by the differences between park and library administrators and local legislators in the same jurisdictions. Accountability is the link between citizen preferences and actions of government officials. Deliberation among government officials, of course, may lead to opinions different from those of citizens who have not been party to discussions. When appointed administrators and elected officials disagree, discussion about the issues is essential to the process of accountability.

CONCLUSION

This essay has been about how to apply analytical measures and planning methods to the equity concept to help public officials make policy about infrastructure. Analysis can provide a basis for deciding whether some areas are below community standards for infrastructure, and whether inequalities are excessive even though all areas may be above minimum standards. Analysis also can enrich deliberations about infrastructure distribution standards. Alleviation of infrastructure inequalities can be complicated by multiple development objectives and inadequate financial resources. The framework for capital allocation policies in St. Paul states well this frequent conflict. The Savannah case illustrates some success in alleviating infrastructure inequalities.

Although not directly discussed, some of the concepts considered here also can be applied by using neighborhood units of analysis to equity issues about sewage treatment plants, reservoirs, landfills, incinerators, expressways, subways, bridges, and airports. Certain neighborhoods may be cumulatively disadvantaged. They may have been bypassed, such as not having a subway stop, or be too close to facilities with undesirable side effects—landfills, expressways, and airport flight paths.

Remedies, of course, are not easily implemented. Once in place, these facilities last for decades. No jurisdiction is likely to follow such a simple decision-rule as having at least one undesirable facility in each neighborhood. Location decisions about these facilities should involve careful consideration of primary and secondary effects (Ortolano, 1988), the extent to which they are cumulative, and whether victims should be compensated.

REFERENCES

Bureau of the Census (1980) Social indicators III. Washington, DC: U.S. Department of Commerce.

GOLD, S. M. (1973) Urban Recreation Planning. Philadelphia: Lee & Febiger.

HANKE, S. (1972) "Pricing urban water," in S. Mushkin (ed.) Public Prices for Public Products. Washington, DC: Urban Institute.

HATRY, H. et al. (1977) How Effective Are Your Community Services? Washington, DC: Urban Institute.

Insurance Services Office (1974) Grading Schedule for Municipal Fire Protection. New York: Insurance Services Office.

LEVY, F. S., A. J. MELTSNER, and A. WILDAVSKY (1974) Urban Outcomes. Berkeley: Univ. of California Press.

LINEBERRY, R. L. (1977) Equality and Urban Policy. Newbury Park, CA: Sage.

LUCY, W. H. (1985) "Accountability and opinions about equity: examples for parks and libraries." State and Local Government Rev. 17, 2: 200-206.

LUCY, W. H., D. GILBERT, and G. BIRKHEAD (1977) "Equity and local service distribution." Public Administration Rev. 37 (November/ December): 687-697.

LUCY, W. H. and K. MLADENKA (1978) Equity and Urban Service Distribution. Washington, DC: National Training and Development Service.

ORTOLANO, L. (1987) "Predicting impacts of infrastructure on land use," in J. M. Stein (ed.) Public Infrastructure Planning and Management (this volume). Newbury Park, CA: Sage.

Saint Paul Department of Planning and Economic Development (1984) "Saint Paul capital allocation policy 1984-85." City of Saint Paul, Minnesota.

SHARP, E. (1982) "Citizen-initiated contacting of government officials and socio-economic status." Amer. Pol. Sci. Rev. 76: 109-115.

TOULMIN, L. M. (1985) "Equity as a decision rule in determining the distribution of urban public services: a case study." Presented at the national conference of the American Society for Public Administration, Indianapolis.

VERBA, S. and N. NIE (1972) Participation in America. New York: Harper & Row.

About the Authors

TIMOTHY BEATLEY is an Assistant Professor in the Division of Urban and Environmental Planning in the School of Architecture at the University of Virginia. He holds a Ph.D. in city planning from the University of North Carolina at Chapel Hill. He currently teaches environmental planning and has written extensively on the ethical and value issues in land use, growth management, and environmental policy.

ANTHONY JAMES CATANESE is Dean of the College of Architecture, University of Florida. He served previously as Director of the Center for Planning and Development, Georgia Institute of Technology, Provost of Pratt Institute, and Dean, School of Architecture and Planning, University of Wisconsin—Milwaukee. He is the author or editor of several urban planning books including *Systemic Planning: Theory and Application* (1970), *New Perspectives in Transportation Research* (1972), *Personality, Politics and Planning: How City Planners Work* (1978), and *The Politics of Planning and Development* (1984).

LEON S. EPLAN heads the urban planning consulting firm of Leon S. Eplan and Associates in Atlanta, Georgia. During the 1970s, he served as Atlanta's Commissioner of Budget and Planning, and later directed the Graduate Program in City Planning at Georgia Tech. He has prepared several park and recreation plans for cities throughout the country, and was a major author of the Department of the Interior's guidelines for their Urban Park and Recreation Recovery (UPARR) program. Mr. Eplan is a past president of the American Institute of Planners.

MARSHALL KAPLAN is Dean of the Graduate School of Public Affairs, University of Colorado at Denver. During the Carter Administration, he served as Assistant Secretary for Urban Policy, Community

Planning and Development for HUD. Kaplan has directed two major Congressional studies: the national study of American infrastructure needs and a study on the health of America's cities. Kaplan's books include: *Community Builders* (with Edward Eichler); *The Land Conversion Process; Urban Planning in the 1960's; A Design for Irrelevancy*; and *The Politics of Neglect: From Model Cities to Revenue Sharing* (with Bernard Frieden); and the recently published *The Great Society and Its Legacy: Twenty Years of U.S. Social Policy*.

DOUGLASS B. LEE is a Principal Investigator at the Transportation System Center in Cambridge, Massachusetts, which is a contract research agency belonging to the U.S. Department of Transportation. Prior to joining TSC, he taught on the faculties of the University of California at Berkeley, and the University of Iowa, in the field of City and Regional Planning. He received his Ph.D. from Cornell University, and currently teaches part time at Boston University. Recent projects he has worked on for TSC include highway user charge responsibilities, transit operating subsidies, major transit investment evaluation, economic and development impacts of transportation, benefit-cost evaluation of air traffic system improvements, and strategic planning for the space station.

JON J. LINES is Senior Research Assistant at the Center for Regional Studies, Department of Environmental Design and Planning, SUNY at Buffalo; and Research Associate, Robert Moses, and Public Works Project, SUNY at Buffalo.

WILLIAM LUCY has taught in the Planning Program of the University of Virginia since 1975 and served as chairman from 1981 to 1985. He is the author of "Accountability and Opinions about Equity: Examples for Parks and Libraries," *State and Local Government Review*, 1985; "Equity and Planning for Local Services," *Journal of the American Planning Association*, 1981; coauthor, with Kenneth Mladenka, of *Equity and Urban Service Distribution*, National Training and Development Service, 1978; and coauthor, with Guthrie Birkhead and Dennis Gilbert, of "Equity in Local Service Distribution," *Public Administration Review*, 1977.

ARTHUR C. NELSON is an Assistant Professor in the School of Urban and Regional Studies and is also the Director, Division of Urban

Research and Policy Studies, the University of New Orleans. He is the editor of a forthcoming "Journal Symposium on Impact Fees," *Journal of the American Planning Association*. Dr. Nelson has published articles in several journals including the *Journal of Rural Studies, Journal of Urban Planning and Development, Urban Resources,* and the *Rural Sociologist.*

KENNETH NEWTON is Professor of Political Science and Social Policy at the University of Dundee, Scotland. He has taught at the universities of Birmingham, Oxford, Pittsburgh, and Madison, Wisconsin, and has written books and articles on urban politics and policy, political sociology, and public expenditure in Western Europe and the United States. Most recently he coauthored *Does Politics Matter?* (with L. J. Sharpe) and *The Politics of Local Expenditure* (with Terence Karran).

LEONARD ORTOLANO, 1907 Foundation Professor of Stanford University, is a water resources engineer and planner with special expertise in the integration of environmental, social, and economic factors into the decision-making process. He played a leading role in creating Stanford's Program in Infrastructure Planning and Management. Dr. Ortolano has been a consultant to the U.S. Army Corps of Engineers, the Environmental Protection Agency, and the International Institute for Applied Systems Analysis. In 1979, he was a Fulbright Fellow and Visiting Professor at the Istituto di Ricerca sulle Acque in Rome. His textbook, *Environmental Planning and Decision Making*, was published by John Wiley & Sons in 1984.

ELLEN L. PARKER is the Administrative Assistant, Center for Regional Studies, Department of Environmental Design and Planning, SUNY at Buffalo; and Research Associate, Robert Moses, and Public Works Project, SUNY at Buffalo.

JOHN E. PETERSEN, Senior Director of the Government Finance Research Center (GFRC), has served as financial adviser to many federal agencies, state governments, and municipalities, including the U.S. Treasury, the U.S. Environmental Protection Agency, and the Department of Transportation. Dr. Petersen is recognized as an expert in the evaluation of financing alternatives, as well as in the structuring, rating, and marketing of municipal debt.

CATHERINE ROSS is an Associate Professor in the Graduate City Planning Program at Georgia Institute of Technology. Dr. Ross teaches courses and consults in transportation planning. She has received research funding from the National Science Foundation, U.S. Department of Transportation, and the Community Services Administration. Dr. Ross is the author of numerous articles, including "Perceptions of a Proposed Rail System" (with Jay M. Stein) in *Transportation Quarterly* (1985).

JAY M. STEIN is Chairperson and Professor in the Department of Environmental Design and Planning, SUNY at Buffalo. He served previously as a faculty member in the Graduate City Planning Program of Georgia Institute of Technology and as Visiting Professor of Infrastructure Planning and Management, Stanford University. The author of numerous articles and papers, he also serves on the Editorial Board of the *Journal of the American Planning Association.*

NOTES

NOTES